D1616734

Bareface

Bareface

A Guide to C. S. Lewis's Last Novel

Doris T. Myers

University of Missouri Press
Columbia and London

Copyright © 2004 by
The Curators of the University of Missouri
University of Missouri Press, Columbia, Missouri 65201
Printed and bound in the United States of America
All rights reserved
5   4   3   2   1   08   07   06   05   04

Library of Congress Cataloging-in-Publication Data

Myers, Doris T.
  Bareface : a guide to C.S. Lewis's last novel / Doris T. Myers.
    p.   cm.
  Includes bibliographical references (p.) and index.
  ISBN 0-8262-1497-5 (alk. paper)
    1. Lewis, C. S. (Clive Staples), 1898–1963. Till we have faces.
2. Psyche (Greek deity) in literature.   3. Eros (Greek deity) in
literature.   4. Mythology, Greek, in literature.   5. Psychology in
literature.   I. Title.
PR6023.E926T5436   2004
823'.912—dc22   2003024715

♾™   This paper meets the requirements of the
American National Standard for Permanence of Paper
for Printed Library Materials, Z39.48, 1984.

Designer: Jennifer Cropp
Typesetter: Phoenix Type, Inc.
Printer and binder: The Maple-Vail Book Manufacturing Group
Typefaces: Palatino, Diotima, and Caligraphy

For

Tom,
Thomas,
and Liz

Contents

Acknowledgments

This book grew out of a paper presented in May 1998, at the international symposium in Erlangen, Germany, in celebration of the centenary of C. S. Lewis's birth. It was sponsored by the *Inklings Gesellschaft für Literatur und Ästhetik* together with the Institut für Anglistik and Amerikanistik and Institut für Systematische Theologie der Friedrich-Alexander-Universität Erlangen-Nürnberg, and the papers from the symposium were later published in the 1998 edition of the *Inklings Jahrbuch.* At a (much) later stage, portions of this manuscript were presented to the Southern California C. S. Lewis Society's Twenty-Eighth Anniversary Summer Workshop (July 29–August 2, 2002). I am especially grateful to Dietrich Petzold and Edie Dougherty for organizing these two opportunities to meet and talk about C. S. Lewis.

Peter J. Schakel and Paul A. Olson read the manuscript and took time from their own heavy publication schedules to offer extensive suggestions and generous encouragement. The comments of the readers for the University of Missouri Press were especially helpful. I am also grateful for the encouragement and editorial help of Beverly Jarrett, Clair Willcox, Jane Lago, and Sara Davis.

It is almost impossible to do research on C. S. Lewis without the gracious, patient assistance of the staff of the Marion E. Wade Center at Wheaton College, Wheaton, Illinois. As always, I am especially grateful to Christopher Mitchell and Marjorie Lamp Mead.

Mary Kingsbury commented on the manuscript from an Orual-loving engineer's point of view; Rosamond K. Sprague commented on Greek and Roman agriculture; and the Rev. Canon Louise Blanchard offered me friendship and personal guidance throughout.

The contribution of my husband, Tom, is literally immeasurable. He read all three versions patiently and carefully; offered encouragement, cogent criticisms, and whatever praise could be spoken without actual dishonesty; performed all sorts of tedious tasks of verifying, proofreading, and translating German sources (of which only Otto appears in the final version); and kept the household together when I was stuck in Glome.

List of Abbreviations

AGO	A Grief Observed
AM	The Abolition of Man
AMR	All My Road before Me
CR	Christian Reflections
DI	The Discarded Image
Exp	An Experiment in Criticism
FL	The Four Loves
GID	God in the Dock
HHB	The Horse and His Boy
LAG	Letters of C. S. Lewis to Arthur Greeves
LAL	Letters to an American Lady
LB	The Last Battle
Let	Letters of C. S. Lewis, rev. ed.
LetChil	Letters to Children
LM	Letters to Malcolm
LWW	The Lion, the Witch, and the Wardrobe
MC	Mere Christianity
Mir	Miracles
MN	The Magician's Nephew
OOW	Of Other Worlds
Pere	Perelandra
Poems	Poems
PoP	The Problem of Pain
PR	The Pilgrim's Regress
Refl	Reflections on the Psalms
SbJ	Surprised by Joy
SC	The Silver Chair
ScL	The Screwtape Letters
SIOL	Spenser's Images of Life
SLE	Selected Literary Essays
THS	That Hideous Strength
TWHF	Till We Have Faces
WLN	The World's Last Night

Bareface

Introduction

"Bareface" — Why a Book about a Book?

"Far and away the best I have written"—this is how Lewis described *Till We Have Faces*, or, as he originally titled it, "Bareface." He added ruefully, "That book . . . has been my one big failure both with the critics and with the public" (*Let*, 492).

Certainly *Till We Have Faces* is a radical departure from the beautiful fantasies and religious teaching that loyal readers are accustomed to associate with Lewis. The reader who picks it up expecting a mental holiday in a strange and wonderful place like Narnia—or Perelandra, for that matter—instead finds a squalid little "kingdom" where two "princesses" play in the barnyard, sliding on the frozen urine of the domestic animals. Similarly, the reader who expects witty, poetic, inspiring arguments for Christianity will be disappointed. Orual, the narrator and main character, was born before Christianity existed. She alternates between cynical disbelief in her tribal religion and hatred for its gods. Her opening lines are quarrelsome and abrasive; many people read no further.

Other people love the novel and read it over and over; for a few, it is not just Lewis's best novel, but the only one they enjoy. It would be arrogant and schoolteacherish of me to define why others love this book, but I can speak for myself. From the first, I became deeply involved in Orual's personality and experience. She is so ugly, and so ashamed of her ugliness, that she wears a veil; she never goes bareface. She is angry. In her father's eyes, she is a worthless female, not even marriageable. She is frustrated with the narrowness of her environment, the barbarian kingdom of Glome. She loses the love of her life, her half-sister Psyche. She will never have a man of her own or be a real wife and mother. It is not that these specific things

1

happened to me, but that my experience has the emotional resonance of hers.

It also has the emotional resonance of Lewis's experience. In his nonfiction books about Christianity, and especially in his letters, Lewis seems very frank, very open; those who read these writings come to feel that he is a personal friend. Yet there is something hidden about him. He refused to go bareface, so successfully that one friend commented that his autobiography, *Surprised by Joy,* should have been entitled, "Suppressed by Jack." In Orual we see much of the real Jack Lewis—his loss of his mother, his disrespect for his father, his desire for closeness, his struggles with disbelief.[1] Again, although Orual's experiences are quite different from his, they ring true. Something similar happened to him.

It is Lewis's last novel, and in some sense he worked on it all his life. He first read the story of Cupid and Psyche from Apuleius's Roman novel, *The Golden Ass,* when he was eighteen. After World War I, as an undergraduate at Oxford, he tried twice to write his own version of the story, "once in couplets and once in ballad form" (*AMR,* 266). As he wrote to one friend, "So, though the version you have read was very quickly written, you might say I've been at work on Orual for 35 years. Of course in my pre-Christian days she was to be in the right and the gods in the wrong."[2] From the beginning his attention centered on the elder sister as narrator, but her motivations became more complex as Lewis matured. For example, in the poetic versions she was not jealous, but simply unable to see Psyche's palace. In the mature version, she was not only unable to see the palace, but also blinded by jealousy. And in his remark about his pre-Christian assessment of Orual we see why the novel consists of two parts, the story as Orual first experienced it, and then the same story retold.

1. George Sayer, *Jack: C. S. Lewis and His Times,* 327–28. A reviewer in the *Church Times* (Nov. 20, 1964), ix, said, "Lewis kept so strict a control over his personal emotions that a hasty reader might suppose he thought in depth but felt rather on the surface." Cited by Walter Hooper, *C. S. Lewis: Companion and Guide,* 177. Kath Filmer, in *The Fiction of C. S. Lewis: Mask and Mirror,* agrees: "the book is Lewis's own, and, in a sense, an attempt at spiritual autobiography." She also notes "the same process" at work in the poem "Because of Endless Pride," from *PR* (111, 119).
2. Quoted in Hooper, *Companion,* 251. See *Companion,* 246–47, for excerpts from the early versions.

Besides becoming involved with the emotional resonances of Orual's experience, I began to notice the book's literary patterning. Its intricacy seems natural, like the dappling of an owl's back, not conscious and mannered like a tapestry. For example, the style is different from any of Lewis's usual rhetorical stances—confident debater, creator of brilliant metaphors, avuncular guide to Narnia— because it is not Lewis's style, but Orual's. She shares his lucidity but none of his other trademarks. Glome is rustic, isolated, backward; thus, Orual uses dialect words from Scotland and semi-obsolete words. She is a tough, unsentimental person; thus, she prefers coarse words, terms more usually applied to animals than to human beings. However, she has been schooled in classical rhetoric, so her plain, rough words are placed into sentences using common rhetorical patterns, such as isocolon, parallelism, and antithesis.[3] The style is the woman herself, and Lewis has immersed himself so completely in her personality that the book at first seems to have no style.

There is an analogous intricacy and naturalness in the plot. Orual apparently has an orderly mind, and one event appears to follow another so inevitably that no narrative skill seems to be involved. Close examination of the plot, however, gives a different impression. I have attempted to deal with the complexity by analyzing the author's specific narrative task in each of his chapters.

Till We Have Faces, then, is a difficult book. One early critic says it is like "an Homeric or Icelandic saga written by Henry James."[4] On the one hand it is a historical novel, a realistic portrait of life just outside Hellenistic civilization based upon Lewis's masterly knowledge of the ancient world. On the other hand, it is a modern novel, with an unreliable narrator and characterizations based on the new psychological paradigms of Freud and Jung. The combination is strange—and strangely compelling. In order to appreciate it fully, we must put aside our expectations of myth and fantasy and take up the assumptions of all realistic fiction: Glome is a real place—at least as real as Thomas Hardy's town of Casterbridge; Psyche and Orual are real women, as individual as George Eliot's

3. Doris T. Myers, *C. S. Lewis in Context*, 201–3.
4. Stella Gibbons, "Imaginative Writing," 94. We should remember that Homer and the Icelandic sagas are based on history. Schakel, *Imagination*, 53n, does not go so far as to call *TWHF* a historical novel, but he does say that it is not "romance, fantasy, or fairy tale."

Dorothea and Rosamond; and the events narrated by Orual, though not mentioned in history books, could plausibly have occurred in the ancient world. As Lewis occasionally pointed out, once "a man" has accepted the idea that supernatural events can happen, there is no reason to believe that they happened only to the Hebrews, never to the pagans.

It cannot be overemphasized, then, that *Till We Have Faces* is not allegory, but a realistic modern novel written according to the expectations of the first half of the twentieth century. The reading skills appropriate to it are the ones appropriate to Hardy's *Tess of the D'Urbervilles* or John Steinbeck's *Grapes of Wrath*. To attempt to use the reading skills appropriate to a neomedieval allegory just multiplies difficulties.[5]

Admittedly, Lewis's source story is thoroughly allegorical. A beautiful mortal named Psyche, or Soul, marries the god Cupid, or Love. He will not allow her to see him and comes to their marriage bed only in darkness. At the insistence of her jealous sisters, Psyche brings a lamp into their bedroom. Cupid leaves her, and she falls into the power of his mother, Venus (raw sexuality). But after many sufferings Psyche is reunited with her husband, becomes a goddess, and gives birth to a daughter named Pleasure. (See the American edition of *Till We Have Faces* for a more complete plot summary and Lewis's comments on his response to the story, 311–13.)

The names of the characters promote allegorical reading: Cupid is erotic love; and as we all know, the experience of falling in love must be accepted with trust, not examined with a lamp of analysis. It leads to many trials, but also, if one is lucky, to pleasure. On another level, it is an allegory of the soul's desire for union with God and the struggles of the spiritual journey. Although Apuleius's version is the earliest one extant, a previous understanding of the allegorical meaning is attested by many artifacts showing a girl with a winged god.[6]

5. For example, one early reviewer wrote, "The religious allegory is plain to read" (*Saturday Review* 40 [Jan. 12, 1957]: 15); and R. J. Reilly, in his valuable study *Romantic Religion: A Study of Barfield, Lewis, Williams, and Tolkien,* called Orual and Psyche "not 'real' persons but rather adumbrations of real persons" (125–26), that is, shadows who fill a couple of slots in an allegory.

6. See Jane Ellen Harrison's *Prolegomena to the Study of Greek Religion,* 644 *et passim.*

The bare outline of the story has fascinated poets, philosophers, and ordinary readers throughout the centuries. It is more than allegory; it has all the mysterious resonance of a myth. That is, the meaning, though clear, is yet somehow beyond our grasp.[7] We think we have understood the story, but there is always something beyond, inviting us to ponder it more deeply. The originality of Lewis's approach is to ignore allegory, to deemphasize the mythic literary tradition, and to treat it as something that could, perhaps did, really happen.

To appreciate the realistic novel Lewis wrote, then, one must tentatively accept the story as something that really happened in a specific time and place. Even in Lewis's own day the knowledge of Greek and Roman culture that had been common to everyone with a college preparatory education was fading. In Lewis's time, English literature was relatively new as a university major. The Greek and Roman classics were considered more intellectually respectable, but Lewis's first-class degree in ancient literature, history, and philosophy did not assure him of a position, so he took an extra year to become qualified in English.

In the United States today, and even in Europe, education in the classics is rare. The clues to time and place that Lewis provides are based on the assumption that his readers will have some fairly accurate ideas about the ancient world: the dominance of Greek art, literature, and philosophy; how Greek culture spread even as the Greeks lost political autonomy, first to Alexander the Great and then to the Romans; and the birth of Jesus Christ in Roman times. As we shall see later, those who "[have] read the right books" (*VDT*, 69) can appreciate Glome as a remarkably accurate "little barbarous state on the borders of the Hellenistic world" (*Let*, 462).

However, we readers of the twenty-first century miss the clues to time and place and misclassify *Till We Have Faces* as a fantasy or allegory. The literary genre it most resembles is that of the historical novel. The historical novel maintains realism in the details of daily life, and in *Till We Have Faces* these details are realistic to the point of squalor. A historical novel is also attached to some important historical period or event, showing us how it must have felt to be a member of Julius Caesar's army or Katharine of Aragon's court.

---

7. See "Myth," 183–87, for a fuller discussion of this vexed term.

Till We Have Faces does not at first seem to fulfill this criterion of the genre, but I believe it is attached to the Incarnation, the historical birth of Jesus Christ.

The god husband of Psyche is something like an angel of God or even the Second Person of the Trinity might have appeared to pagan eyes, and at the end of the book it is hinted that human views of deity will undergo a radical change: "Nothing is yet in its true form" (*TWHF*, 305).

The novel shows, very indirectly, how it might have felt to have been present at the Incarnation. Orual's jealousy and her struggles with Psyche's marriage to a god are comparable to what Jesus's family might have felt when he was being hailed as the Messiah. Jesus's apparent rejection of his family in the synoptic Gospels hints at such feelings, and Lewis himself explicates this aspect of *Till We Have Faces* in a letter to Clyde Kilby.[8]

All these clues to the meaning of the novel were becoming hidden even in Lewis's own day, as a more extensive reading of English literature replaced the study of the Greeks and Romans. As a result, for most of us today, the experience of reading *Till We Have Faces* is like deciphering a document in which every fifth word is missing. The story is so powerful that a good reader can enjoy it, but it is hard going. I hope that this book will restore some of those missing words.

The setting in the classical world and the analogy between Jesus and Psyche do not, however, make *Till We Have Faces* an inspiring, religious novel. Like all of Lewis's work, even his most objective scholarship, the book is pervaded by his faith, but the story is specifically pre-Christian, and any overt theologizing would be inappropriate. Those who turn to Lewis for something to strengthen their faith will not find it in *Till We Have Faces*. However, believers may be led to examine the strength of their own acceptance of Christ, and nonbelievers their own tendency to discount the religious convictions of others. Lewis is asking his readers to put away any grim determination to read something that will "do them good," and

---

8. Matt. 12:46–50, Mark 3:31–35, and Luke 8:19–21. Lewis cites Luke 2:48 rather than these passages, but he describes a family's reaction to a religious vocation in these terms: "The others suffer a sense of outrage. What they love is being taken from them! The boy must be mad! and the conceit of him!" (*Let*, 463).

simply let themselves be carried into the intensity of Orual's experience as she struggles with the ultimate questions of the spirit.

Method of Study

The project I originally had in mind was a Glomian parallel to John Livingston Lowes's *Road to Xanadu*, but I soon realized that I could not begin to handle the multiplicity of Lewis's associations. His whole lifetime of intellectual curiosity and disciplined study went into this novel; not even a one-volume encyclopedia could do it justice. I did not relinquish my desire to get to know Lewis by reading what he read, but I narrowed my scope by choosing just a few key authors in each field: Freud and Jung in depth psychology, William James and Rudolf Otto in religious psychology, and J. E. Harrison, Gilbert Murray, Robert Graves, and Edwyn Bevan in commentary on the classical world. There is documentary evidence that Lewis read all of these authors, and insofar as possible, I have used the editions available in his time. I have paid relatively little attention to Lewis's biographers, even those who knew him personally. The picture of Lewis that emerges complements rather than contradicts the biographers; the emphasis and tone are different. I hope that it will renew and enliven the interpretation of his other fiction in addition to *Till We Have Faces*.

The Organization of the Guidebook

Bareface consists of three parts: "Chapter by Chapter," "Further In," and "Glossary," cross-referenced for easy browsing.

Part I. Chapter by Chapter

As the title suggests, part 1 takes the reader through the novel a chapter at a time. The novel is divided into two books, with twenty-one chapters in book 1 and four chapters in book 2.

Each chapter is discussed from four viewpoints:

"The Art of Story" comments on what Lewis has to accomplish in the chapter and the techniques he uses.

"Context" provides background information on topics directly relevant to the individual chapter. Larger topics, and those relevant to several chapters, are treated in part 2.

"Love" traces Orual's relationships, but with some comments on other characters.

"Faith" points out the problems of religion raised in the chapter.

These four divisions are designed to be read separately if the reader so desires. "The Art of Story" and "Context" are fairly informational; for some people, it may work best to read them first, and then read Lewis's chapter. The sections on love and faith are interpretative, designed to be read in an interactive fashion, possibly after reading Lewis's chapter. I have provided a chapter title (mine, not Lewis's) to indicate the focus of each chapter and subtitles for the four sections to facilitate browsing. Some of the subtitles also suggest particularly applicable "Further In" essays. The independence of each section entails some unavoidable repetition.

Part II. Further In

Part 2 consists of brief articles on key topics. Some readers may find in them all the help they need for resolving difficulties with the book.

"Further In" has a wider focus than "Chapter by Chapter." Often the article applies to the whole novel, or to several chapters rather than a single one, and some articles contain cross-references to others. Several articles are helpful in understanding Lewis's life or his other writings apart from *Till We Have Faces*. My intention is to smooth over difficulties while allowing each reader to skip unneeded information.

Part III. Glossary

One of the most striking aspects of *Till We Have Faces* is the style. Lewis uses dialectal and obsolete expressions to give Orual a rough, countrified, unladylike way of speaking. The glossary contains words that are odd because of their rarity in modern prose, because they are used in a special sense, or because they are particularly characteristic of Orual's personality. Page references to the novel are provided so that words may be studied in context. In addition to focusing on Orual's style, the glossary will help readers whose first language is other than English. Finally, the glossary is a tribute to Lewis's concern with intelligent reading based on exact under-standing of the nuances of words.

Each of the three divisions makes its own contribution to putting the reader in touch with this unique novel and the man who wrote it.

Documentation

References to Lewis's works appear parenthetically in the text, using abbreviated titles and page numbers. A list of abbreviations is found in the front matter. Biblical citations, also parenthetical, are normally taken from the King James Version, the one most widely used in the 1950s. All other references are contained in footnotes.

Part I

Chapter by Chapter

Book One
The Way It All Happened

Chapter 1. Welcome to Glome

A. The Art of Story: Getting Started

Speaking to the open-minded Greek who will, she hopes, read her book, Orual, the narrator, introduces most of the main characters and three main issues. The troubling, ambiguous nature of love is suggested by her description of Ungit, the Glomish equivalent of the love goddess Aphrodite (Venus). In addition, Orual tells of her ugliness, which separates her from others and makes it hard for her to find love. The problem of faith is introduced when the Fox calls stories about the gods "lies of poets," implying that the gods do not really exist. Finally, without being aware of their significance, Orual refers to the blood sacrifices offered to the goddess Ungit, thus suggesting Lewis's conviction that pagan sacrifices foreshadowed the sacrifice of Christ.

In the opening lines Lewis establishes Orual's narrative voice, telling the reader a great deal about her personality and circumstances: "I am old now and have not much to fear from the anger of gods. I have no husband nor child, nor hardly a friend, through whom they can hurt me. My body, this lean carrion that still has to be washed and fed and have clothes hung about it daily with so many changes, they may kill as soon as they please. The succession is provided for. My crown passes to my nephew."

If *Till We Have Faces* were a film, it might open with a panning shot of Glome, perhaps showing Orual walking around the palace

This chapter refers to *TWHF*, pp. 3–12.

grounds or sitting on her throne, accompanied by music to signal the mood of the story. All this would be background for the listing of credits and might take five minutes. In these first five sentences Lewis accomplishes more, and more quickly, in seventy-four words.

In the first sentence, the reference to gods who might be personally vengeful establishes the setting as a prescientific time and the speaker as one who is brave enough to defy the power of the gods. In the second sentence, the reader learns that the speaker is a woman but not a mother ("no husband nor child") and a very lonely person. In the third sentence, the phrase "lean carrion" expresses the character's low opinion of herself. Carrion is dead flesh for animal or bird scavengers, but the narrator's flesh is too "lean" to offer even them much nourishment. The long sentence builds up to a challenge: she dares the gods not just to hurt, but to kill her.

By contrast, sentences four and five are short and direct. The words "succession" and "crown" show that the author is a queen, and the sentence rhythms show that she is domineering and decisive.

The second paragraph announces the purpose of the book as the narrator sees it: "I will accuse the gods, especially the god [of] the Grey Mountain." Like Job, she sees herself as a plaintiff against the god, but she does not hope for a divine answer. Instead she appeals to Greek philosophers who speculate about everything, even the nature of the gods. Of course she cannot realistically hope that Greek philosophers will ever send an answer back to her.

In the third paragraph she introduces herself by name. She also introduces Ungit, the goddess of Glome. The geography of Orual's small world is almost a diagram of her conflict with the gods: her city is on one side of the river Shennit, about a mile from the banks; the temple of Ungit is on the other side of the river, also about a mile from the banks. Ungit's son is beyond, away from Glome but still somehow involved in its affairs.

The rest of the chapter moves quickly with the death of Orual's mother, the coming of a Greek slave—the Fox—to be her tutor, the king's second marriage, and Orual's discovery that she is ugly. These events point to three major themes of the book: Orual's need for love, her struggle with the faith of the Old Priest versus the enlightenment of the Fox, and the meaning of Glome's paganism within the larger context of the Incarnation of Christ.

B. Context: The Trojan War and
Disordered Love ("Glome," 163)

Glome is a barbarian kingdom—that is, a place where the people do not speak Greek. It is outside the Greek colonies that lined the Mediterranean in the Hellenistic period. It was probably in Scythia, but that does not say much, for the Greeks gave the name "Scythia" to everything that was outside civilization and north of the Black Sea, but not far enough north to belong to the Hyperboreans. They used it in the same vague way that English-speakers in the early twentieth century used "Africa," and, in fact, Lewis's Glome is analogous to the African locales of John Buchan or Rider Haggard.

The Fox brings Greek culture, especially literature, to Glome, and in so doing, he brings the tradition of the Trojan War. When he tells about the mating of Aphrodite and Anchises, he is putting the story of Orual's dealings with Ungit and her son into the context of the Trojan War, for the son of this mating was Aeneas, the hero who escaped from burning Troy and founded Rome. The Trojan War is the starting point of the Homeric epics and also the basis of several great tragedies of the Greek golden age. For Greek culture, this war was not just a military operation, but the very prototype of disordered, destructive love, the craving that ignores the good of individuals, families, and the whole society. The story became a central feature in European culture.

Lewis believed that pagan culture was a preparation for what he regarded as the central event in history, the Incarnation of Christ. In *Till We Have Faces* he shows that literature, philosophic enlightenment, and superstition all played a part in this central event. Each one posed questions for which the Incarnation of Christ was the only answer.

C. Love: Orual's Plight

The story opens with the death of Orual's mother, leaving Orual in a loveless environment, for she gets little affection from her nurse and none from her father. Because she is so ugly, even the slaves prefer her sister Redival, and it is unlikely that any man will ever

want her. The Fox brings some love into this environment, responding with pity to her ugliness and with appreciation to her sharp
mind. He teaches her reading, writing, and philosophy, but the Greek
wisdom he brings does not meet her need. The philosophy consists
of a dull striving after virtue and Stoic detachment, and the poetry
depicts the ambiguous, troubling nature of love.

Orual's first response to love in poetry is far from positive. She
ignores the pastoral beauty of how Aphrodite sends the animals to
the delights of love; instead she identifies with Anchises' horror at
learning the identity of his lover. She concludes, "[I]f the goddess
was more beautiful in Greece than in Glome, she was equally terrible in each" (*TWHF*, 8).

Quotations from two of the Fox's favorite poems also hint at the
dangers inherent in love. "Take me to the apple-laden land" is line
742 in the *Hippolytus* of Euripides. In this tragedy, Aphrodite, offended by the virginity of Hippolytus, son of Theseus, afflicts his
stepmother, Phaedra, with passionate love for him. She commits
suicide, and Theseus, blaming Hippolytus, curses his son and brings
about his death. The line, which occurs in a chorus expressing a
longing for something beyond human struggles with sex and love,
for the transcendence represented by the Garden of the Hesperides,
is probably Lewis's own translation. Here is Gilbert Murray's translation of the stanza in which it occurs:

> To the Strand of the Daughters of Sunset,
>   The Apple-tree, the singing and the gold;
> Where the mariner must stay him from his onset,
>   And the red wave is tranquil as of old;
>   Yea, beyond that Pillar of the End
>   That Atlas guardeth, would I wend;
> Where a voice of living waters never ceaseth
>   In God's quiet garden by the sea,
> And Earth, the ancient life-giver, increaseth
>   Joy among the meadows, like a tree.[1]

The other quotation, "The Moon's gone down," is from the lesbian
poet Sappho, who wrote passionate songs to Aphrodite and was

---

1. Euripides, *Hippolytus*, tr. Gilbert Murray, 39. See "Faith: Belief and Faith"
below.

supposed (erroneously, scholars now believe) to have killed herself for love.[2] We remember that Dante called Love "the god of terrible aspect" and suspect that Orual's experience of love will bring
suffering.

D. Faith: Belief and Faith ("Stoicism," 214)

In "On Obstinacy in Belief," a paper first delivered to the Oxford
Socratic Club, Lewis distinguished between *Credere Deum esse*, believing that God exists, and *Credere in Deum*, putting one's trust in
God.[3] At this point in the story, Orual believes that Ungit and her
son exist, but she emphatically does not trust them. Nor should
she. In her experience, Ungit is ugly—a black, featureless stone—and
the worship she requires is fearsome and cruel. She sits in a dark
temple that smells of blood, for animals and sometimes people are
sacrificed to her. Some of the worship involves sacred prostitution,
and girls are kept in the temple for that purpose.

The Fox's problem with faith is more subtle than Orual's fearful
reaction to Ungit. Like many educated Greeks, from Socrates on, he
does not believe literally in the gods of epic and tragedy. As a Stoic,
he believes in the laws of nature and the importance of virtue, but
it is poetry about the gods, not Simonides on virtue, that brings the
lilt to his voice.[4] His situation is much like Lewis's during his years
of study at Bookham: "[He cared] for almost nothing but the gods
and heroes, the garden of the Hesperides . . . and believe[d] in nothing but atoms and evolution and military service" (*SbJ*, 174).

Although the *Hippolytus* as a whole can be seen as a reference to
the difficulties of love, the Chorus's song, "Take me to the apple-
laden land," expresses longing for the beyond. As Lewis tells us in
Surprised by Joy, he first felt this longing when he saw a toy garden
that his brother had made in "the lid of a biscuit tin," and he adds,

2. *Oxford Classical Dictionary*, 3rd ed., s.v. "Sappho." Hereinafter cited as
OCD 3.

3. The date on which "Obstinacy in Belief" was read before the Socratic
Club is unavailable. It was published in *Sewanee Review* 63 (Autumn 1955):
525–38; and reprinted in *WLN* (1960), *They Asked for a Paper* (1962), and *Screwtape
Proposes a Toast* (1965).

4. *OCD* 3, s.v. "Simonides." See also Schakel, *Reason and Imagination*, 16.

"As long as I live my imagination of Paradise will retain something of my brother's toy garden" (*SbJ*, 7). During the year he was studying for his English degree, while still believing in "nothing but atoms and evolution and military service" he reread the *Hippolytus*, and that song was an important step in his adult conversion. He recalls, "*In one chorus* all that world's end imagery which I had rejected when I assumed my New Look rose before me....I was overwhelmed... off once more into the land of longing, my heart at once broken and exalted" (*SbJ*, 217; emphasis added). When the Fox sings this song to Orual, we can infer that she—and the Fox—will eventually experience something beyond the ugliness and facelessness of Ungit.

Chapter 2. Enter Psyche

A. Art of Story: Colors

The king's second wife—her name is never mentioned—dies giving birth to Psyche, who will become the center of Orual's life. Even as a newborn, Psyche is luminous and beautiful, but her birth bitterly disappoints King Trom, who had hoped for a son. In his rage he kills a slave, swings Orual around by the hair, threatens to kill the Old Priest, and says he will send the Fox, who will not be needed to tutor his son, to the silver mines.

Orual's terror, at the birth itself and the king's rage, dominates the first half of the chapter. She is so frightened by the screams of the woman in childbirth that she does not mention the sound until it stops, to be replaced by the sound of women bewailing the mother's death. In addition to sounds there are colors. Various reds contend with the darkness of the night. Orual sees the red flames of the torches "sway[ing] and gutter[ing]," the Priest's processions around the great fire, the blood on the floor, first from the animal sacrifices and then from the spilling of wine and a boy's blood.

In the second half, Orual summarizes the good years she had as Psyche was growing up. White and blue contrast with the red and black of the night when Psyche was born. Instead of the wavering torch flames in the drafty hall, there are boughs of white blossoms "rocking and dancing against blue-and-white skies." But the chapter ends in another fear—that the Fox's praises of Psyche's beauty will arouse the enmity of the gods.

See *TWHF*, pp. 13–24.

B. Context: Facing Death ("Stoicism," 214)

When the king threatens to send him to the mines, the Fox decides to forestall such misery by committing suicide, for "to depart from life of a man's own will...[is] according to nature." Orual fears that "those who go that way" are punished in the afterlife by being forced to "lie wallowing in filth," but the Fox says that at death the physical body is merely dissolved into its elements (*TWHF,* 17). He does not quite state the Stoic belief that the bit of divine reason within his body ("the god within me") will return to the Divine Reason, but he does assure Orual that death is as natural as birth and should be accepted with the same equanimity.

It is striking to compare the Fox's situation with that of Jesus. In the synoptic Gospels it is recorded that Jesus said, "The spirit indeed is willing, but the flesh is weak"; that "Horror and anguish overwhelmed him"; and "My heart is ready to break with grief." Also, Luke says that "his sweat was like clots of blood falling to the ground."[1] As Lewis pointed out, Jesus did not demonstrate the bravery of the noble pagan: "God could, had He pleased, have been incarnate in a man of iron nerves, the Stoic [*sic*] sort who lets no sign escape him. Of his great humility He chose to be incarnate in a man of delicate sensibilities who wept at the grave of Lazarus and sweated blood in Gethsemane.... He has faced all that the weakest of us face, has shared not only the strength of our nature but every weakness of it except sin" (*Let,* 383). The Fox is ashamed of his emotions; Jesus accepted his.

In the Fox, Lewis shows us a man who aspires to be a true Stoic but falls far short of his goal. His enlightenment has theoretically freed him from the fear of death, but he is shaking with fear. He almost paraphrases Jesus' words, "The flesh is weak" when he says, "The body is shaking. I needn't let it shake the god within me" (*TWHF,* 18). Paradoxically, in his fear, his failure to be a perfect Stoic, the Fox was a precursor to Jesus. Lewis explains it this way: although "it sounds odd to attribute to perfect man a fear which imperfect men have often overcome," only "He who [fully] lived a human

---

1. Matt. 26:41, RSV; Mark 14:33–34, NEB; Luke 22:45b, NEB. For similar comments by Lewis on Jesus' suffering, see *Let,* 431; *LM,* 42–43; *GID,* 149.

life (and I presume that only one did) can fully taste the horror of death" (*Let*, 303, 305).

C. Love: Rapture—And Disorder

Chapter 2 explores several facets of disordered love. First, there is the oblique reference to the Trojan War in the Fox's reaction to baby Psyche: "Helen herself, new-hatched, must have looked so" (*TWHF*, 21). "New-hatched" reminds us that Helen was supposedly born from an egg, because Zeus took the form of a swan to ravish her mother, Leda. Helen was beautiful and terrible like Aphrodite; and like Helen in Troy, Psyche will be the center of conflict in Glome.

Second, Orual's rapturous love for Psyche is also disordered. She says, "I wanted to be a wife so that I could have been her real mother. I wanted to be a boy so that she could be in love with me. I wanted her to be my full sister instead of my half sister. I wanted her to be a slave so that I could set her free and make her rich" (*TWHF*, 23). The adoration Orual feels for Psyche is like a stem cell—undifferentiated, capable of being any kind of specific relationship, whether mother to child, lover to beloved, sister to sister. But there are two evidences of disorder in all these imagined roles: Orual craves a greater closeness to Psyche than she actually has, and in each imagined role, she sees herself as the dominant one—mother, male, older sister, master.

The lack of respect for females, however, cannot be cited as an example of disordered love. It is simply historical realism. Females may have received worse treatment in Glome than in the Greece of the classics, but not by much. Orual observes that in Glome, slave boys are valued, but girls are dehumanized—often bedded by the king, and if not objects of his lust, sold away from the only home they have ever known, or given to the temple of Ungit (goddess of love and fertility) for ritual prostitution. Orual refers offhandedly to "when they were ripe," as if they were fruit. Although her personality contains much of Lewis's own, this passage should not be cited as evidence for Lewis's misogyny, but as proof of his zeal for producing historical fiction.

D. Faith: Control by Sacrifice ("Pagan Religion," 204)

In our post-Christian era, many people turn to prayer and sometimes offer sacrifices to persuade whatever is controlling the universe to accomplish what they desire or desperately need. Glome is no different. When Trom's wife (and more important, the child) is in danger, the king orders more sacrifices, and Orual awakes to the "smell of slaughtering" (TWHF, 14). To the king, the sacrifice is a business transaction; as the Latin ritual has it, Do ut des—I give (this sacrifice) so that you will give (what I want). When his wife dies and the child is seen to be a girl, he turns to the Old Priest and demands, "You had better recover what [Ungit] owes me" (TWHF, 15).

As a Stoic, the Fox's perspective is closer to Lewis's Christian view. His goal is not to obtain things through prayer and sacrifice, but to conform to the Divine Nature. In The Abolition of Man, Lewis compares modern applied science to magic, because the goal of both is "to subdue reality to the wishes of men." In contrast, "[f]or the wise men of old the cardinal problem had been how to conform the soul to reality, and the solution had been knowledge, self-discipline, and virtue" (AM, 88).

Chapter 3. Hard Times in Glome

A. The Art of Story: Gradually Downhill

In this chapter Orual traces the diminishment of her happiness with Psyche, step by step. She begins, "It was Redival [the second sister] who ended the good time" (*TWHF*, 25), but the attentive reader will note a discontinuity between actual events and Orual's evaluation of them.

How many of the diminishments may be attributed to Redival? First, she had nothing to do with forming the alliance with Caphad, which drags down Glome's prestige. King Trom made the alliance to marry Psyche's mother, and it "proved a snare" (*TWHF*, 26). Redival did flirt with the young officer Tarin, but it was King Trom who had him castrated. This caused Tarin's father to stir up a rebellion against the king, but Redival's flirting did not actually cause the rebellion.

Redival was jealous of Psyche's beauty, and she did tell the Old Priest (or someone else at the temple) that Psyche was being worshipped. However, if the kingdom had not had a run of bad luck, perhaps nothing would have come of it. When Psyche nursed the Fox through the plague, Batta gossipped about it, and people came to believe in Psyche's healing hands, but this sequence of events is not Redival's doing.

To sum up, certainly Redival, along with gossiping Batta, caused some of the mischief; the king caused some; some just happened. Just as certainly, Psyche caused some of it by being beautiful and

See *TWHF*, pp. 25–34.

being a healer. Her nature, which she could not change, was her doom. To have Orual begin the chapter by accusing Redival of ending the good time establishes Orual as an unreliable narrator, thus modernizing the story with a modern fictional technique.

B. Context: Judea and Troy

This chapter increases Psyche's importance and stature by implying that she is first like Christ and then like Helen of Troy. She is like Christ in her determination to touch the people who need healing; indeed, one meaning of "Savior" is "Healer." The New Testament says that Jesus' ministry was sometimes so demanding that he and his disciples had no time to rest, or even to eat. Psyche's ministry, too, is physically demanding; she grows paler and paler, and "[h]er walk [becomes] a stagger" (*TWHF*, 32). Her willingness to sacrifice herself is equaled only by her compassion for the people.

Psyche is like Helen in her great beauty. Psyche had the beauty of Ungit "in mortal shape," just as Helen had the beauty of Aphrodite. "Ah, no wonder," sings the Fox, quoting the *Iliad*, "if the Trojans and the Achaeans suffer long woes for such a woman. Terribly does she resemble an undying spirit" (*TWHF*, 33). Just as Helen's presence in Troy brought on a twenty-two-year war, so Psyche's presence will bring trouble to Glome.

Psyche is Christ-like, not a symbol for Christ, just as she is Helen-like, and not a symbol for Helen. To say that Psyche is "a Christ figure" is a subtle distortion of the text. As Lewis said in his letter to Clyde Kilby, "She is in some ways like Christ not because she is a symbol of Him but because every good man or woman is like Christ. What else could they be like?" (*Let*, 462). Christian tradition describes Jesus as perfect Man, and Orual describes Psyche as a perfect human being, in language that could be applied to Jesus in character and Helen in physical beauty: "[S]he was ... what every woman, or even every thing, ought to have been and meant to be, but had missed by some trip of chance" (*TWHF*, 22).[1] Spiritual beauty and physical

---

1. Compare what Lewis says in *MC*: "If we let him ... [Christ] will make the feeblest and filthiest of us into a god or goddess, dazzling, radiant, immortal creature" (175).

beauty coalesce in one image: Orual says, "I remember her going out, slim and straight as a sceptre, out of the darkness and cool of the hall into the hot, pestilential glare of that day" (*TWHF*, 32).

C. Love—Several Kinds

Chapter 3 provides examples of several different kinds and degrees of love. The first is Redival's flirtation with Tarin, an officer of the guard. It is nothing more than normal sexual interest, but Orual introduces it, oddly, with the words, "It was Redival who ended the good time" (*TWHF*, 25). She blames her giddy sister for the lessening of her joy in Psyche, because Redival's presence hinders the cozy, exclusive friendship she has enjoyed with Psyche and the Fox.

Orual's love for Psyche is not only exclusive but protective. When Redival hits her half-sister, Orual goes into a blind rage, bloodying Redival's face and choking her. As Psyche's foster mother, Orual is expressing mother-love out of control, the dark side of an emotion we share with the animals. Her love for Psyche also intensifies her fear of Ungit and the Old Priest who is supposed to know Ungit's mind. Redival's veiled threat to tell the priest how the people worship Psyche makes Orual perfectly willing to give Redival a necklace she craves. Certainly Orual's love for Psyche is possessive; does she also worship Psyche? Perhaps she does in a sense, for Lewis says "the deep, narrow devotion" of mother-love can become idolatry (*FL*, 18).

However, lest our understanding of nurturing, possessive love become too simplistic, Lewis shows us that Psyche's love of the Fox is also intense and possessive. When he came down with the fever, Psyche nursed him, even though she had been forbidden to risk her life for a slave. Orual recollects, "She would fight, yes, and bite, any who stood between her and his door" (*TWHF*, 30).

The difference between Psyche's love and Orual's is that Psyche's love includes compassion, a compassion broad enough to encompass all the needy people of Glome. She also feels a royal obligation: "They are our people" (*TWHF*, 30). For British readers, the situation is reminiscent of Wat Tyler's Rebellion in 1381, when the boy-king Richard II was sent out to speak to and calm the mob. King Trom, of course, feels no such compassion or royal obligation, and no love for Psyche. He exposes Psyche to the dangers of the crowd to prevent a rebellion in which he might lose his power or even his life. Orual protests, "It will kill her," but the king merely answers, "They'll kill us all if she stops" (*TWHF*, 32). He is willing for Psyche to die if he is saved.

D. Faith: Spiritual Healing or Superstition?

By allowing Orual to blame Redival for "the bad times," Lewis conceals, for the time being, the depth of the philosophic question he is raising. Are Glome's troubles and Psyche's apparent power to heal entirely the result of natural causes, as the Fox says, or are some things caused by the gods? It is important for Orual's complaint against the gods that the issue be raised but not resolved, and Orual's seemingly straightforward, definite remark attributing the kingdom's ills to Redival subtly prevents resolution.

In describing her radio drama, *The Man Born to Be King*, in which she treated the life of Jesus historically rather than mythically, Dorothy L. Sayers remarked that in some things the ancients' thought was quite different from that of moderns, but in other respects it was the same.[2] Today the scientific, experimental method has given doctors great power over illness, but many people still seek cures through prayer and other nonmedical means. And frequently the efficacy of these alternative approaches is validated experimentally. Of course, it is not necessary to believe that nonmedical healing is spiritual or divine. The Fox, who does not admit the existence of supernatural causes or events, says that Psyche's touch may have healed him. He says, "It might be in accordance with nature that some hands can heal" (*TWHF*, 31).

Orual, thinking not of the Fox's recovery, but of the crowds who pressed Psyche for healing, sees that no cause-effect relationship can be established: "Only the gods know if those who recovered were those whom Psyche had touched, and gods do not tell" (*TWHF*, 33). She fears most a chain of natural causes: Batta, by gossiping about the Fox's recovery, and Redival, with her many trips to the temple, may draw the attention of the Old Priest, who will punish

2. Dorothy L. Sayers, *The Man Born to Be King*, 8.

Psyche in the name of Ungit. But Orual equally fears the supernatural: Ungit may become offended by the people's worship of Psyche and harm her. The Fox makes fun of what he regards as Orual's superstitious fear, but Orual knows that "it is not good to talk that way about Ungit" (*TWHF*, 24). Thus the Fox and Orual struggle with natural versus divine causation, just as modern people do. Lewis, like Sayers, is treating his subject realistically rather than mythically.

Lewis's own position was that the Scriptures affirm spiritual healing, but any particular instance of it might be due to chance or fraud. His open-mindedness on such matters was balanced by his insistence that one should focus on practical duties instead of trying to solve abstract theological questions. About five years before the writing of *Till We Have Faces*, he wrote to one inquirer, "[M]y own mind is v. far from clear" on the boundaries between "faith and superstition" and urged the person to seek information from a professional theologian, "if it is a *practical* problem for you." To another he wrote, "On the whole my attitude wd be that any claim *may* be true, and that it is not my duty to decide if it is" (*Let*, 401, emphasis added; *Let*, 402, emphasis in original).

Chapter 4. Psyche the Accursed

A. Art of Story: Alien Shadows

Chapter 4 is a transition leading up to the confrontation with the Old Priest in chapter 5. An important image expressing the transition occurs while Orual, worried because Psyche has gone out into the street alone, waits with the anxiety of a mother for her to come home. She watches the sun move and the shadows of the pillars change position. They look alien to her, their movement a visual expression of her fear that her world is changing (*TWHF*, 38). The chapter consists of three scenes and a summary of worsening conditions in Glome, leading up to the arrival of the Old Priest.

The first scene is the protest and near-riot in front of the palace; it shows the reader how precarious the king's position has become. He can respond to the jeer, "Barren king makes barren land" only by having the speaker killed. The second is Orual's conversation with Batta and Redival in which Orual is frightened to learn that Psyche has left the palace alone.

Both of these lead up to the central scene, in which Psyche reveals that people are calling her "the Accursed." The scene's tension peaks when Orual furiously threatens to get the king to punish the people who have insulted Psyche. She does not realize, or has forgotten, that the earlier confrontation before the palace door demonstrated the king's weakness and inability to punish people. Psyche proposes that the two of them have supper together and be happy for the time being. Her words remind one of Jesus' saying, "With

See *TWHF*, pp. 35–43.

desire I have desired to eat this passover with you" (Luke 22:15) and provide a subtle hint of what is to come.

B. Context: The Holy Smell ("The Holy," 168)

When the Old Priest enters the Pillar Room, the formal hall of justice in the castle, he brings with him "the Ungit smell," and Orual says the room "became very holy" (*TWHF*, 43). What Orual means by "holy" is the same as the word *numen* coined (or, more accurately, adopted from Latin and applied in a new way) by Rudolf Otto.

Otto uses *numen* to refer to people's awareness of a presence that is either far above or far below conscious reason. It has nothing to do with moral purity, or love, or any of the qualities we naturally attribute to God. It is the unknowable, the uncanny, the otherworldly, and we respond to it with a shudder. Otto emphasizes the numinous to counterbalance what he sees as twentieth-century Christianity's overemphasis of a concept of God that is primarily intellectual, abstract, and focused on morality. He asks people not to try to cut God down to our size, not to "sanitize" God.

Certainly Orual's childhood experience of divinity is not sanitized by rationality, or even by soap. She remembers that she was afraid of the priest of Ungit because of "the holiness of the smell that hung about him—a temple-smell of blood (mostly pigeons' blood, but he had sacrificed men, too) and burnt fat and singed hair and wine and stale incense" (*TWHF*, 11). When, at the conclusion of chapter 4, the Old Priest comes to the palace, Orual reacts to "the smell of old age, and the smell of the oils and essences they put on those girls, and the Ungit smell. . . . It became very holy" (*TWHF*, 43).[1]

C. Love: Psyche Growing Up

When Psyche comes home from visiting her old nurse, she is tired and frightened. She had gone innocently, to offer her healing touch, but the people called her "the Accursed" and threw stones at

---

1. Lewis himself was very sensitive to smells. In discussing how he got his ideas, he spoke of seeing mental pictures that had "a common flavour, almost a common smell" (*OOW*, 32).

her. She needs comfort. The picture of Psyche beside Orual, hiding
her head on her sister/foster mother's knees, is a visual expression
of need-love as described in Lewis's *Four Loves*. But she is not a little
girl anymore, and she no longer looks to Orual for guidance. When
Orual says that Psyche "had done very wrong," she "neither accepted the rebuke like a child nor defended herself like a child, but
looked at me [Orual] with a grave quietness, almost as if she were
older than I." And Orual adds, "It gave me a pang at the heart"
(*TWHF*, 39).

D. Faith: The Reproaches

Lewis's point that every good person is like Christ includes a call
to suffering. Just as the multitudes followed Jesus, begging to be
healed, and then called for him to be crucified, so also those who
"were worshipping [Psyche] not six days ago" (*TWHF*, 37) avoid
her and even throw stones at her. Psyche's question to Orual, "What
did I do to them?" suggests the Reproaches from the traditional
Good Friday liturgy: "O my people, what have I done unto thee? or
wherein have I wearied thee? answer unto me."[2] The question is
repeated over and over, and in each case the answer is one of Christ's
mercies to his people. The devotion is an expansion of Micah 6:3–4,
in which the answer is, "For I brought thee up out of the land of
Egypt," etc. Thus Orual's words, "You healed them, and blessed
them, and took their filthy disease upon yourself" (*TWHF*, 39) suggest the liturgical replies.

Although the Reproaches were not much used by the Church of
England in his time, Lewis would almost certainly have known about
them, for he had written a definitive study of English literature of
the sixteenth century, a time when much poetry was based on de-
votional exercises. In any case, he would have known the passage
in Micah. It might be argued that the liturgical echo leads us to a
mythic rather than a realistic reading of the novel. This is cogent,
but in their own way the Reproaches reflect everyday life, in which
anger and cruelty are often the response to goodness.

2. The text of the Reproaches is found in *The Annotated Book of Common
Prayer...of the Church of England*, 286, as part of a discussion of ancient customs in relation to the Reformation.

Chapter 5. The Condemnation of Psyche

A. The Art of Story: The Trial

The author's task in this chapter is to combine the mythic, traditional story of Aphrodite's anger toward Psyche with the realism of early twentieth-century anthropology about sacrifice in a primitive society. Lewis is faced with what could be a block of dreary explanation; however, he presents the necessary background in the course of a struggle between the Old Priest and the Fox for the mind of the king. The Old Priest lays out the evidence that Ungit is offended by the presence of the Accursed in Glome. Granted his premises, his argument is reasonable. The Fox, fighting for Psyche's life, argues that the Old Priest's explanation is illogical and self-contradictory.

The king is not really responsive to either of them; he is not interested in theology, but in his own survival. When the Old Priest tells him that the Accursed One is in the royal palace, he is angry and frightened until he learns that the victim is Psyche, not he. Likewise, Orual is not interested in the theological battle, but rather in the fate of her beloved Psyche. She clings to her father's knees, begging him to spare the girl. King Trom responds with blows and kicks. His youngest daughter's fate is sealed.

B. Context: Sacrifices and Offerings
("Pagan Religion," 204; and "The Holy," 168)

When an ordinary sacrifice was performed, an animal would be dedicated to the god, killed, and then butchered. The blood was

See *TWHF,* pp. 44–56.

poured out on the altar, the god's portion (usually skin, bones and fat) burned, and the rest used for a sacred banquet, a fellowship between god and mortals. C. S. Lewis apparently meditated repeatedly on sacrificial customs, for he believed that the blood sacrifices of both pagan and Jewish religion prepared for the coming of Christ. In "A Cliché Came out of Its Cage," first published in 1950 (before the writing of *Till We Have Faces*), he responds to the suggestion that our world is lapsing into paganism with "O bright / Vision!" (*Poems*, 3).[1] He is implying, perhaps, that just as ancient paganism prepared for the Messiah, so a lapse into paganism would give modern Christendom a new start. In *Reflections on the Psalms*, published in 1958, he writes, "Every temple in the world, the elegant Parthenon at Athens and the holy Temple at Jerusalem, was a sacred slaughterhouse," and, he continues, "If temples smelled of blood, they also smelled of roast meat; they struck a festive and homely note, as well as a sacred" and adds that the sacrifice was a celebration in which "God gave himself to men" (*Refl*, 93, 45).

But the Great Offering described by the Old Priest is quite different from ordinary celebrations. It is a propitiatory sacrifice, offered to appease the god's anger and to cleanse the people of wrongdoing. The sacrificial victim is tabu (or, as the Old Priest says, accursed). If the victim were an animal, it would not be eaten, but burned completely—i.e., offered as a holocaust.[2] The seriousness of the offense is measured by the fact that the sacrifice must be human. In backward, benighted Glome, human sacrifice is still practiced, even in the Hellenistic age.

In both Jewish and pagan traditions, there was a memory of human sacrifice, but it was considered horrible. Thus Abraham's intention to sacrifice Isaac was prevented by the Lord's messenger. An actual human sacrifice is recorded in the book of Judges, in which Jephthah sacrificed his daughter, but the author is careful to record

---

1. "Cliché" was published in *Nine: A Magazine of Poetry and Criticism* 2 (May 1950): 114. According to Hooper, Lewis wrote his prose works in a single draft but worked and reworked his poems. See *Companion*, 174–75.

2. This is a simplification of both Greek and Hebrew customs, but it highlights the point Lewis is making in chapter 5. See also Vergilius Ferm, *An Encyclopedia of Religion*, 681; and J. R. Dummelow, *A Commentary on the Holy Bible*, 87–90. These older sources are closer to what would have been familiar to Lewis. A useful modern source is Walter A. Elwell, *Concise Evangelical Dictionary of Theology*, 352–55.

that he was really an outsider and that it happened in a time of disorder, when "there was no king in Israel: every man did that which was right in his own eyes" (Judges 21:25). Lewis notes that the pre-Exilic Jews were tempted to sacrifice babies to Moloch "in times of terror" but were usually conscious that the Torah set forth a higher standard of morality than that of the "nations" (*Refl*, 63, 54).

In Greek and Roman literature, human sacrifice "occurred only in myth and scandalous story."[3] For example, Iphigenia's death at the hands of her father was a consequence of the disordered love that led to the Trojan War. Another example is the sacrifice of Psyche in the original story as told by Apuleius. He relates the event but emphasizes that it is a "Milesian tale" (i.e., a voluptuous or scandalous romance).

Since Jesus also lived during the Hellenistic period, presumably human sacrifice was no longer practiced; yet the New Testament authors refer to his death as a sacrifice, and the language is too familiar to shock twentieth-century readers. Lewis describes Psyche's sacrifice in language that echoes Christianity but is just different enough to be troubling. The Old Priest speaks of the Holy Tree, just as the cross is sometimes called "the tree." "The Brute's Supper" parallels "the Lord's Supper." The paradox of the god's identity— the Brute is Ungit herself, Ungit's son, or the god of the mountain— hints at the Christian mystery of the Trinity. The marriage of man or woman to the god recalls the language of mystics through the centuries. The purpose of using language in this way is not to assert that Psyche symbolizes Christ but simply to startle the reader, as Lewis did in such apologetic works as *Mere Christianity*, and also, by yoking two universes of religious discourse, to increase one's imaginative grasp of the fear of the Holy.

C. Love: The Goddess and the Shadowbrute
("The New Psychology," 196; "Pagan Religion," 204)

About Ungit and her son the Old Priest says, "nothing that is said clearly can be said truly about [the gods]" (*TWHF*, 50). Certainly

3. *OCD* 3, s.v. "Sacrifice, Greek." *OCD* 1, s.v. "Sacrifice," mentions that the Athenians "felt ashamed of the sacrifice of Persian prisoners before the battle of Salamis."

this is true of the human experience of love as imaged in Aphrodite and Cupid. Insofar as the following discussion is clear, it will not be the truth, for Lewis is drawing on complex mythic material, and he hints at more than can be put into words.

The Fox calls Ungit the Glomish Aphrodite, but she is not the classical goddess of love. She is a fertility goddess, not a goddess of sexual pleasure. The primitive society of Glome is interested in survival—that enough plants and animals grow and enough children are born to sustain the tribe. The fertility required for survival involves sexual attraction; thus, Eros is the son of Aphrodite. However, he is not a god of sex but of being in love. Over the time between Homer and Lewis, there developed a large body of literature dealing with people's perceptions of the relationships between sex and being in love, between physical fruitfulness and spiritual growth. If the son of Ungit is the Glomish Eros, he should be the god of transcendent desire—the Dantean emotion praised by Lewis's friend Charles Williams and allegorized by his beloved Renaissance poet Edmund Spenser. It is the desire that begins, says Lewis, as "a delighted pre-occupation with the Beloved" (FL, 142, 133). Instead, Ungit's son is introduced as the Shadowbrute. What, then, is the relationship between the deities of Glome and the classical tradition?

Throughout book 1, our information about the gods comes only from Orual, the unreliable narrator. In book 2, however, the Fox says that everyone, "even Psyche," is "born into the house of Ungit" (TWHF, 301). Perhaps he is saying that everyone is subject to the forces of Nature, and also to the workings of human nature, for Lewis understands the Greek gods as "products of the total system of things" (Mir, 13).

Renaissance authors such as Spenser made much of the concupiscible passions, the motivations of love that are necessary to survival in humans and animals alike. They also recognized the irascible passions, motivations of anger. These too are necessary, for the irascible passions give animal or human the will to fight for survival and to endure hardship. In this respect Ungit represents something that is morally neutral, although humans (but not animals) are obligated to govern these passions by reason. That is what the Fox attempts to practice in his life.

But Lewis knew by experience that the concupiscible passions and their manifestations in affection, erotic love, and friendship cannot always be controlled by reason, for as Jung said, there is an "abyss of darkness in human nature." Thus, Lewis personifies the abyss of darkness and the terror of it as Ungit's son, the Shadow-brute. In the Shadowbrute he connects the Renaissance psychology of love with Carl Jung's concept of the shadow. Jung defines the shadow as "the thing a person has no wish to be."[4]

Renaissance and Jungian psychology can also be reconciled with Christianity. For example, a Christian monk who is also a Jungian explains the passions and the shadow in this way: The shadow carries the "disagreeable and ruthless element in myself," the "rejected bad qualities" that otherwise we would recognize as our own, the shortcomings that corrupt and taint all our loves. Our attempts to escape facing up to our shadow bring down God's wrath, which is not anger, but "unrelenting opposition" to whatever damages us.[5] Orual's love for Psyche does not appear tainted at this point, but as the Old Priest insists, the Shadowbrute cannot be ignored. Jungians agree. The introduction of the Shadowbrute here illuminates Orual's opening assertion that the god of the Grey Mountain, the son of Ungit, "hates me" (*TWHF*, 4) and also looks forward to her encounter with the shadow side of her nature when she feels the god's wrath, but finds "no anger . . . in his face [or] voice" (TWHF, 173).

D. Faith: The Old Priest
("Pagan Religion," 204; "Stoicism," 214; "James," 175)

The confrontation of the Old Priest's belief in Ungit with the Stoicism of the Fox invites Lewis's readers to consider the difference between superstition and strong conviction. To the Fox, the Old Priest's faith is superstition, but Orual sees that there is something more in his words and behavior. His knowledge of deity is based on sixty-three years of dealing with Ungit. His experience of daily sacrifice and worship is quite different from the Fox's abstract meditations on the Divine Nature.

---

4. Andrew Samuels, et al., *A Critical Dictionary of Jungian Analysis,* 138–39, citing Carl Jung, *Collected Works* 16, para. 470, hereinafter *CW.*
5. Christopher Bryant, *Jung and the Christian Way,* 75–76; *Depth Psychology and Religious Belief,* 38.

The Old Priest also knows how Ungit, who lives in the temple, is related to the Shadowbrute, the god of the holy mountain, and why the sacrifice must be made to the Brute. But the most important thing he knows is that the gods are inscrutable, nonrational, beyond ordinary experience; the gods are ineffable, "and nothing that is said clearly can be said truly about them" (*TWHF*, 50). To all the Fox's objections that the Old Priest's faith is self-contradictory and illogical, the priest replies only, "It is a mystery." What he calls a mystery, the Fox calls superstitious nonsense, rejecting not only the Old Priest's concept of Ungit, but also the Olympian gods of Homer and the other Greek poets. The poetry is beautiful, but the stories are not true.

As Orual listens, she loses hope. The Fox's enlightened logic seems thin and weak, for the room has become filled with "the holiness and horror of divine things" (*TWHF*, 49). Furthermore, the Old Priest counters with a realistic assessment of the power of religious belief. The people will fear the Shadow; they will mob the palace and burn it down; nobody, not even the priest of Ungit himself, can stop them. Religion's power does not depend on "Greek wisdom" (i.e., reason and logic), nor can those who remain on the level of naturalistic explanations grasp holy mysteries.[6] To get in touch with divine power, there must be sacrifice, a depth of seriousness expressed in the spilling of blood. It is sacrifice, not Greek wisdom, that brings the rain and makes food grow. He taunts the Fox for having surrendered to slavery instead of fighting to the death as a free man.

He then proves the depth of his own conviction by remaining still when King Trom thrusts his dagger through his clothes and into his skin. He is indifferent to death because he is wholly Ungit's servant, wholly obedient to her will, and he has faith that her will cannot be circumvented. Orual, watching, knows and fears: "The Fox had taught me to think—at any rate to speak—of the Priest as of a mere schemer [who made Ungit say] whatever might most increase his own power.... I saw it was not so. He was sure of Ungit" (*TWHF*, 54). The offhand phrase, "to think—at any rate to speak—" is very revealing. Up to this point Orual's skepticism concerning Ungit is a surface conviction, adopted to please her teacher. Now

---

6. Cf. the necessity of blood sacrifice as announced by the Old Priest with 1 Cor. 1:18–25.

the Old Priest's conviction, expressed in his behavior, makes her aware of the numinous in a new way. The Fox's skepticism is an inadequate refuge from the overwhelming horror of the Holy.

In Glome there are only two possibilities: superstitious belief in the personal goddess who demands blood or rational belief in the impersonal Divine Nature that does not give one the courage to die. The attitude of contemporary Christians perhaps falls somewhere between. They may agree with the Old Priest that faith gives them "life and strength, not knowledge and words" (*TWHF*, 50); however, they are also aware that it is our rational approach to nature, not sacrifice, that enables us to predict the weather, to grow larger crops than Hellenistic farmers could dream of, and to manipulate the processes of human fertility. Lewis leaves Orual caught in the dilemma, as indeed he must, for she lives in the Hellenistic age.

Chapter 6. Fighting for Psyche

A. The Art of Story: Ordinary Violence

The fight to save Psyche falls into three stages:

1. The Fox urges political finagling, even to the point of bargaining away the kingdom.

2. Orual tries to shame the king with "[hiding] behind a girl" (*TWHF*, 60).

3. Orual begs to take Psyche's place, but the king shows her that her ugliness makes her unworthy to be the Great Offering.

Defeated in her fight to save Psyche, Orual goes to the prison room and asks to see her beloved sister. When Bardia refuses, she tries to get her way by violence. Untrained girl that she is, she obtains a sword and tries to fight Bardia. Deeply moved by her courage, he takes the risk of disobeying the king's orders and lets Orual into the prison room.

Chapters 5 and 6 contrast two kinds of force that confound human existence—the transcendent and the ordinary. In chapter 5, Orual felt "[t]he holiness and horror of divine things" (*TWHF*, 49). The Old Priest dominated the king by means of his ceremonial garb, his faith in Ungit, his strength in weakness, and his prophetic blindness, with which he caused the presence of divine power to be felt. When he speaks of mythic things, Glome becomes the locus of tragedy. In chapter 6, Lewis shows the situation's ordinary side. Instead of the king's monstrous anger, there is his shamefaced suggestion that Orual treat her bruises with raw meat. Instead of the Old Priest's

See *TWHF*, pp. 57–66.

solemnity, there is the Fox's cleverness and Redival's sniveling fear. When Orual, in her grief, wishes that Bardia had killed her, saying, "I'd be out of my misery now," he matter-of-factly replies, "You'd be dying, not dead. It's only in tales that a man dies the moment the steel's gone in and come out" (TWHF, 65). The situation is merely sad, not mythically tragic.

Part of the contrast between the two chapters is due to the difference in rhythm. Chapter 5 begins with the Old Priest's entrance and works steadily to a climax. Chapter 6 is a series of conversations between different people, interrupted by relatively long passages of description: of the great mirror, the servants' behavior, Redival's personality, the layout of the palace, of how Orual chose the sword. These interruptions slow down the rhythm of the chapter, turning the narrative into an everyday experience of misery rather than storybook tragedy.

B. Context: Psyche Like Iphigenia

The sacrifice of Psyche raises the issue of humanity's relationship to deity within the context of disordered love. The king's remark that the Greeks also sometimes sacrificed daughters enhances the realism of Lewis's historical novel by connecting it with actual Greek literature. It also reminds the reader again of the Trojan War and the whole constellation of ideas surrounding that primary example of disordered love. Agamemnon sacrificed his daughter in order to make the winds blow favorably so that he and his men could join the war in Troy. It was the beginning of the curse on his house, which worked out as the Fox says.[1] Perhaps it is not too much to suggest that when one is pursuing a purpose dictated by disordered love, as Agamemnon was, it is impossible to carry out divine purposes. For the same reason, King Trom is unable to have any insight into the Old Priest's commitment to Ungit. He merely gibes, "That's just like the gods.... Drive you to do a thing and then punish you for doing it" (TWHF, 58).

1. It is the beginning of the curse with respect to the Trojan War and its consequences. In a larger sense, the House of Atreus had been cursed since Atreus caused his brother Thyestes to commit cannibalism. The enmity between those two was also caused by disordered love. See OCD 3, s.v. "Atreus."

C. Love: Everyday Love

In chapter 5, the Old Priest's knowledge of Ungit and the Shadow-brute brings focus to the symbolic, deeply psychological aspect of love. In chapter 6, the same kinds of love are expressed, but in everyday, nonmythic behaviors. For example, Orual offers herself as a sacrifice in place of Psyche. In this she is like an ordinary mother, for she longs to take on her child's suffering. I have heard a mother standing by her child's bed in the hospital say, "If only I could be sick instead of him." And the Fox, like an ordinary father, says, "But, Master, I'd lose not only my throne but my life to save the Princess, if I were a king and father" (*TWHF*, 59).

Bardia, too, says "I'd give my own life for the girl in there, if it would do any good" (*TWHF*, 65). He loves both Orual and Psyche for their good qualities—one is brave, the other beautiful—but also because of long acquaintance, the *storge* (affection) of Lewis's *Four Loves* (53–83). Bardia remembers when Psyche was little and sat on his lap. At first, he can express his love only through homely kindness, by standing guard over Psyche himself. But then he does actually risk his life: he breaks military discipline and allows Orual to visit Psyche against strict orders to the contrary. In this primitive society, and with an angry goddess involved, he could easily face execution for his disobedience.

King Trom, in contrast to Orual, Bardia, and the Fox, shows neither the love of a parent nor the courage of a soldier. In chapter 5, he shows himself relieved, even happy, when he learns that Psyche is to die instead of himself. In chapter 6 he even claims that his is the greatest grief because Psyche belongs to him: "She's mine, fruit of my own body. My loss" (*TWHF*, 60). He suspects that Orual's love for Psyche springs from some selfish motive, for no ugly woman could possibly love a pretty half-sister so deeply. At this point it is unclear whether he is simply judging Orual in terms of his own selfishness, or if Lewis is foreshadowing some quality of Orual's love that will be revealed later.

Whether or not Orual is like her father, Redival certainly is. Her first concern is that she will not suffer. She is a little less selfish than he; at least she says, "Oh, poor Psyche!" Apparently she intended only to get Psyche into trouble, not to bring about her death. Orual feels that Redival's emotions are "not wholly feigned," but certainly shallow (*TWHF*, 62, 63).

D. Faith: Psyche Like Christ ("Myth," 183)

Lewis repeatedly asserted that the pre-Christian myths about gods taking on human form were precursors to the Incarnation, and contrariwise, that the story of Jesus summarized and validated the stories about pagan gods: "Myth became fact."[2] Christ died and then lived again like Bacchus the wine god; he was the light of the world like Apollo the sun god, and a wise healer like Aesculapius the son of Apollo (or indeed Apollo himself). Jesus as myth-become-fact also validated human life—its joys and loves, its frustrations and vulnerabilities, its nobility. Living in a time before the Incarnation, Orual, the Fox, and Bardia all express willingness to give their own lives to save Psyche, just as Jesus gave his life for his friends.

Two speeches vividly make the point. First, the king says, "It's only sense that one should die for many. It happens in every battle" (*TWHF*, 61), echoing the speech of Caiaphas the high priest (John 11:49). Then Bardia says, "I wonder do the gods know what it feels like to be a man" (*TWHF*, 66). His words imply that the Immortals can afford to be detached, even cruel; but God as myth-become-fact does know what it is to be human, to love one's friends and want to protect them.

2. This is the title of Lewis's essay in *World Dominion* 22 (Sept.–Oct. 1944): 267–70. Rpt. *GID*, 63–67.

Chapter 7. The Night
before the Offering

A. The Art of Story: The "Child's" Goodbye

Throughout the chapter, Psyche's broad, philosophic speculations are set beside Orual's narrow, highly focused love for her.
Orual has always acted as Psyche's mother; she comes to cuddle
and comfort her sister, but finds that her "child" is the strong one.
The challenge for Lewis as an artist is to let Orual tell the story in
her own words while planting hints that she does not understand
her own feelings and motives.

During their conversation the two sisters sit, comforting one
another by turns. The decisive point comes when Psyche kisses
Orual's hands, flings them away from her, and stands up. In a film,
this action would make a meaningful close-up. Psyche expresses
affection by kissing Orual's hands, but then she frees herself from
them. She is ready to stand on her own. Orual realizes that Psyche
is now "out of my reach, in some place of her own" (*TWHF*, 74).

B. Context: Like Socrates and Jesus ("Plato," 210)

In Lewis's time, Socrates and Jesus were the most frequently cited
examples of people who suffered unjustly for their nobility. Both
were put to death for supposedly false teachings. Socrates was accused of corrupting the youth, teaching them to scorn conventional
wisdom about the gods. Jesus was accused of stirring up the crowds

See *TWHF*, pp. 67–76.

and blaspheming by calling himself the Son of God. Both Jesus and Socrates accepted their deaths with patience, and so did Psyche. In the Tower Room, the night before her sacrifice, Psyche resembles first one, then the other.

Like Socrates the noble pagan, Psyche is the image of dignity, "tall and queenly and still." Like him, she is concerned with seemly behavior. Socrates directed his friends to make sure the cock he had promised to Aesculapius was duly offered. Psyche directs Orual in the disposal of her effects, and tells her to say whatever is proper to the king, for "[o]ne would not seem rude or ignorant at the last." Socrates spends the day talking of philosophy; Orual records—with anger—that Psyche "spoke so steadily and thoughtfully, as if we had been disputing with the Fox" (*TWHF*, 68, 69, 71).

Some of Psyche's words parallel those of Jesus. She says, "How can I be the ransom for all Glome unless I die?" (*TWHF*, 72), just as Jesus said that a seed must fall into the earth if it is to produce fruit (John 12:24). Jesus forgave those who crucified him, saying, "Father, forgive them; for they know not what they do" (Luke 23:34, RSV). Psyche forgives Redival's betrayal, saying, "She also does what she doesn't know" (*TWHF*, 69).

Like both Socrates and Jesus, Psyche suggests that there is something beyond death. She says "other Greek masters," non-Stoics, teach "that death opens a door out of a little, dark room... into a great, real place where the true sun shines" (*TWHF*, 73). This can be seen as a veiled reference both to the *Phaedo* and to Jesus' words about the many rooms in his Father's house.

Lewis's use of the familiar comparison between Socrates and Jesus and applying the features of both to Psyche is not done to establish Psyche as a "Christ figure" in a literary structure. *Till We Have Faces* is a realistic novel; what happened to Socrates, Jesus, and Psyche is simply what happens to good people in the real world, a place where there is no Aslan, no Merlin, to rescue them. In *Reflections on the Psalms,* Lewis cites a passage in *The Republic,* in which Plato imagines "a perfectly righteous man treated by all around him as a monster of wickedness" who remains perfectly righteous "while he is bound, scourged, and finally impaled." This is not prophecy and not coincidence, says Lewis, but simply an insight into the way the world is. Both Socrates and Jesus were executed for the same reason: "because goodness is what it is, and because the fallen world

is what it is" (*Refl*, 104–5). The vivid, unsettling resemblance between Psyche and Christ is not a mere trick of literary technique,
but the expression of fundamental truth as Lewis sees it.

C. Love: Mother and Child

In her first ecstatic days of loving Psyche, Orual says, "I wanted
to be a wife so that I could have been her real mother" (*TWHF*, 23).
Mothering Psyche is the only fulfillment available to Orual, for she
will never be a wife. And her motherly love is flawed. Most mothers reconcile themselves to the reality of losing their children as
they become adults. As Psyche says, even if she had not been the
Great Offering, she would have been "given to some king in the
end" (*TWHF*, 73); she would have left Glome; she would have lost
Orual and the Fox and been lost to them. But Orual's love for Psyche is disordered; it arises from the deficiency in her own life as an
ugly woman. In her passionate devotion to the only beauty her life
has ever held, she is not ready to free Psyche to be an adult.

Throughout the chapter, Psyche shows herself to be different from
the way Orual wants her to be. First, she calls Orual "Sister" instead
of "Maia" (which means "mother"). Then Psyche pets and comforts
Orual, making her "the child and the victim" instead of letting Orual
be the comforter. When she does shift to calling Orual "Maia," it is
because "she was so quick and tender" that she knew Orual was
disappointed by her grown-up behavior. As Orual says, "It was so
unlike the sort of love that used to be between us in our happy
times" (*TWHF*, 67).

Worst of all, Psyche wastes time by insisting that Orual tell her
about the beating. Instead of childish pity, she responds to the story
by advising Orual to follow the Stoic teachings of the Fox. She says,
"We have been three loving friends" (*TWHF*, 69), implying that she
cares for Orual and the Fox equally.

Thus Psyche's strength is a disappointment to Orual. She is glad
when finally Psyche does weaken, does confess her fear that her
death will be one of slow starvation because there is no Shadowbrute. Now, Orual feels, she has her child back. Throughout their last
evening together, she interprets Psyche's courage as hard-heartedness
and a lack of love for herself. Orual is the center of her own universe, as who is not?

D. Faith: Faith and Doubt
("The New Psychology," 192; "The Holy," 168)

This chapter shows that doubt is not the opposite of faith, but rather its environment. Psyche wavers between steadfast acceptance that her death is somehow marriage to the god and her fear that there is no god. In this she portrays faith as a dynamic balance rather than an absolute dogma. Her questions and answers are ones that people have dealt with over the centuries.

First, is there a God, and if so, is God good? Both Psyche and Orual hark back to the Fox's teaching. The Fox believes that gods like Ungit do not exist. He insists that either there are no gods at all or they rise above the petty jealousies that human myths ascribe to them. Psyche finds light in his teaching, but Orual vehemently denounces it as false comfort. For Orual, the world is worse than the Fox's teaching. She declares that the gods do exist, and that they are "viler than the vilest men." Psyche suggests two other answers; perhaps both the Fox and Orual are wrong. Perhaps the gods are real, but they do not perform the cruelties ascribed to them. Or perhaps "they do these things and the things are not what they seem to be" (TWHF, 71).

For Psyche, both the Fox's philosophy and the Old Priest's faith contain part of the truth. She expresses it in a Jungian image: the world is a city, but it is built on earth. The city is the conscious, reasoning mind; the earth is the subconscious, the source of human creativity and the human experience of God.[1] She seeks the kind of religion that Lewis believed Christianity provides—a combination of rationality and the suprarational sources of creativity (SbJ, 235–36). And despite her doubts, Psyche ends with faith. Her experience of longing, of what Lewis sometimes calls Sehnsucht, calls her to the mountain. It is her home, the source of all beauty, the place of the god of the Grey Mountain who has wooed her all her life. In the final analysis, it is her experience of longing that forms her belief, not reasoning or observable evidence.

---

1. See Bryant, Jung and the Christian Way, esp. p. 48.

Chapter 8. Psyche Is Gone

A. The Art of Story: A Problem in Viewpoint

At the opening of this chapter, Psyche is still in Glome; at the end she is gone. Lewis needs to describe the change quickly and briefly, but he also needs to show how devastating it is to Orual. Both needs are obstructed by his original decision to tell everything from Orual's viewpoint and in her voice. She has promised to "tell all...from the very beginning" (*TWHF*, 3), and in her own mind she has established herself as a very objective, emotionless narrator. Lewis accomplishes the swift change from Psyche here to Psyche gone by allowing Orual to fall ill and to become conscious of Psyche's absence only after many days. Her sickness also shows that the loss of Psyche is more than she can endure. It is the outward expression of her inner grief.

To appreciate what Lewis did, it is useful to again compare it with film. Each choice of medium and viewpoint has its own advantages and disadvantages; with the resources of the camera the artist could make something very different of this chapter. In film it would be relatively simple to express the emotional intensity of the change between Psyche present and Psyche gone by music and picture. Orual's struggle to follow Psyche to the sacrifice, her final look at her beloved "daughter" from the staircase, and her obsessive dreams of Psyche the torturer would all make good images. Music and lighting would briefly express the difference Orual finds when she regains consciousness.

See *TWHF*, pp. 77–87.

However, the print medium is better for presenting the central philosophic and religious problem of the chapter: the fact that the Great Offering seems to have solved Glome's problems. Orual wonders if Ungit is real after all, but the Fox denies that there is any connection between the Great Offering and Glome's recovery. However, he is not comforted by his own philosophy; he and Orual turn to poetry instead. This development is further discussed in sections B and D below.

B. Context: Chance and the Nature of Things

In pointing out that Glome's troubles began to disappear as soon as Psyche was sacrificed, Orual commits the post hoc fallacy of believing that if Y came after X, then X must have caused Y. The Fox replies, "Cursed chance, cursed chance," and adds, "It is these chances that nourish the beliefs of barbarians." Then Orual reminds the Fox, "How often, Grandfather, you have told me there's no such thing as chance" (*TWHF*, 85). He has to admit that she is right. In the Hellenistic period many people had come to worship the goddess Tyche—Fortuna to the Romans—that is, Lady Luck. The Stoics rejected Tyche. They taught that since the Nature of Things is good, nothing can be other than it is. Orual can only conclude that Psyche died for nothing, because prayer and sacrifice cannot change anything.

At this point the Fox recovers his orthodox Stoicism by turning to virtue as the only reality. Life or death, prosperity or adversity, the world's praise or blame—all are matters of indifference. Only virtue is good. Anyone can achieve virtue, for it is a matter of will. Human beings cannot control what happens to them, but they can control their will. Thus the Fox praises Psyche for having lived well and having died with courage and patience. But then "love got the better of his philosophy," and he cries out in pain, "Aiai! Aiai—oh, Psyche, oh, my little one" (*TWHF*, 85).

The next day Orual asks the Fox to recount the tragedies of Iphigenia and Antigone, for she knows that there is comfort in poetry— or as she somewhat cynically describes it, "words coming out of his own mouth" (*TWHF*, 86). Some, if not all, of Lewis's readers would see that Orual and the Fox are like Boethius in mistakenly turning to tragic poetry as an escape from pain and an unsolved philosophical problem.

Boethius (about A.D. 480 to 524) is little known today, but his *Consolation of Philosophy* was a primary text throughout the Middle Ages and Renaissance. Because it was considered necessary to the training of a wise and virtuous king, *The Consolation of Philosophy* was translated into English three times during this period: into Old English at the behest of Alfred the Great, into Middle English by Geoffrey Chaucer, and into Renaissance English by Elizabeth. As an expert in this period, Lewis was thoroughly familiar with it.

The Consolation is based on Boethius's own life story. Everything seemed to be going his way, but then he was framed for a crime and thrown into prison. All his worldly goods and comforts were taken from him, and he knew that sooner or later he would be executed, as he was. The book is a dialog with Philosophy, who comes to him in prison as a beautiful lady. The first thing she does is to wean him from tragic poetry. With her help, Boethius learns what the Fox as a Stoic asserts: that Chance does not exist, because Nature is a seamless web, foreordained.

But with the help of Lady Philosophy, Boethius is able to argue logically that human beings have free will and that God hears and answers prayer without breaking the seamless web.[1] He approaches the contradiction between the "seamless web" and the freedom of human action in terms of God's knowledge. If everything is foreordained, then God must know what will happen beforehand. Since human beings cannot do something that God does not know about, they cannot act freely. But Boethius looks at it this way: Suppose a man is standing on a hill looking at a chariot race on the plain below. He foresees that because of their course and speed, two chariots are bound to collide. But his foreknowledge does not cause the collision; the charioteers are acting freely in driving their vehicles.

Just as the man on the hill can see the whole chariot race at once, God sees the whole history of the universe. To human beings there is past, present, and future, but to God all is present. Human prayers and choices are just one more aspect of the seamless web. We pray

1. Boethius calls the reality behind everything "God" instead of using the Fox's term, "the Divine Nature." He was probably a Christian, but the book is written to show what a person can learn about God through philosophy alone, without revelation.

in the present; God hears and answers in the present, for everything is present to Him.

To solve the problem in this way is, of course, beyond the capacities of Orual and the Fox. But Boethius's argument was very important to Lewis, and he expresses it in his own words on several occasions.[2]

C. Love: A Loving Hatred

Orual's hunger for love cannot be satisfied by any of the people around her. When she regains consciousness, she finds the Fox caring for her, even though he is still weak from his own illness. He was "very loving and tender, . . . and so were [her] women [servants]." She concludes, "I was loved; more than I had thought" (*TWHF*, 82–83).

However, the waking dreams she had during her illness tell another story. In the dreams, Psyche mocks her, leaves her out of games, and even tortures her. Psyche prevents her from having a lover, taking the man from her "on the very threshold of the bridal chamber, or from the very bedside." Significantly, the man looks like either Tarin, Redival's boyfriend, or Bardia, another woman's husband. Through all the dreams Orual holds a "determination to be avenged" (*TWHF*, 81).

When she recovers, she remembers that Psyche is everything to her, although she is not everything to Psyche. She minimizes her resentment by describing it like this: "[I]t hurt me somewhat" that on their last night together Psyche talked "so little of me" and "so much about the god of the Mountain, and the King, and the Fox, and Redival, and even Bardia" (*TWHF*, 82). She describes her feeling accurately but fails to call it "possessiveness" or "jealousy."

D. Faith: Knowing God

The Old Priest and the Fox have different impressions of the divine character. The Old Priest believes that Ungit is personal,

---

2. *ScL*, 127–28; *Mir*, app. B, 174–81; *Let*, Oct. 20, 1952, Aug. 3, 1953; and *LM*, 110.

capable of both anger and response to sacrifice; the Fox believes in an impersonal Divine Nature. How can these two concepts be reconciled, as Lewis believes is done by Christianity?

In "The Efficacy of Prayer," an essay written after *Till We Have Faces*, Lewis says directly what he shows dramatically in the novel. After citing two examples of answers to prayer in his own life he says, "The thing we pray for may happen, but how can you ever know it was not going to happen anyway? Even if the thing were indisputably miraculous, it would not follow that the miracle had occurred because of your prayers. The answer surely is that a compulsive empirical proof such as we have in the sciences can never be attained."[3] He solves the problem by putting it in the context of human relationships. We believe that a person did something in response to our request because we know what that person is like. Or as he says in *Letters to Malcolm*, almost the last thing he ever wrote, the connection between prayer and result cannot be established by experiment. We believe the connection exists "because we have from deep acquaintance a certain impression of [God's] character" (*LM*, 49).

3. First published in *Atlantic Monthly* (Jan. 1959). Rpt. *WLN* (n.d.), 6–7; and *Fern-seed and Elephants* (1975), 97.

Chapter 9. Life without Psyche

A. The Art of Story: Achieving Realism ("Apuleius," 145)

Chapter 9 is a transition between the loss of Psyche in Glome and the reunion with her in the mountain country. There Psyche will tell Orual an incredible story about being married to a god and living in his palace. Lewis's source, the "Cupid and Psyche" segment of *The Golden Ass,* is frankly a fairy story; Apuleius, the author, does not even try to make it realistic. Lewis's narrative method is designed to take the story out of the realm of fantasy and make it sound like history.

One method of creating realistic fiction is to supply exact numbers and times. Thus Lewis shows Orual, the sober, down-to-earth sister, calculating carefully that it will take her sixteen hours to go to the sacrificial tree and return and that she will need warm clothes and food for camping out overnight. Apuleius merely says, "The sisters enquired the situation of the rock where Psyche had been abandoned and hurriedly made their way there."[1]

Both fictional modes account for certain facts before they are needed in the plot. Orual will need to know how to use a sword later on; Lewis plants a plausible explanation here: Bardia taught her in an effort to overcome her depression. It helps, too, if the fact is down-to-earth and dull. Apuleius plants the older sisters' ability to jump off the cliff and float down to Psyche's palace on the West-Wind. The explanation is that Cupid has ordered the West-Wind to

See *TWHF,* pp. 88–101.
1. Apuleius, *The Golden Ass,* 5.7.1.

obey Psyche. Later, when they jump on their own, they fall to their deaths.

Both traditional fantasy and modern realistic fiction use the environment to express moods and suggest meanings beyond physical facts. Significant alternations of light and dark are, in fact, common in all literature; Lewis uses them in chapter 9 and continues the pattern in chapter 10.

The journey starts in a gloom that is "almost as dark as full night." When Orual and Bardia pass the house of Ungit, traveling east, it is still dark, though Orual feels "as if the air were sweeter as we got away from all that holiness" (TWHF, 93, 94). They turn away from the Holy Road and climb a ridge going toward the Holy Mountain. At the top there is sunlight, and Orual is tempted to respond with delight.

When they attain "the last rise before the real Mountain," the sunlight is very strong, but they look down on a "cursed black valley" (TWHF, 97). They approach the Holy Tree gradually. Orual speaks of "the bad part of the Mountain," by which she means "the holy part" and the "gods' country" beyond the sacred tree (TWHF, 100).

Lewis builds up their approach to the "perilous land," "the secret valley of the god," "the small valley bright as a gem" (TWHF, 100–101) by well-chosen sensory images: first the slight dizziness, as though they were walking off into the sky; the visual contrast between the brightness and greenness of this place and the black valley; the sounds, of bees and running water; the smell of the air, and the touch of its warmth. It is an Eden, so hospitable that Orual almost lays aside her veil. They descend to the valley, and there they meet Psyche.

B. Context: Orual the Tragedy Queen

In this chapter Orual first begins to see herself as a tragic heroine. When Stoic philosophy fails to comfort the Fox for the loss of Psyche, Orual distracts him by asking him to recite some tragic poetry, just as Boethius sought consolation in literature when Lady Luck failed him. The poetry suggests to Orual a final act of love toward Psyche—to seek out the bones and bury them properly. She says,

"Grandfather, I have missed being Iphigenia. I can be Antigone" (*TWHF*, 86). Antigone was persecuted—in some versions slain—because she was determined to carry out the burial ritual for her brother against the king's decree. By deciding to bury Psyche's bones, Orual identifies herself with Antigone, assuming the stance of a tragic heroine.

And literature has the same effect on her that it had on Boethius the character in *The Consolation of Philosophy*. It leads her into depression and self-pity. As she and Bardia travel toward the mountain, she deliberately turns away from the beauty of the day, closes herself to the possibility that the universe might be based on joy underneath the grief. She deliberately sulks instead of using the proffered moment of delight as a rest from sorrow, as a means of strength for the ordeal ahead. She struggles to maintain her tragic gloom, telling herself "over like a lesson the infinite reasons [her heart] had not to dance" (*TWHF*, 96).[2]

Certainly Lewis does not support such an attitude. As a survivor of the trenches in World War I and of the Home Guard and food shortages in World War II, he regarded cheerfulness as a religious duty. Human life cannot be secure, he said, but it can be "merry" (*PoP*, 115).

A further insight into Orual's choice of gloominess is found in Lewis's earlier novel *Perelandra*. In it the Un-man, an embodiment of Satan, encourages Tinidril, the yet-unfallen Eve of the planet, to think of herself as a tragic heroine. He believes this mood will make it easier for her to disobey Maleldil (God). Similarly, as *Till We Have Faces* develops, Orual's choice to see herself as a tragedy queen leads her to do much harm, both to herself and Psyche.

C. Love: Bardia's Love for Orual

The previous chapter focused on the Fox's love for Orual; chapter 9 focuses on Bardia. Just as the Fox tried to help Orual by teaching her philosophy and reciting tragic poetry to her, Bardia expresses his love—fatherly, or perhaps brotherly—by teaching her to fight

---

2. Schakel, *Imagination*, 115, sees the lack of dancing in *TWHF* as a reflection of "the joyless and disordered affections of the narrator."

with the sword. He shows her the resources of the human body in enabling one to deal with sorrow, and she learns that sweat is "far better than philosophy, as a cure for ill thoughts" (*TWHF*, 91).

He also volunteers to help her go to the Grey Mountain to give Psyche a decent burial. More precisely, he offers to go to the mountain in Orual's place, to save her from danger. When she insists on going, he simply assumes that he must go with her. Near "the bad part of the Mountain," both of them are afraid, but Bardia first offers to go on alone, and then says firmly, "I'll go where you go, Lady" (*TWHF*, 100). He is as loyal as a beloved dog.

It is too bad that Orual cannot accept the depth and worth of Bardia's disinterested love, his steadfastness toward her. She overhears him say to another soldier, "Why, yes, it's a pity about her face. But she's a brave girl and honest. If a man was blind and she weren't the King's daughter, she'd make him a good wife" (*TWHF*, 92). Orual's reaction is self-pity: this is the only "love-speech" she ever got. Bardia shows true worth in that he perceives her bravery and honesty and loves her despite her ugliness, but Orual does not truly appreciate his goodness.

D. Faith: Ritual without Awe ("The Holy," 168)

On the way to the Grey Mountain, Orual and Bardia pass the temple of Ungit. According to the priests, the house of Ungit either "resembles, or (in a mystery)...really is, the egg from which the whole world was hatched" (*TWHF*, 94). Her description of it would perhaps mean more to well-educated British readers of the fifties than to most readers, British or American, of today. Lewis could expect many readers to know about the Universal Egg from Pliny's *Natural History* and Homer's *Iliad*. In addition, some classics scholars had become what we would call anthropologists, and studies like Frazer's *Golden Bough* would arouse numerous memories and half-memories of ancient religions.[3]

Orual also describes the ritual of spring in which the priest is shut into the temple of Ungit and fights his way out as a symbol of

3. Robert Graves, *The Greek Myths*, 27n, cites Pliny, *Natural History*, 4.35 and 8.67, and Homer, *Iliad*, 20.223.

new birth. The description reminds the classicist of another myth in which Eros, who "set the universe in motion" hatched from the egg, and as readers we remember that the priest wears a bird mask on ritual occasions.[4]

Orual's description of both temple and ritual is flat and factual; there is no sign that she responds to the mystery of creation and re-birth with awe and wonder. She describes the "holy" shape of the temple as "like a huge slug" and presents the priest's symbolic strug-gle to hatch from the egg as merely make-believe (*TWHF*, 94). Her temperament seems to be completely prosaic; she is interested only in the material, the factual, not the possibility that the things visible may be keys to invisible, transcendent realities. Of course, her lack of curiosity and imagination is useful to Lewis the novel writer, for it enables him to dodge the question about whether Ungit's son, the god of the Grey Mountain, is the same as Eros, the son of Aphrodite, and also dodge the question of whether the god is somehow to be identified with the Second Person of the Christian Trinity.

4. Graves, *Greek Myths*, 30.

Chapter 10. Over to the Other Side

A. The Art of Story: Psyche's Story

In this chapter Psyche tells what happened to her and how she survived being sacrificed at the Holy Tree. The artistic problem is to show her as transformed, a goddess, but still the Psyche that Orual has always known.

Part of the process is accomplished in the previous chapter as Orual and Bardia courageously go beyond the Holy Tree to "the edge of the perilous land." There is a certain giddiness, "as if [they] were walking straight into the empty sky" (*TWHF*, 100). Then they come to the slope leading to Psyche's valley. It is a place of flourishing plants, flowing waters, and sweet air. They go down the slope. At the bottom, there is a stream and Psyche is standing on the other side, looking like a goddess in her rags.

Lewis intensifies the emotion of this meeting by setting up an implicit comparison with other literary works. The stream between them and Psyche is a subtle allusion to Dante's meeting with Matilda in *The Divine Comedy*, which occurs in the Garden of Eden. Lewis uses this same allusion in *Perelandra*, in which Ransom first sees and speaks with the Green Lady, the Eve of the planet, across water.[1] Psyche's valley is an Eden, and she is mistress of it. Bardia responds with awe, saying, "This is a very dreadful place" and "It is a goddess." But Orual feels "no holy fear" (*TWHF*, 103, 102); she recog-

See *TWHF*, pp. 102–16.
1. Matilda: Dante, *Purgatorio*, 28.11.34–42 and 33.11.118–19; the Green Lady: *Pere*, 34–35. See Myers, *Context*, 65–66.

nizes Psyche as the one who had been her baby. Indeed, Psyche, even though she has slept with a god, assures Orual, "I'm your own true Psyche still" (*TWHF*, 115). But perhaps Orual dismisses Psyche's transformation too easily, for she does not receive what her younger sister tells her.

B. Context: Pagan Miracles? ("Myth," 183)

The incredible events that Psyche relates may invite us to conclude that the novel is meant as a fantasy after all. However, we will miss the point of *Till We Have Faces* if we do not accept Psyche's story as fact—history—rather than myth or allegory.

It is fact, not in the sense that it actually happened, but that it could have happened. It could have been the sequence of events out of which the original myth arose. Psyche's experiences seem beyond the realm of literal possibility, but as Lewis said in *Miracles*, "I am in no way committed to the assertion that God has never worked miracles through and for Pagans or never permitted created supernatural beings to do so" (*Mir*, 138). He believed that pagan mythology came from many sources: allegory, ritual, the mere fun of telling a good story. But some sources, not excluding the supernatural, were "true history" (*GID*, 132).

Since the story is told from Orual's point of view, there is no need, indeed no way, to be specific about the identity of Psyche's god-lover. He could be one of the kinds of beings described as the "Longaevi" in *The Discarded Image*. Lewis uses this tradition in *That Hideous Strength:* Jane Studdock sees Venus, and Ransom tells her that she has seen the wraith of the planetary being he met in Perelandra. Or Psyche's god-lover might be a heavenly messenger like the ones met by Abraham and others in the Old Testament. These are sometimes referred to as angels and sometimes simply called God after the one they represent. About the pre-Incarnational period Lewis said, "What you get is something coming gradually into focus" (*GID*, 58). Since the events of *Till We Have Faces* occur in this period, we can be sure that Psyche's love somehow represents God Incarnate, who will come into full focus as Jesus of Nazareth. And knowing Lewis's speculations about God's ways with the pagans, we know that we—and Orual—should at least keep an open mind about the factuality of Psyche's story.

C. Love: Mother Love Again

Orual loves Psyche with everything she has to give, but she loves Psyche as Maia, the mother, not as Orual the sister. Throughout Psyche's story of being wedded to the god, Orual wants to make "plans" for getting Psyche back to Glome. Psyche wants only to tell her wonderful story. The two do not engage in conversation; they merely take turns talking.

Orual shows the love of a mother, determined to be with her child at all costs, for she says, "I'd go if the river flowed with fire instead of water." But she thinks of Psyche as a half-grown girl, not a woman. In crossing the stream, she thinks, "She *will be* a stronger woman than ever I was" (*TWHF*, 103; emphasis added). She uses the future tense *will be* even though she sees that she could not get across the river without Psyche's physical support. Because Psyche is just her girl-child, she sees Psyche's offering of food and wine as a childish game of make-believe.

But Psyche refuses to play child to Orual's motherliness. She gently mocks Orual's efforts to plan for her safety, and while acknowledging that Orual reared her well, puts aside her childhood days "with one light kiss" (*TWHF*, 105). Then she takes control of their exchange by beginning to tell what it is like to be the sacrificial victim. Orual is impatient with the story, but she is glad when Psyche says she lost all her childhood longing for the gold-and-amber palace—not because it was childish, but because it was "unnatural and estranging" (*TWHF*, 109). Of course, children's dreams and aspirations often seem that way to parents.

D. Faith: In Another Person, in a Higher Power

1. In Another Person

Out of Psyche's story comes Orual's problem of whether to trust the younger woman. It is a repetition, in different terms, of the question of faith raised in *The Lion, the Witch, and the Wardrobe*. Lucy returns from Narnia with a strange tale about her experiences there. Peter and Susan do not know whether to believe her. Professor

Digby's answer is, "There are only three possibilities. Either your sister is telling lies, or she is mad, or she is telling the truth" (*LWW*, 48). In *Till We Have Faces* Psyche insists that the two of them are standing in full view of her palace, but Orual can see nothing of the sort. What is Orual to do? Is Psyche mad, or lying, or telling the truth?

In the telling of her story, Psyche shows that she is not mad. She distinguishes carefully between the dreamlike state she was feeling when the sacrificial procession left Glome and the clarity of hearing the iron being fastened around her waist. She distinguishes between her childhood fantasy of the gold-and-amber palace on Grey Mountain, which she could not believe no matter how hard she tried, and the reality of the things she never thought of disbelieving—the rain, her glimpse of West-Wind, her invisible servants. She argues logically that the god's palace is not a dream, because it is so completely beyond anything she could imagine.

Furthermore, she shows none of the megalomania of the religious fanatic; instead of thinking herself a goddess, she describes the shame of mortal flesh before supernatural beings. She is not angry or defensive when Orual doubts her but says calmly, "You shall see gods for yourself" (*TWHF*, 111). Her story is detailed, and all the details fit together.

She is obviously not mad, and Orual knows she has been truthful from childhood. Why, then, does Orual not believe her? Perhaps there is a hint in her response at the end of Psyche's story: "If this is all true, I've been wrong all my life. Everything has to be begun over again" (*TWHF*, 115).

2. In a Higher Power

Psyche's dream of the gold-and-amber palace was neither belief nor faith, but imagination. Powerful as it was, it had occupied a shallow place in her personality compared with the faith that she could hold on to, the faith that came from "somewhere deep inside." She says it contained both the abstract, highly moral philosophy of the Fox and the Old Priest's blood-and-earth understanding of sacrifice and that she did not so much hold it as "just let it hold onto [her]" (*TWHF*, 109–10). Lewis here dramatizes his belief that Christianity is the only religion to combine philosophy and the mythic meaning of sacrifice in this way.[2] He states it directly, without drama, in his letter to Kilby: "Psyche is an instance of the [naturally Christian soul] making the best of the Pagan religion she is brought up in and thus being guided . . . towards the true God" (*Let*, 462).

2. *PoP*, 22. See Gilbert Meilander, *The Taste for the Other*, 228n60.

Chapter 11. Mixed Emotions

A. The Art of Story: Physical Struggle, Mental Decision

This chapter presents a response to Psyche's fantastic story—Orual's response, and perhaps the reader's. Why can't Orual see the palace? If *Till We Have Faces* were a fairy tale, an allegorical fantasy, a typical reason might be that she had not plucked the blue flower or said the magic word. But if it is a realistic novel, then the explanation must be realistic also. The realism is especially important in that it maintains the credibility of Psyche, so carefully demonstrated in the previous chapter.

Film could capture, better than the text, the way Orual and Psyche face each other like "two enemies met for a battle to the death," how they stand, "each with eyes fixed on the other in a terrible watchfulness." Orual screams at Psyche with "my father's own fury"; Psyche grabs her hands, trying to make her touch the palace wall; and Orual shakes her sister "as one shakes a child" (*TWHF*, 117, 118). Film could record the "sharp, suspicious" look on Psyche's face as they begin to speak and realize that they are not seeing the same thing.

But film could not record the subtlety of Orual's thought processes—her uncanny fear that the palace is really there, her emotional response to Psyche's efforts to cuddle her, her decision to see Psyche's experience of sexual love as something dirty. And how could film give sufficient importance to her confession, like an adverb modifying the action to come, that she does not really know

See *TWHF*, pp. 117–29.

what she saw and thought? She says, "By remembering it too often I have blurred the memory itself" (*TWHF,* 117). Even a careful reader might well skip over this important sentence.

B. Context: How Dreadful Is This Place ("The Holy," 168)

Orual's first response to learning that the palace is invisible is to say, "This is a terrible place" and later, "This valley was indeed a dreadful place; full of the divine, sacred, no place for mortals" (*TWHF,* 117, 120). She is experiencing "the fear of the Lord" as described by Rudolf Otto, who says human beings react with horror to contact with the divine because they are in touch with the *living* God rather than the *"philosophic* God of mere rational speculation."[1] He says we mortals rationalize God in order to reduce our fear. Orual rationalizes when she remembers that Psyche may be mad. She says, "At the very name *madness* the air of that valley seemed more breathable, seemed emptied of a little of its holiness and horror" (*TWHF,* 122).

However, contact with living divinity is not all horror. Otto says it is also marked by fascination and joy. Psyche has described the fear and shame she felt at being invited into the god's house, but when she tells of meeting her lover in "the holy darkness" her eyes express "unspeakable joy" (*TWHF,* 123). And just as theologians have sought to reduce the horror by rational speculation, Lewis seeks to get a handle on the unspeakable joy by imaginative speculation.[2] He loves to imagine, and describe, Heaven and the wonders of grace. In the preceding chapter, Psyche's account of how she came to the Happy Valley is shot through with Lewis's love of imagination.

---

1. Compare Jacob's words, "How dreadful is this place!" and his fright at the presence of the divine: "Surely the Lord is in this place and I knew it not" (Gen. 29:17a, 16b). Rudolf Otto, *The Idea of the Holy,* 23. Hereinafter cited as *Holy.*

2. For a careful, scholarly tracing of the complementarity of rationality and imagination in Lewis's life, see Peter Schakel's *Reason and Imagination.* In *Imagination and the Arts in C. S. Lewis,* he defined Lewis's understanding of the imagination as "the mental, but not intellectual, faculty" and as "an avenue leading toward the spiritual" (4, 11).

C. Love: Losing Psyche Again

Again "Maia" experiences the loss of her beloved "daughter." The emotions Orual describes are many-layered. There is the self-less, rapturous appreciation of Psyche's beauty—her perfect throat, her deep, rich voice, her queenly bearing, the perfection of a woman fully alive. But Orual also feels sexual jealousy. She thinks of Psyche in bed with her lover and reviles her as a temple prostitute. On another level, she feels "inconsolable grief" because "the world had broken in pieces and Psyche and I were not in the same piece" (*TWHF*, 120). She blames the gods for taking Psyche away from her so completely, so irretrievably. The hatred and fear of deity that she has carried from her earliest childhood is confirmed by her loss.

Just one sentence, one metaphor, reveals that she could think differently: "A thought pierced up through the crust of my mind like a crocus coming up in the early year" (*TWHF*, 121). She thinks that perhaps the gods ought to have Psyche, because her sister is herself godlike.

But the crocus is a transient flower; Orual reverts to her belief that the gods are cruel and unfair in taking her child away from her. She speaks to Psyche like a cross mother to a five-year-old; she calls Psyche a slut, like a frustrated mother addressing a teenager. Psyche is neither. Orual's loss of her child becomes final when she orders Psyche to come with her, adding, "Psyche, you never disobeyed me before," and Psyche replies, "I am a wife now. It's no longer you that I must obey" (*TWHF*, 126–27).

D. Faith: Seeing Is Believing—or Is It?

Why can not Orual see Psyche's palace? At first it seems that Orual is too hardheaded, too much of a realist, too scientifically objective, to enter into Psyche's fantasy. Hearing Psyche's story, she responds, "You have told me so many wonders. If this is all true, I've been wrong all my life. Everything has to be begun over again" (*TWHF*, 115). Surely this sounds like the scientist who is willing to discard a theory when the facts as observed and measured do not support it.

Another factor, however, is the choice of which data Orual will pay attention to, and which she will ignore. One datum is Psyche's track record for truthfulness; as she says, "I have never told you a lie in my life" (*TWHF,* 123). Another is her physical well-being, which is inconsistent with the theory that she is out of her mind with terror, loneliness, and suffering. But what Orual fixes on is the rain. She sees Psyche as wet and getting wetter, while Psyche insists that she is indoors, and dry. True scientific objectivity would dictate being slow to draw a conclusion and asking oneself what additional tests or facts would be needed to reconcile the contradictory data.

Much research on processes of perception has been done since Lewis's day, but Lewis himself summarized what we know very simply in *The Magician's Nephew:* "For what you see and hear depends a good deal on where you are standing: it also depends on the sort of person you are" (*MN,* 125). But when Psyche suggests that her husband will enable Orual to see, the response is, "I don't want it. I hate it. Hate it, hate it, hate it" (*TWHF,* 124). Her vehement emotion prevents her from keeping an open mind.

Furthermore, human emotions are greatly influenced by language, and Orual's word choices facilitate a rejection of her sister's story. For example, when she compares Psyche to "one of Ungit's girls," her words reduce the rapturous union with the god to ritual prostitution. She sees Psyche's indifference to the rain as that of the "cattle" of the field, thus reducing her sister to an animal. This language influences her more than she realizes. Before she chooses, she has already chosen. The verb forms show it: "I *saw* in a flash that I *must choose* one opinion or the other; and in the same flash knew which I *had chosen*" (*TWHF,* 126; emphasis added).

Thus Orual's unbelief can be explained psychologically. Faith, however, is not a matter of belief or unbelief, but a matter of trust. In "The Obstinacy of Belief," Lewis describes situations when "we can do all that a fellow creature needs if only he will trust us": getting a dog out of a trap, rescuing someone who is drowning, helping a novice mountaineer over a bad spot. "We are asking them to trust us in the teeth of their senses, their imagination, and their intelligence." He then asserts that Christians trust God because they have "a knowledge-by-acquaintance of the Person [they] believe in" (*WLN,* 23, 25). Orual claims to know Psyche better than anyone else in the world, but her knowledge does not result in trust.

Chapter 12. Guesses — And a Glimpse

A. The Art of Story: The Twilight Zone

Patterns of light and dark were used to establish moods and meanings on the trip toward the mountain. The events of the period after Orual's visit with Psyche are set off by patterns of twilight and dark. It is just before sunset when Psyche sends Orual back across the stream. There, on the "human" side, it is already deep twilight, and in this twilight Orual looks back across the stream and sees the formerly gemlike valley as "[Psyche's] terrible valley" (*TWHF*, 129). Has a physical twilight fallen on the valley, or is this simply Orual's dark mood? Since the other references to light and dark are realistically coordinated with the time of day, it is probable that Psyche's valley is also dark; however, Orual's mood may also cause her to see it as darker than it is.

On the "human" side Bardia makes camp. The darkness deepens, but the fire he builds carves out a cozy, homelike place from the surrounding darkness. After they lie down to sleep the fire presumably goes out, though Orual does not mention it. In the early morning she leaves their bed, walking up and down along the stream in the gray twilight. There are "dark holes" in the stream, the deeper gray of the pools. And there she sees the god's house, also gray. Orual is literally in a twilight zone, a place of ambiguity.

The journey back to Glome is also sunless. It was morning twilight when they left Glome the day before, and it is evening twilight when they return. From now on, Orual will live in a spiritual twilight.

See *TWHF*, pp. 130–39.

B. *Context: Plain Speaking and Godhood*

After her vision of the palace Orual turns to address her future readers, calling on them to agree with her that the gods are unjust. The vision she has been given is ambiguous; the answer to her puzzle is just another puzzle. She forgets what the Old Priest said: "[N]othing that is said clearly can be said truly about [the gods]" and demands that they speak plainly, saying, "Psyche could speak plain when she was three; do you tell me the gods have not yet come so far?" (*TWHF*, 50, 134).

But some language scholars argue that religious language is normally ambiguous, paradoxical, and antithetical. Prickett calls it "the language of contradiction," and illustrates it with the well-known picture that can be seen either as a chalice or as two people facing each other. Orual's confusion, like Dante's at the top of Mount Purgatory, is "a metaphor of a certain kind of religious experience where the same event must be seen in two very different ways *at the same time* if either is to be understood at all."[1]

Similarly, Orual's demand that the gods speak plainly, like the three-year-old Psyche, sounds like Prickett's description of the goals of modern Bible translators: "to [convey] the 'correct meaning' of the original in 'language that is natural, clear, simple, and unambiguous.'" Modern English, says Prickett, is "separate[d] from the critical sensibility of its past [by] an intolerance of ambiguity." The tendency to resolve ambiguities leads the translators to omit numinous language, like the phrase "still small voice" (1 Kings 19:12) in the King James Version. Both Catholic and Protestant translators in the seventeenth century believed "that oddities in the . . . texts were there for a divinely ordained purpose." In contrast, modern translators, both Catholic and Protestant, "responding to the unstated assumptions of the scientific revolution," fail to suggest that the "inherent peculiarity" of what Elijah heard "might indicate a quite *new* kind of experience."[2]

1. Stephen Prickett, *Words and "The Word": Language, Poetics and Biblical Interpretation*, 161–66.
2. Ibid., 6, 8, 9. Prickett's discussion of Matilda in Dante's Earthly Paradise (157–60) reminds us that Psyche's home is a kind of Eden—"a new world" (*TWHF*, 100–101) and a place of ambiguity.

Since Lewis apparently went to so much trouble to provide his novel with a modern, realistic narrative surface, Orual's frustrated cry against ambiguity is surely not without deep significance. Lewis gave a lot of thought to the nature of language, and his conclusions were similar to those of Prickett. In "The Language of Religion" he posited three types of language: scientific language, unambiguous and tending toward the mathematical; poetic language, which appeals to the senses and arouses the imagination; and ordinary language. He classified scientific and poetical language as "two different artificial perfections of Ordinary" and concluded that anyone who tries to express religious experience in ordinary language is forced toward either theological language, in its exactness a species of the scientific, or poetic language, which is less clear but has great power to "use factors within our experience [as] pointers to something outside our experience" (*CR*, 129, 135). By demanding that religious experience possess the clarity of ordinary speech, Orual is closing herself off from the possibility of having such experience.[3]

C. Love: For Bardia, for Psyche

In the valley near the holy mountain, two couples sleep, one on each side of the stream. Just as in Glome, where the river Shennit divides the city from the house of Ungit, here the stream divides Psyche's invisible palace from the camping-place of Orual and Bardia. On the human side of the stream the horse is cropping grass, Bardia has made a fire, and "two rocks close together [make] the next best thing to a cave." Orual rejoices in the mortal, nonmagical food, the warmth of the fire, and the company of that "wonderful creature" (*TWHF*, 131, 130), the man and soldier Bardia.

As the narrator of the story, Orual conceals most of her thoughts about Bardia, but one can read between the lines. When he proposes that they "lie close, back to back," he is somewhat embarrassed and says, "I'm no more to you, Lady, than one of your father's big dogs" (*TWHF*, 131). Indeed the comparison to a dog is apt, for his loyalty toward Orual is as faithful, as humble, as nonjudgmental, as any

3. See Myers, *Context*, 203–4.

dog's for its master. But his embarrassment is evidence that he does think of Orual as a woman. At the time Orual was surprised that Bardia thought of her as a woman, but as she looks back on it while writing her accusation of the gods she concludes that Bardia had simply overlooked her gender, because of her ugliness. Her terse comment conceals—from the reader or herself?—her fantasies, her girlish crush on Bardia.

However, as she lies awake, thinking "about Psyche...and also of another thing" (*TWHF*, 132), the reader can infer that her thoughts involve a comparison between her situation and Psyche's. She is lying close to a mortal man, a man already married to someone else; Psyche is lying in the arms of her god-husband. Orual is deprived of a man's love, and now, as she sees it, of Psyche's love also; Psyche has a love that brings her inexpressible joy. Orual is empty, Psyche is fulfilled.

The next day, on the trip back to Glome, Orual asks Bardia why Psyche's lover forbids her to see his face. Bardia's answer, "[because his] face and form would give her little pleasure if she saw them" (*TWHF*, 136). On this basis, added to her previous thoughts, Orual decides, weeping under her veil, that she must kill Psyche. She argues, "I perceived now that there is a love deeper than theirs who seek only the happiness of their beloved. Would a father see his daughter happy as a whore? Would a woman see her lover happy as a coward?" (*TWHF*, 138).

Her words paraphrase what Lewis says in *The Problem of Pain*: "[T]he mere 'kindness' which tolerates anything except suffering in its object is, in that respect, at the opposite pole from Love. When we fall in love with a woman, do we cease to care whether she is clean or dirty, fair or foul?" But in the essay Lewis goes on to say that this kind of love is appropriate to God's love for his creatures, but egotistical and possessive in human beings. When God became a man and lived "as a creature among his own creatures in Palestine" he was nonegotistical and supremely self-sacrificing (*PoP*, 46, 49).

D. Faith: "What's Really" ("The Holy," 168)

In the twilight before the dawn, Orual goes to the stream for a drink, and looking across the stream, she momentarily sees Psyche's palace in the mist. The glimpse conquers her. She responds with the fear and awe that Otto describes as horror. The next day, without telling him what she has seen, Orual asks Bardia if there really was an invisible palace in the valley. He replies cautiously, "I don't well know what's *really*, when it comes to houses of gods" (*TWHF*, 135). In his own way, he is stating the puzzle of anyone who wonders what to believe.

We say, "Seeing is believing." But is it? The sight of the palace makes such a strong impression on Orual that she temporarily loses her self-centeredness and with it, her disbelief. For the moment, it is more important to cross the stream and ask forgiveness than to save herself from drowning. There is also the fact that the palace is not something she could have imagined. Just as Psyche believed that the West-Wind was real and not a dream "because one's never seen things like that" (*TWHF*, 111), so the strangeness of the house is good evidence for its reality. But instead of trusting her own perceptions as Psyche did, Orual thinks, "Perhaps it [is] not real" (*TWHF*, 133).

Although the building is strange to Orual, Lewis's readers can see that it is like a Gothic cathedral—something not to be built for another fourteen centuries. Pillars and architraves are features of classical buildings, but buttresses and incredibly tall, slender pinnacles come from the Age of Faith. The very shape attests that it is a god's house, because as Otto says, the Gothic cathedral is "to us of the West" the most holy of all types of art.[4]

On the journey home Orual tells Psyche's story to Bardia. She omits her brief glimpse of the palace, but even without this bit of data, Bardia's answer to the riddle is fairly correct: Psyche obviously is not mad; he would not dare say she lies; therefore, she must be telling the truth in calling herself a bride. He does not know exactly what to believe, but he trusts Psyche and therefore recommends letting her alone.

---

4. Otto, *Holy*, 67. See Schakel, *Imagination*, 151–52, for an overview of Lewis's use of architecture in *TWHF*.

Chapter 13. Orual's Soul-Searching

A. The Art of Story: The Fox's Interpretation

Lewis must show Orual telling the story of Psyche, which the reader already knows, without undue repetition; at the same time he must advance the action. He accomplishes both tasks by focusing not on her narrative, but on the Fox's interpretation of it. The Fox applies his Stoic philosophy to put each thing Orual says within the framework of nature, of ordinary cause and effect. His conclusion that Psyche is mad and her mate a mountain man holds together plausibly enough.

Again Lewis uses the technique of contrasting Orual's two advisers. In chapters 8 and 9 they comforted her—the Fox by philosophy and Bardia by teaching her to swordfight. In chapters 12 and 13 they interpret Psyche's story. Bardia's implied advice, to let the god and his bride go about their own business, is based on pious behavior—observing the taboos and offering due sacrifices. The Fox's advice is based on a Stoic's judgment that reason and nature are sufficient to understand the situation. But he is not all Stoic. When Orual threatens to kill Psyche to break a shameful union, the Fox condemns her violence (the violence of disordered love in Greek tragedies) as "detested impieties." Both men advise her not to meddle.

B. Context: Wedding the Divine Nature? ("Stoicism," 214)

As a Stoic, the Fox does not believe in the gods, but only in the Divine Nature. Nevertheless, in thanksgiving that Psyche is alive,

See *TWHF*, pp. 143–53.

he "make[s] a libation to Zeus the Saviour" (*TWHF*, 140), just as earlier he had thanked Zeus for Orual's recovery and the breaking of the drought. Since he believes the Divine Nature is a seamless web, so that the sacrifice of Psyche had nothing to do with the change of Glome's fortunes, it would seem illogical for him to exclaim, half praying and half cursing, "Oh Zeus, Zeus, Zeus, if I had ten hoplites and a sane man to command them!" (*TWHF*, 147). Perhaps the Fox is calling on the Divine Nature while using the name of Zeus.

At the same time, he is deeply offended at the idea that the Divine Nature—or a manifestation of It in a "god"—might be Psyche's lover. He calls the very idea "profane, ridiculous" and adds, "You might as well say the universe itched or the Nature of Things sometimes tippled in the wine cellar" (*TWHF*, 143). Here Lewis is repeating an effect he previously used in *The Horse and His Boy*. The horse, Bree, says, "Even a little girl like you, Aravis, must see that it would be quite absurd to suppose [Aslan] is a *real* lion. Indeed it would be disrespectful. If he was a lion he'd have to be a Beast just like the rest of us. . . . [H]e'd have four paws, and a tail, and *Whiskers!*" (*HHB*, 200). (At this point Aslan comes up behind the horse and tickles him with his catlike whiskers.)

The Fox's reaction should not, of course, be read as a hint that Psyche's lover is literally the eternal Son of God. Instead, Lewis is setting up an analogy, making the idea of Incarnation strange, so that the jaded post-Christian readers for whom he wrote may experience it as if for the first time.

C. Love: Passion and Compassion

Orual is furious at the suggestion that Psyche may be pregnant by a mountain man. Her passion stems partly from her motherly possessiveness and partly from her disgust at Psyche's adult sexuality. Believing that only she can save Psyche, she threatens again to kill her sister rather than allow her to continue in such dishonor. The Fox is shocked and replies bluntly, "There's one part love in your heart, and five parts anger, and seven parts pride" (*TWHF*, 148). He loves Psyche too, but his love expresses itself in willingness "to be a runaway—to risk the flogging and impaling—for your [Orual's] love and hers." Then the Fox suggests, "A good man might be an outlaw and a runaway" (*TWHF,* 149), but it means nothing to Orual. The contrast between love that is expressed in force and love expressed in self-sacrifice is clear to us as readers, but it goes over Orual's head.

D. Faith: Orual's Prayer

Exhausted, the Fox proposes that they talk again in the morning. This is good problem-solving technique, but Orual interprets it first as lack of love for her and second as masculine weakness. Like Tinidril in *Perelandra,* she is romanticizing herself as the queen of a tragedy—creating an image of herself as "the tall slender form, . . . stepping forth fearless and friendless into the dark" and of "the other sex" as "pitifully childish and complacently arrogant" (*Pere,* 126). Feeling that the Fox has deserted her, she prays fervently to the gods, but she prays from behind her mask, as a queen of tragedy rather than as herself.

Her prayer is a complex mixture of ancient religion and modern psychological introspection. It has five features:

1) She prayed as an individual, not as a member of the community.

Today people think of prayer as a private matter, but in *Reflections on the Psalms,* Lewis reminds us there was little or no separation in the ancient mind between private and public worship (*Refl,* 44). For Orual, praying without sacrifice and the temple ritual are evidence of how desperate and sincere she is in her loneliness. But by whose doing is she abandoned? She has had Bardia's counsel: Don't meddle with gods' business. The Fox's counsel is not fully ripened, but he has not abandoned her. Although she cannot depend on the community of Glome, who sacrificed Psyche in the first place, to support her in her search for right action, the smaller community of her two friends has responded lovingly and honestly to her.

2) She "called upon" the gods with her whole heart.

In chapter 15 of *Letters to Malcolm,* Lewis discusses the difficulty of entering into prayer. The conscious mind, he says, is a façade; no matter how hard he tries to turn his attention inward, his awareness "turn[s] out to be the thinnest possible film on the surface of a vast deep" (*LM,* 79). And what does Orual know of the "vast deep"?

She knows only how intensely she desires to have Psyche back with her. Some of the Greek philosophers in the Hellenistic period said the gods were simply images of God, the Great Unknown. Lewis's concept is similar, but he gives it a modern psychological spin. His own image of God is "a bright blur"; like his own true nature, the true nature of God remains unknown, and "The real I has created them both—or rather, built them up in the vaguest way from all sorts of psychological odds and ends" (*LM*, 78).

3) She "took back" all the accusations and criticisms she had previously made against the gods.

Orual's hatred and distrust of the gods is much deeper than a simple recantation can wipe out. Her first reaction to learning that the lions have returned is "so Ungit has played us false after all" (*TWHF*, 145). As she will realize later, however, the appearance of the lions enables her to go to Psyche again.

Her second reaction is a cynical generalization that shows she does not really expect an answer to her prayer. She says, "Not a word will come to you until you have guessed wrong and they all come crowding back to accuse and mock and punish you for it" (*TWHF*, 150). A prayer that does not reflect *metanoia*, a change in thinking, does not really take back previous accusations and criticisms.

4) She tried to bargain with the gods, promising to do anything they asked in return for a sign.

What if they had asked that she leave Psyche alone?

And is it true that there is no sign? The breaking of the drought has been welcome to Glome, and Psyche has seen it as a sign: "I knew quite well that the gods really are, and that I was bringing the rain." The rain continued to fall. It was falling when Orual began her prayer, and when she finished, "the rain drummed on as before" (*TWHF*, 110, 150).

5) Nothing changed as a result of her prayer. Whether the gods answered or not, prayer brought no wisdom to Orual.

Chapter 14. Back to the Mountain

A. The Art of Story: A Skillful Plot ("Apuleius," 145)

Orual's determination to separate Psyche from her mysterious, perhaps monstrous, lover necessitates a second trip to the mountains. This is something Orual must do alone, in secret, and in plausible circumstances. In Apuleius's fairy tale, the two older sisters zoom from Psyche's palace to their own homes, back to the palace, to their parents' home, and then back to Psyche to set in motion the plan to reveal Cupid. Then they go home again. Ships are somehow involved, and Zephyr (the West-Wind) brings them from the sacrificial rock to the palace, but their movements are vaguely sketched in, and their only motivation is unprovoked malice.

In contrast, Orual's movements and motivations are explained by careful plotting. From an author's point of view, the royal lion hunt solves several problems. It gives Orual a small window of opportunity—"two days at least" (*TWHF*, 145)—so that she feels justified in returning to Psyche the very next morning, without waiting for the Fox's counsel. It provides a reason—the king's order—that Bardia cannot go with her and be a witness to what will happen. It explains how she can get away with concealing what really happens: Gram, the soldier Bardia sends with her, is noted for his silence.

The reason Psyche gives in to Orual's persuasion is also carefully plotted and psychologically credible. In Apuleius's fairy story, Psyche is the typical innocent younger sibling who believes what she is told. Lewis's Psyche behaves much more plausibly—and intelli-

See *TWHF*, pp. 154–67.

gently. When Orual tries to assert her motherly authority over her half-sister, Psyche replies that she no longer owes obedience to Orual, but to her husband. When Orual poses the syllogism that Psyche's lover must be either monster or felon, and asserts that the Fox and Bardia agree with her, Psyche replies, simply but firmly, "How should they know? I am his wife. I know" (*TWHF*, 161).

Orual then argues paradoxically that if Psyche really believed in her husband, she would be willing to test him. Psyche replies that she will not disobey him. Finally Orual sets her power against the god's. She threatens to kill Psyche and then herself, and stabs herself with the dagger to show that she means it. After they have bandaged Orual's arm, Psyche agrees to light the lamp and get a look at her sleeping husband—not because she distrusts him, but to keep Orual from killing herself.

Apuleius's evil sisters prey on Psyche's innocence and simplicity; Lewis's Orual wins by subtle logic, half-truths, and finally by the impious threat of suicide. Psyche will not let Orual's blood defile the threshold of her dwelling. Unlike Apuleius's silly Psyche, she knows what she is doing and knows that she will suffer for it. She says, "This is the price you have put upon your life. Well, I must pay it" (*TWHF*, 166).

B. Context: Psyche's Fall

Although Orual has visualized herself as the queen in a tragic drama, forced to act alone to save her beloved "daughter," it is Psyche whose situation is truly tragic. Her decision to disobey her husband will lead to her banishment from the palace and her Happy Valley, just as Adam and Eve were banished from Eden.

Her disobedience is comparable to that of Milton's Adam in *Paradise Lost*. Milton's Adam did not for a moment believe the serpent's lie about the fruit; he went along with Eve and took the fruit, "not deceived, but fondly overcome with female charm."[1] In the same way, Psyche is not deceived. She says, "I know what I do" (*TWHF*, 166), and her words are tragic. In the abstract, it is easy to see that the love of her husband should take priority over her love for Orual,

1. John Milton, *Paradise Lost*, 9.998–99.

but the physical ties of affection for the woman who cared for her as a baby, like Adam's physical tie of sexual love, cannot be denied. As she says, "It goes down to my very roots and cannot be diminished by any other newer love" (*TWHF*, 165).

C. Love: The Hidden Lover

The purity of Psyche's love for her husband contrasts strongly with Orual's love for "her child." Whereas Psyche's love for Eros makes her love everyone and everything more, Orual's obsession with Psyche causes her to judge Bardia and the Fox wrongly. Psyche is sure of her husband; it does not matter what Orual, Bardia, and the Fox think, nor what all of Glome might say. She accepts her husband's prohibition, not out of fear, but simply because it is her pleasure to trust and obey him. When Orual says, "[We] can think of one reason only for such a forbidding. And of one only for your obeying it," she is implying that Psyche is out of her mind, but Psyche replies, "Then you know little of love" (*TWHF*, 162).

D. Faith: Two Views of Orual's Self-Deception

When Psyche refuses to obey Orual with the words, "Dear Maia, my duty is no longer to you," Orual proclaims, "Then my life shall end with it" (*TWHF*, 164). It is good drama, or perhaps melodrama, but how serious is it? Instead of stabbing herself in the heart, Orual thrusts the dagger into her arm. She holds out her arm to let the blood drip onto the ground, but she has brought bandages to stop the flow. She has no intention of bleeding to death. She does not even intend to maim herself, for she admits that she might not have stabbed herself if she had realized how delicate and complicated the functioning of the human arm is. Psyche believes her threat to kill herself; should we?

The idea that Orual's threat of suicide is at least partly motivated by her view of herself as a tragedy queen is perhaps suggested by Lewis's own skepticism concerning the clarity of one's intentions. In *Letters to Malcolm* he speaks of "the façade...I call consciousness" (*LM*, 78) and in *The Screwtape Letters* of how human beings feel "blameless and ill-used . . . with no more dishonesty than comes natural to a human" (*SL*, 123).

However, Peter J. Schakel's explanation also makes sense: "She didn't *want* to die—she wanted to live and have Psyche back. This radical gesture, she thought, would lead to that result. What if Psyche had refused? As I read the chapter, I believe Orual was fully ready to kill Psyche and then herself—better Psyche be dead than belong to another, and what did Orual have to live for without Psyche?"[2]

The fact that two such different interpretations are possible is good evidence of the subtlety and psychological depth of Lewis's portrayal of Orual. It reflects his perception of the difficulty of being honest to God, which permeates the whole novel and finally leads to the key words, "How can [the gods] meet us face to face till we have faces?" (*TWHF*, 294).

2. Personal communication, used with permission.

Chapter 15. Meeting the God

A. The Art of Story: The Physical and the Supernatural

By its literary structure, this chapter asks the reader to believe in Orual's experience. The first three pages prepare for the appearance of the god by grounding Orual—and us, the readers—firmly in the physical world. As she waits on the other side of the stream, Orual gives herself up to fantasy, wishing that genial, affectionate Bardia were with her instead of Gram, imagining how Psyche, devastated by disappointment and shame, will fall into her arms for comfort; visualizing her own funeral, and that "[e]veryone loved me once I was dead" (*TWHF*, 170). But each time she begins to daydream, she is confronted with physical sensation—the cold, the throbbing of her arm, and finally, the deep darkness and the first and second lightings of Psyche's lamp.

When the god does appear, the mental event is enveloped in physical sensation. Orual hears his stern, "golden" voice, and it sends through her body "a wave of terror" so intense that "it blotted out" the pain in her arm. She sees lightning, hears thunder, and is drenched by the sudden rise of the river, the "tyrannous pelting rain" (*TWHF*, 171). Then she sees the god as a man-shape within a light and hears his pronouncement, that Psyche must suffer in exile, and Orual must, in some mysterious way, be Psyche. Orual struggles physically against the storm, struggles to cross the stream. The physical action is an expression of her refusal to accept the separation from Psyche that the god has said must be. Not until daylight

See *TWHF*, pp. 168–76.

comes to show the destruction of the Happy Valley does she give up and prepare to return to Glome.

Now that the struggle with the god is over, the weather turns fair; the physical environment for the supernatural experience has done its work. On the way down the mountain Orual thinks, "I'd proved for certain that the gods are and that they hated me" (*TWHF*, 175).

B. Context: Love and Wrath

1. The Lord of Terrible Aspect in Greek Tragedy

Dante calls Love "the lord of terrible aspect." Many Greek tragedies say the same thing. For example, in Euripides' *Iphigeneia at Aulis* the Chorus muses on the double nature of love. They sing: "Aphrodite is a great power," and being "touched by her" is the best blessing life can offer; nevertheless, the singers beg to be touched "Only lightly, to be free of . . . the lust that drives men mad." Concerning the self-centered desire of Paris they sing,

> And your own desire gives you wings.
> And out of this comes . . . war . . . and more war
> Driving Greece with spear and ship to the walls of Troy.[1]

In Greek there is a pun: "desire" (*eros*) and "war or strife" (*eris*). Orual's description of Psyche's joyous childhood certainly bears out the Chorus's assertion that love is the best blessing life can offer. Her desire to have Psyche for her own is not erotic in the modern sense, but it is a disordered, self-centered emotion.

Concerning Eros, Aphrodite's son (in Glomish terms, Ungit's son, the god of the mountain, and Psyche's lover) the Chorus sings that he has two kinds of arrows, gold-tipped and lead-tipped, love and hate, happiness and "heart's turmoil." It concludes

> Let the touch of desire be light and pure,
> Let me know Aphrodite but, oh, in part only,
> Not all, not totally.[2]

1. Euripides, *Iphigeneia at Aulis*, phrases from ll. 543–46, ll. 585–87.
2. Ibid., l. 551, ll. 554–57.

2. God's Wrath, Greek and Jewish

Although Lewis saw foreshadowings of the Incarnation in pagan literature, he saw a direct preparation for the coming of Christ in the Jewish Scriptures. Thus both Greek and Hebrew concepts of God's anger are relevant to Orual's experience of judgment.

Orual sees the god looking at her with "passionless and measureless rejection." It is not "what men call anger," but it hurts worse than mortal anger. His voice as he pronounces her sentence is "unmoved and sweet; like a bird singing on the branch above a hanged man" (*TWHF*, 173). Her experience bears out the Fox's teaching that the Divine Nature is beyond and above the sometimes petty emotions of the Olympian gods.

In contrast, the Old Testament most often portrays God as deeply passionate as well as august and majestic. When his people betray him, he exclaims,

> What shall I do with you, O Ephraim?
> What shall I do with you, O Judah?
> Your love is like a morning cloud,
> like the dew that goes early away. (Hosea 6:4, RSV)

He longs for them to love him steadfastly and not transiently, personally and not through ritual sacrifices alone (Hosea 6:6). And in Genesis, when God pronounces judgment on Adam and Eve, he also pities them, providing clothes for their nakedness (Gen. 3:16–19, 21).

C. Love: The Pain of Love

Waiting on the other side of the stream, Orual experiences love as pain. She asks, "How could [Psyche] hate me, when my arm throbbed and burned with the wound I had given it for her love?" (*TWHF*, 169).

For Psyche, too, love leads to hurt. Because she loves Orual so much, she risks offending her lover, her god. Her Happy Valley is destroyed, and Orual hears her weeping, weeping more grievously than a child, or a man wounded in the palm, a tortured man, or a girl dragged off into captivity from a conquered city. The depth and bitterness of Psyche's grief is a measure of how much she loves both Orual and her god, for now she is losing both.

And her god-husband, does he also suffer for love? In *Miracles,* Lewis asserts that the principle of vicarious suffering is at the heart of the universe: "The Sinless Man [Christ] suffers for the sinful, and, in their degree, all good men for all bad men. And this Vicariousness . . . is also a characteristic of nature" (*Mir,* 123). In *The Lion, the Witch, and the Wardrobe,* Aslan, the redeemer of that world, suffers because of Edmund's wrong choice. Even in *The Golden Ass* of Apuleius, the comic source of *Till We Have Faces,* Eros suffers, although it is only a burn from the oil of Psyche's lamp. Nothing is said about the god's suffering in *Till We Have Faces,* but we know that Psyche's wrong choice leads at the very least to his loss of her companionship in the Happy Valley.

Even though Lewis may have believed that the god suffers, it is impossible to show it, for he is telling the story from the viewpoint of Orual, who understands little of deity and hates what she does understand. She does not understand the god's mysterious words, "You also shall be Psyche" (*TWHF,* 174) as an expression of divine pity for her and her sister. Her experience at this point is very far from Psyche's hopeful words that ended her previous visit: "All will be well; all will be better than you can dream of" (*TWHF,* 128–29).[3]

D. Faith: Belief without Faith

Although "faith" and "belief" are considered synonyms, "faith" carries connotations of trust, while "belief" refers more specifically to mental acceptance of something as true. For example, Psyche breaks *faith* with her husband by failing to obey him, but she continues to *believe* that he is a god. She must break faith with him in order to keep her promise to Orual. Ironically Orual thinks to herself, "indeed once I had her oath I never doubted her *faith* to it" (*TWHF,* 170, emphasis added).

In return, Orual breaks faith with Psyche when she makes her sister's love into "a tool, a weapon, a thing of policy and mastery"

---

3. These serene words echo Julian of Norwich's *Showings,* 149. Lewis was reading it in 1940, amidst the desolation of World War II (*Let,* 352).

(*TWHF,* 165). She has no faith in Psyche's husband, and her belief about him rises and falls. As she waits on her side of the river, she wonders if he could really be a god, but she forces herself not to think about it. When the god appears she knows that he is real; in his presence it seems that she had known it all along, that her "doubtings, fears, guessings, debatings, questionings" (*TWHF,* 173) were nothing but self-deceptions.

Through the rest of the night she does not consider whether she believes; all her energy is devoted to trying to cross the stream, trying to go to Psyche before it is too late. As she and Gram begin their journey toward Glome, her belief hardens. She says, "I'd proved for certain that the gods are and that they hated me" (*TWHF,* 175). This is certainly not faith. Instead of trusting the gods, she determines that she will survive their punishment, whatever it is and whenever it comes.

The separation between belief and faith was played out in Lewis's own life, for he says in *Surprised by Joy* that he began to attend daily prayers in the chapel of his college when he became a Theist, but before he believed "Jesus Christ is the Son of God." It was a matter of faith, of thinking that he "ought to 'fly [his] flag'" (*SbJ,* 237, 233). He acted in faith, and belief followed. Perhaps at least some of Orual's actions in her subsequent life will be her version of this kind of faith.

Chapter 16. Waiting and Building

A. The Art of Story: The Queen Is Born

The speaker began this novel by identifying herself as a queen. But before she was a queen, she "was Orual the eldest daughter of Trom, King of Glome" (*TWHF*, 4). Throughout the first fifteen chapters, she is Orual. Chapter 16 describes the beginning of the transition from Orual to queen of Glome. In losing Psyche, Orual has lost the very center of her life, for she has lost her identity as Maia, Psyche's foster mother. Now, as she waits for the god to punish her, she also begins to build a new identity.

Transitional chapters normally present a technical problem for the author. Lewis's way of handling the transition is to interweave identity-building episodes with episodes in which Orual mourns for Psyche and waits for the gods to strike. The first episode of waiting/mourning comes when Orual must endure the Fox's questioning about what happened between her and Psyche. Although she does not state the connection, her decision to veil her face is surely a response to his sorrow over what she did to Psyche.

Identity-building is mainly a matter of breaking free from the king. These episodes are as follows:

1. The king commands her to remove her veil. When she does not obey, he begins to "[work] himself into one of those white rages" (*TWHF*, 182) like the one that led to his killing the slave boy on the night Psyche was born. Orual shows no fear; she faces him down with her veiled facelessness.

See *TWHF*, pp. 177–90.

2. After she wins this first clash of wills, her fearlessness is no longer a show but real. She is able to set boundaries with him, making him choose whether she and the Fox must guard Redival or work in the Pillar Room.

3. The king breaks his thigh in a fall, and Orual orders six men to hold him down while Arnom (the second priest) sets the bone. Instead of the king's torturing her, she is, in effect, torturing him. He cries out in fear of her, "I know who she is" (*TWHF*, 186).

4. Finally, by making a deal with Arnom in the king's name, she takes the first step in establishing herself as queen. When she is left alone in the great hall, she thinks that being queen will help her endure the waiting and mourning, but what really comforts her is the thought that King Trom will be dead. She says, "I drew in a long breath, one way, the sweetest I had ever drawn. I came near to forgetting my great central sorrow" (*TWHF*, 189).

After Orual establishes her right to wear the veil and loses her fear of the king, the narrative focus shifts to mourning and waiting. She closes Psyche's room and begins to fill in the waiting time by studying philosophy with the Fox and physical training with Bardia. Finally, after she establishes her queenship with Arnom, the Fox, and Bardia, she hears the sound of weeping—really just the chains of the well. Immediately her fantasies of freedom and queenship give way to "a torture of hope" and the "bitterness of intense disappointment" (*TWHF*, 189–90).

B. Context: The Virgin Queen

Orual as queen resembles Elizabeth I, the Virgin Queen of a period of prosperity, exploration, and high culture for England. Elizabeth was the daughter of Henry VIII, who married six women in the effort to sire a male heir to his throne. Trom's second marriage was made for the same purpose, and he did not marry again only because none of the neighboring kings would give him their daughters. Like Henry, Trom is sensual, gross, and undisciplined. Orual sometimes shows a temper like his or echoes his voice, but (like Elizabeth) she is more inclined to justice and compassion, as her decision to cede the Crumbles to the House of Ungit shows. Objective reason tells her that the land should belong to Ungit, despite her resentment against the goddess. Compassion also comes into it: if the temple had enough land, perhaps the priests could be prevented from "wringing so much out of the common people by way of gifts" (*TWHF*, 188). Later we will learn more of her wisdom as a ruler.

C. Love: More Suffering

This chapter focuses on the Fox's intense suffering for love. The shifts in his emotions are subtly reflected in the names he uses to address her. At first he gently protests against her going off without waiting for further talk, and he calls her "child." Then in response to her stinging rebuke he addresses her more formally as "Lady." And when he realizes that Psyche is lost, his expression becomes "very haggard," and he switches back to calling Orual "child" and "daughter" (*TWHF*, 178).

He realizes that her account of what happened on the mountain is heavily edited, that her secrecy is a break in their relationship. As he looks at her, Orual is reminded of her childhood and the way he used to sing "The Moon's gone down." Then she was alone because of her ugliness, but now she is isolated by her action. And her break with the Fox leaves him alone. For him, this is the latest in a series of losses—of his family, his place in Greek society, his freedom, Psyche. He reacts by accepting the half loaf that Orual is willing to give. He says, "I'll not lose you" (*TWHF*, 180).

The depth and truth of his affection contrast with Orual's love for Psyche. Whereas the Fox allows Orual to keep her secret, to make her own decision as an adult, Orual gets rid of Psyche's adult clothes and the hymn Psyche had written about her longing for the god of the mountain. The Fox affirms Orual's freedom, but Orual puts Psyche's things in a locked room. She suffers for love, but the one she loves is not the real Psyche.

D. Faith: The Fudge Factor ("Stoicism," 214)

Orual avoids faith by avoiding facts. She carefully explains the reasons for her actions as she accomplishes the transition from Orual to "the Queen," but these reasons will not bear close examination. She is fudging.

She does not tell the Fox that she tried to persuade Psyche by saying that he and Bardia agreed about the unknown lover, because he will call it a lie. She tells the reader that she meant only that they both thought the lover was evil. But did they? What Bardia really said was that perhaps—only perhaps—Psyche's lover concealed his appearance because it would give Psyche no pleasure. To be horrible looking is not necessarily to be evil. What the Fox said was that Psyche's lover was an outlaw, probably a villain, but that he might, nevertheless, be a good man. The depth of her lie (or self-deception) is revealed when she says, "I wondered . . . whether I had never at all believed her lover was a mountainy man" (*TWHF*, 179). She omits the fact that her lamp plan would have been equally unreasonable if Psyche's lover had been the Shadowbrute. What had she really believed about Psyche's situation?

After being shamed by her conversation with the Fox, Orual writes, "I never told Bardia the story of that night at all" (*TWHF*, 180). As a loyal, respectful servant of the royal family, he would not presume to ask, and it has already been established that Gram would not volunteer any information. Thus, by telling the Fox a half-truth and Bardia nothing, Orual keeps her secret. She admits to herself that she has seen the god, saying, "No one who had seen and heard the god could much fear this roaring old King" (*TWHF*, 181). But her factual experience does not lead to faith, for she will not face the facts to the best of her ability. Instead, she avoids her memory of what happened by becoming very busy.

Her avoidance is graphically represented in her decision to wear the veil. By concealing her face, she hides her deceit in concealing her self-wounding from the Fox. She knew that by using emotion to bend Psyche's will she was denying the primacy of Reason, the basis of the Fox's whole universe. Ideally, the Stoic avoided all appeal to the emotions. Stoic rhetorical theory held that arguments should be based on facts and reason (inferences from facts) alone; it even taught that losing a debate was preferable to an appeal to the emotions.[1]

1. George Kennedy, *The Art of Persuasion in Greece*, 292.

Finally, Orual's explanation of the veil is a fudge. She calls it "a sort of treaty made with my ugliness." Although she speaks frankly about her "shames and follies" as a young girl, when she believed she could make herself less ugly, this frankness is meant to distract herself and us from the deeper reason, her shame in lying to the Fox. After all, it was after their conversation that she assumed the veil. He was "the last man who ever saw [her] face" (*TWHF,* 180, 181).

Chapter 17. The Queen Grows Stronger

A. The Art of Story: Do It Fast! ("Time," 219)

In chapter 17, Lewis shows his power as a writer by moving over many events, making them seem natural, even inevitable, given Glome's circumstances and Orual's character. The speed of the narrative helps to distract us as readers from the loss of Psyche, and our admiration for "the Queen"'s quick, sure decisions moderates our tendency to dislike Orual for her treatment of Psyche.

The narrative reads so fast that most people (perhaps) will not notice two errors in detail. Bardia's speech, "I've played chess too long to hazard my Queen" (*TWHF*, 197), is an anachronism; there is no evidence that the game existed before A.D. 600, while the story takes place in "sometime" B.C.[1] The other error is grammatical: Orual says, "And none of you can think of a better way out of our dangers" (*TWHF*, 199). She should say "neither," since "none" implies that she is talking to three people, as in the previous conversation outside the king's door. But at this point she is talking to only Bardia and the Fox; Arnom has already left the palace. The use of "none" caused me to look back (on a subsequent reading, not the first) to determine whether Arnom really had gone, as I thought I remembered. Readers are less aware of such niceties of grammar than they were when Lewis was writing the book, and the speed of the narrative makes the error even easier to overlook.

See *TWHF*, pp. 191–202.
1. Game pieces from a time earlier than A.D. 600 have been found in Russia, China, India, Central Asia, and Pakistan, but they probably came from "earlier, distantly related board games." *New Encyclopedia Britannica*, s.v. "Chess."

Despite that speed, at least one of Orual's expressions helps to establish her queenship by subtly reminding us of Elizabeth I. Her trick of speech in using a noun as a verb, "I'd queen it with the best of them," first became common in English during the Elizabethan period.[2]

B. Context: The Queen's Two Bodies

Orual's perception that she has become two people, "the Queen" and "Orual," illustrates the medieval doctrine of "the king's two bodies." Orual wonders "if this [is] how all princes [feel]" (*TWHF*, 199), and medieval political science answers "yes." It was observed that the king in his public person was powerful, God's chosen instrument of justice; as a private person he was subject to weakness, illness, and death. This concept is expressed in the stone, coffin-shaped monuments found in many European churches. On top, there is a carved replica of the ruler (who may be a bishop or a lord rather than a king) in his ceremonial garb. On the side, there is the wasted, naked, perhaps skeletal form of the private person.[3]

In this chapter Orual is forced to become "the Queen" at a moment's notice. Fortunately for Glome, she has a natural ability to lead. She shows it in her quick response to the crisis of Trunia. Although she says that his "news struck [her] almost stupid" (*TWHF*, 192) she thinks on her feet. Her attention to detail is shown when she asks him to conceal his face; like an American president of today, she controls information to keep her options open.

Then as she discusses the situation with Bardia and the Fox, the idea of engaging Trunia's brother Argan in single combat "[comes] scalding hot" (*TWHF*, 195) into her head. Bardia and the Fox approve until they learn that she plans to do the fighting herself. Then they argue against it—the Fox because it is immodest, Bardia because it is too risky. But these are not their strongest reasons; instead their love for her makes them unwilling to take the chance of losing her.

Their love is for the private person, for "Orual," not "the Queen." Carried forward by the exhilaration of being queen, she ignores

---

2. Myers, *Context*, 201.
3. See Ernst H. Kantorowicz, *The King's Two Bodies*, figs. 28, 30, 31.

their misgivings, overrides their objections, and gives the necessary orders. "The Queen" radiates confidence that she can kill Argan. Not until after Bardia and the Fox have left her alone does "Orual" think more personally, think about her mortal danger, and wonder if she can be brave enough to carry through the plan.

For Orual, the situation is complicated by her personal relationship with her father, who must die if she is to be queen in fact. She does not pity his suffering, but thinks only of the freedom his death will bring. In chapter 16, she made her first political deal as queen-to-be, and then experienced almost a vertigo as she thought of "the largeness of a world in which he was not" (*TWHF*, 189). In chapter 17, her taste of queenship is so sweet that after business is over, she seeks his bedchamber and is comforted to think, "Even if he lives, he will never have his mind again" (*TWHF*, 202).

What are we to make of Orual's determination to dissociate the public persona so completely from the inner person? The clear description of how private and public persons are combined into one individual applies, of course, to every ruler, male or female. That it occurs in Orual's life is not good evidence that Lewis allows his character to be a strong woman only by forcing her to become mannish. Orual resolves to "vanish altogether into the Queen" and perhaps thereby "almost" cheat the gods (*TWHF*, 201). On the one hand, this attitude will permit her to do her job, to fulfill her destiny, but on the other hand, there will be enormous loss of integrity and individuality.[4] Her decision is spiritual, not a matter of sexual politics.

C. Love: Substitutes for Love

In this chapter, Orual begins to experience the kind of love available to a queen: first, attention and flattery. Trunia calls her "pretty," and although she knows the compliment is misplaced, she enjoys it. She calls her natural impulse to draw out the flirtation "a fool's

---

4. Colin Manlove, in "Caught Up into the Larger Pattern," comments, "The whole book refuses us certainties, even the certainty that Orual has done wrong" (273).

wish" and puts it aside. "I came to my senses," she says (*TWHF*, 191). Minor as this incident is, it reflects her determination to become hard and unfeeling.

Second, she gets the caring and loyalty that a top military man gives to his leader. Bardia knows what her face is like; despite that, he cares so much for her that he cannot "assent in words" to her plan to fight Argan. But he does not offer what she longs for, a response from him to the intimacy she felt when they slept side by side on the mountain. When he says, "Oh, Lady, Lady, it's a thousand pities they didn't make you a man" (*TWHF*, 199, 197) her dismay—comparing his remark to having a gallon of cold water added to one's broth—indicates that toward him she is still more woman than queen.

Almost immediately her hardness shows itself again. The Fox begs her, with tears in his eyes, not to risk losing her life and thus leaving him with no consolation. For a second time he recites the losses of his life: home and freedom, Psyche, and finally Orual. He appeals to her pity as she had appealed to Psyche's love of her on that last night in the Tower Room. She responds with tears, but "tears of pity for myself more than for him," and "she did not let them fall" (*TWHF*, 199; cf. 180).

Perhaps she receives only substitutes for love because in her self-centeredness she remains unaware of her unique self. Her judgments upon herself swing back and forth. First she compares herself with Psyche, "who [will] be far above [her] in everything," and her vow that Psyche will never be above her suddenly shows itself as vehement hatred. Then she blames the gods for putting this hatred in her mind and calls Psyche "my child, the very heart of my heart" (*TWHF*, 200). It is not "the Queen" who speaks, but perhaps it is the Orual who imagines herself as the queen of a Greek tragedy. It is not the self that both Bardia and the Fox love so deeply.

D. Faith: The Sandy Waste

Busy with the affairs of state, Orual has no time to deal with issues of faith. She takes to queenship "as a stricken man takes to the wine-pot." Her quick decisions as "the Queen" have caused Orual

to forget about the "sandy waste" of her inner life, but consciousness of it returns when she has some time to be alone. She thinks
that dying at Argan's hands "would be the best thing in the world"
(*TWHF*, 201), but she is not wise enough to see the sandy waste as a
divine mercy.

Chapter 18. The Eve
of the Battle

A. The Art of Story: Repetition and Comparison

Like any skilled novelist, C. S. Lewis emphasizes themes by patterns of repetition. This chapter presents a repetition of the events surrounding the sacrifice of Psyche, but this time the person to be sacrificed is Orual. Psyche was willing to die to save Glome; Orual puts herself forward to save Glome from being overrun by Phars. The god on the mountain had prophesied that Orual would also be Psyche, and here the working out of that prophecy begins.

A minor event, the making of sober plans for the death, begins the pattern of repetition. When Psyche was to be sacrificed, Orual lay injured on the floor and "heard them talking on, making all the plans for Psyche's death.... They were talking soberly and prudently like men providing for a journey or a feast." A few months later, "Orual" is the one to be sacrificed, but "the Queen" takes an active part in the planning. She remembers, "we went orderly to work on all the conditions of the fight and the hundred small things that had to be agreed on." Although the Fox does not lie injured on the floor, he is the suffering witness, for "all these provisions" are making the risk of Orual's death "more real and more irrevocable at each word"—as real as a journey or a feast (*TWHF*, 56, 205).

Comparing the two preparations not only emphasizes their similarity, but also shows how Orual and Psyche differ in character. Here are four differences:

See *TWHF,* pp. 203–14.

1. Psyche forgives Redival for getting her into trouble with the House of Ungit, saying, "She also does what she doesn't know." At the same time, she sees into Redival's shallowness, directing that Redival be given the jewels that are "big and costly" and without value as remembrances (*TWHF*, 69). Orual promises not to kill Redival for betraying Psyche, but instead of pity, she feels only scorn for her sister and sarcastically promises to find her two husbands.

2. Psyche directs Orual to give the king a polite message, whatever a dying girl should say to her father. Orual ignores her dying father as she prepares for battle.

3. On the eve of her sacrifice, Psyche talks gently, somewhat academically, of death as a door into a better life. In the press of business Orual has no time for philosophy. She must kill the pig, free the Fox, arrange a marriage for Redival, and choose her hauberk.

4. Psyche sits in the Tower Room, "tall and queenly and still," although she admits to a fear that perhaps there is no god, no Shadowbrute, "and those who are tied to the Tree only die" gradually (*TWHF*, 68, 70). Orual turns herself into "the Queen," who acts as if she is immortal while negotiating the terms of the fight, but finds that "Orual would whisper a cold word in the Queen's ear at times" (*TWHF*, 205).

B. Context: Mortal Women and the Goddess of Peace

Ironically, Orual finds herself serving Ungit (Aphrodite) by arranging the marriage between Redival and Trunia. In the Renaissance, Aphrodite was known as one who brought concord between political entities. Elizabeth I, the Renaissance ruler of England, did not have a sister to marry off, but she used the possibility of her own marriage as a political weapon. Orual, the Glomish Elizabeth, uses a marriage to bring peace between Phars and Glome.[1] Her duel with Argan is, or at least could be, the sacrifice of her life. Psyche also brought peace to Glome; being offered to the Shadowbrute, she was both bride and sacrifice.

1. The idea of sexual love as a facilitator of peace goes back much further. For example, in Old English, one word for "wife" or "woman" translates as "peace-weaver."

C. Love: The Fox's Terrible Choice ("Stoicism," 214)

The way they love contrasts the characters of Orual and the Fox. Orual has no love for her father, and indeed he has abused her both physically and mentally. She is in the royal bedroom when the king dies, but she is so busy with choosing armor for her fight that she ignores his passage. In contrast, the Fox sits by the king's bedside, watching through the last hours. Orual thinks, "It was not possible that he should love his old master" (*TWHF*, 213). Perhaps his Stoic detachment enabled him to maintain a certain ironic affection for the rough old king, even though Trom "addled [his] brains with beating [him] about the ears" (*TWHF*, 141). In any case, the Fox's Stoic principles require that he treat all human beings as worthy of respect, for all bear within themselves sparks of the Divine Nature.

Both Orual and the Fox find their identities in the ones they love most deeply, and again their behaviors form a telling contrast. Orual's deepest identity was as Maia, the mother of Psyche. Now she has lost Psyche and, therefore, her identity as Maia. The mythic personage that she now resembles most is Niobe, the mother who grieves and mourns. But the hurly-burly of "the Queen's" decision-making distracts "Orual," makes her forget her grief, and she decides against forcing/allowing herself to feel her sorrow. One part of her says, "Orual dies if she ceases to love Psyche," but another part says, "Let Orual die. She would never have made a queen" (*TWHF*, 211).

The Fox had lost his identity as a Greek when he became a slave. He had developed a new identity as the girls' grandfather, but now he, too, has lost Psyche. Still, his love for Orual is so deep that he freely remains (in effect) a slave and renounces his identity as a Greek. When Orual proclaims his manumission, he thinks of his former life, of being free to go where he chooses, of eating the tuna and olives that are not available in Glome, of feeling the intellectual excitement of philosophic conversation with his peers. But almost at the same time he sees Orual devastated by the thought that he really might go away. He gropes his way out of the Pillar Room, unable to see a clear choice.

By evening he has decided to stay with Orual in Glome. He is responding to her neediness, to the weakness of the woman who is "all Orual, even all child" (*TWHF*, 207–8). He gives a Stoic's reason for his choice—the necessity of fitting into the Whole that is the Divine Nature. He bolsters it with the practical consideration of how difficult it would be to reestablish his identity in Greece. But his real reason for remaining as "Grandfather" in Glome is his love for Orual. Terrible words express the depth of his suffering, the cost of his decision: "But that he did not limp, you would have thought he had been in the hands of the torturers" (*TWHF,* 209).

As Orual is choosing to become less compassionate in order to be "the Queen," he is choosing unconditional love.

D. Faith and Institutional Religion
("Pagan Religion," 204; "The Holy," 168; "Stoicism," 214)

When the Old Priest dies and Arnom takes his place, the religion of Glome becomes merely institutional for Orual. It had not always been so. In her childhood, the temple practices and ceremonies were real, even though her emotions could better be described as raw fear, rather than religious awe. She feared Ungit, the strong and terrible goddess; she feared the Old Priest because of his "temple-smell," his weird clothes, and his bird mask. When he came in his paraphernalia to demand the sacrifice of Psyche, his presence made the room "very holy," and she felt "the horror of holiness" (*TWHF,* 43, 54).

After Psyche's sacrifice, Orual has two personal, noninstitutional experiences of the gods: one in her own room, when she attempts to speak with them "myself, alone, in such words as came to me, not in a temple, and without a sacrifice" (*TWHF,* 130), and another when she actually sees and hears the god on the night of the downfall of Psyche's palace. This second experience leaves her knowing for certain "that the gods are and that they hated me" (*TWHF,* 175).

Then, in the midst of Orual's transformation into the queen of Glome, Arnom becomes the chief priest. He comes to the Pillar Room in his sacred garb. At first Orual remembers, like a nightmare, her fear of the Holy. But in putting on the accoutrements of the Old Priest, Arnom has not become holy; "there was no feeling that Ungit came into the room with him" (*TWHF,* 205). He puts on his public, institutional persona, but unlike the Old Priest, he has no private intimacy with Ungit.[2]

2. See chapter 17, section B, "The Queen's Two Bodies."

For many, perhaps most, people of Glome, Arnom is sufficient leader of their worship of Ungit. The institution is part of what gives them a feeling of unity and purpose. They are not sensitive enough to be aware of his lack of conviction. The setting apart of persons, places, objects, garments, gestures, or language has only the power that people ascribe to it. And in Orual's eyes, Arnom does not change when he puts on the symbols of the chief priest. We remember that she was not aware of the depth of conviction in the Old Priest until her father threatened him with a dagger.

Perhaps her experience on the mountain has sensitized her to what the Holy can be. Perhaps it has even caused her to downgrade the once-terrifying bladders and bird mask to a kind of play-acting.

Chapter 19. Triumph and Sorrow

A. The Art of Story: More Comparisons

This chapter establishes the pattern of surface triumph and underlying sorrow that will characterize Orual's reign over Glome. Her defeat of Argan, which establishes her queenship of Glome and Trunia's kingship of Phars, is a triumph, but the victory celebration that follows is disgusting and empty of joy. The previous chapter showed the similarities between the experiences of Orual and Psyche; this chapter emphasizes the differences: the fight and its consequences are worlds away from Psyche's sacrifice and ecstatic marriage.

The chapter is divided into three parts: preparations for the fight, the fight, and the life situation created for Orual by her victory. In each part minor details create contrasts with the sacrifice of Psyche.

Before the fight, both Orual and Psyche hope to be courageous, but Orual wishes to "make a brave show [in the procession through the city] and in the fight." By contrast, Psyche, on her last night in Glome, tries not to weep even in private, for she says, "We must not shame our lineage" (*TWHF*, 216, 70). Neither is much concerned about her own death, for Orual is numbed by the political consequences and Psyche by the drugs she has been given. Both go out with faces covered, for Orual wears a hood covering her whole helmet, making her into a "scarecrow or leper," while Psyche wears a wig and heavy, mask-like makeup, turning her into "an ugly doll" (*TWHF*, 216, 80).

See *TWHF*, pp. 215–25.

98

During the fight Orual, her face hidden by her hood, does "not believe in the combat at all," just as Psyche, with a face stiff and unnatural with paint, "couldn't feel it was [she] who was being sacrificed" (*TWHF,* 219, 106). And when Orual survives the fight, Bardia addresses her as "Blessed," the same title he gave to Psyche, survivor of the sacrifice, on the Grey Mountain (*TWHF,* 220, 103).

After the fight, Orual participates in a feast, a hurly-burly affair, a virtual parody of the feast given to Psyche on her bridal night. Exquisitely dressed, Psyche was delicately served by invisible beings and entertained by music. Orual was frightened and disgusted by the "heat and clamour," the drunkenness, and the men's gross behavior at table—"the gobbling, snatching, belching, hiccuping, the greasiness of it all, the bones thrown on the floor, the dogs quarrelling under our feet." Psyche left her banquet for the god's bedchamber; Orual in drunken loneliness retreats into her "fool's bed" (*TWHF* 223–24), since the man she loves is married.

B. Context: Masculine, Feminine, and Human

Both feminists and nonfeminists are inclined to describe Orual's decision to wear a veil as a rejection of her womanhood, and they blame her author for it. Candice Fredrick and Sam McBride, for example, suggest that Lewis was "uncomfortable with the idea of a woman warrior" and coped with it by "transform[ing] Orual into a man."[1] But that is not what the novel says. Orual became a warrior in a perfectly feminine way, as "a sad and sullen girl" being persuaded to try sword fighting by "a big, kindly man" (i.e., Bardia) who recognized her natural "gift for the sport" and hoped to alleviate her sadness (*TWHF,* 90–91).

Furthermore, within the givens of the novel, it is difficult to argue convincingly that Orual ever rejected womanhood. Her choices of how to be a woman were very much limited by her circumstances. Although the story takes place in the Hellenistic era, when freedom for women in the upper classes was greater than in the classical period, Lewis attributes to the women of Glome a more modest way

1. Candice Fredrick and Sam McBride, *Women among the Inklings: Gender, C. S. Lewis, J. R. R. Tolkien, and Charles Williams,* 151.

of life, one that could be generalized in terms of continuity: maintaining the ritual remembrance of the dead, providing the household with woven fabrics and cooked food, bearing children, telling the traditional stories.[2] To do these things a woman had to be married, but as we are told from the beginning, King Trom thinks Orual is so ugly that he will not even try to find a husband for her. Even if the poverty and disorder of Glome had not made neighboring kings unwilling to marry their sons to his daughters, Orual would not have been married.

In the process of becoming queen, Orual does move back and forth between masculine and feminine stereotypes, but she is always human first. Some of her thoughts and actions might seem stereotypically masculine: her cynical observation that the common people are cheering not for her but for the prospect of a free show; her seemingly fearless approach to the fight, made possible by a masculine suppression of feelings; her iron control of grief and rage at the departure of Bardia to be with his wife. However, many others are stereotypically feminine: her opening comparison between the housework for a feast and the preparations for the swordfight; her recollection of Psyche's feminine bravery in going out to heal the people, then going out to be sacrificed; her tears behind the mask when Argan falls. She weeps for joy at having pleased Bardia, but perhaps also for the finality of having taken the life of a man. She feels that the killing must be like the loss of virginity, for neither can be undone.

At the banquet, masculine and feminine behaviors come together. First there is the womanly responsibility of providing food and drink for the company, combined with the ruler's duty of networking with the nobles of Glome and Phars. She thinks in frustration, "If only I could have ridden away from them all and got to the butler...and learned what wine we really had!" (*TWHF*, 221). Despite this worry, she is able to enjoy Trunia's "courteous banter" in a thoroughly feminine way. The banquet itself is a mixed pleasure. Her womanly modesty is shamed by the men's gross behavior, yet she has a manly pride in her victory, at having become a warrior. In her

2. Michael Grant, *From Alexander to Cleopatra: The Hellenistic World*, 194–204; Lesley Adkins and Roy A. Adkins, *Handbook to Life in Ancient Greece*, 408; R. G. A. Buxton, *Imaginary Greece: The Contexts of Mythology*, 115–17.

drunken pride she thinks of herself both as a queen and a warrior, and she classifies herself with the great princes—the rulers, male or female, who take mistresses or lovers. She never intends to suppress her femininity, although her inner pain leads her to suppress Orual.

Thus, wearing the veil is not primarily a rejection of femininity, but of what she has done to destroy Psyche. She put it on after she became so ashamed at having concealed the truth from the Fox, and under it she does what she has to do to maintain her power as queen and the safety of her kingdom. In order to rule well, she puts aside her grief for her lost child, except in the silence of the night, when she hears the weeping and groaning of the chains swinging at the well.

C. Love: Two Who Love Orual

Apparently the Fox had been in a war, had surrendered rather than fight to the death, and had thus lost his freedom. Sensitive and intellectual, he knows what Orual is risking in the single combat with Argan, and he feels it even more vividly than Bardia, who is a fighter by profession. In the tension before the battle Orual sees him "standing with his face set like iron" and knows that "he would have wept if he had tried to speak" (*TWHF*, 218). This is the man she had accused (silently) of not loving her, of preferring Psyche to herself.

As for Bardia, at the fall of Argan he "came running up to me, with tears in his eyes and joy all over his face" (*TWHF*, 220). She, too, is crying behind her veil, and when he courteously kisses her hand, the touch of his lips goes through her like a stroke of lightning. Surely he loves her. But there is a message from his wife that her labor has begun. He asks permission to skip the banquet and rushes away, much to Orual's rage and disappointment. She is left to make do with Trunia's courtly flirtation and to be the only woman at the feast.

D. Faith: The Tragic Mask ("The New Psychology," 192)

Orual has decided to "let Orual die" and become all queen. To do so, she must cling to her mask. On the Greek stage an actor appeared larger than life because of the mask (Greek, *prosopon;* Latin, *persona*) he wore. Chapter 19, beginning with Orual's adamant refusal to fight bareface, ends with the creation of a tragic persona, helped by "the wonderful power of wine." Her sorrow is "glorious and noble," and she is "a great, sad queen in a song."[3] As on the Greek stage, her tragic mask is larger than life: "Psyche, Psyche, my only love. I am a great queen. I have killed a man. I am drunk like a man. All warriors drink deep after the battle. Bardia's lips on my hand were like the touch of lightning. All great princes have mistresses or lovers" (*TWHF,* 224).

To hide one's true self behind the tragic mask cuts off the possibility of contact with deity. As William James says, "in the world of religion, personality is the one fundamental fact"; by being occupied with "personal destinies," religion keeps human beings "in contact with the only absolute realities which we know."[4] In *Mere Christianity,* Lewis put it this way: "[W]hile in other sciences the instruments you use are external to yourself (things like microscopes and telescopes), the instrument through which you see God is your whole self" (*MC,* 144).

This principle is not, of course, original with either James or Lewis; it has been a truism from Socrates' "Know thyself" to Thomas Merton. Merton even uses the mask image: "We can be ourselves or not, as we please. . . . We may wear now one mask and now another, and never, if we so desire, appear with our own true face." But having chosen falsity, "truth eludes us."[5] The medieval *Cloud of Unknowing* puts it vividly: "Swink and sweat in all that thou can'st and mayest for to get thee a true knowing and feeling of thyself as thou art. And then I trow soon after that thou will get thee a true knowing and feeling of God as he is."[6] The author speaks of both "knowing" and "feeling," for the understanding of the Divine Nature is not just feeling as the Old Priest implies, nor yet just know-

3. See Schakel, *Imagination,* 95. Lewis's use of music in this passage of *TWHF* is referring specifically to the sad music of Greek tragedy, which Orual knows only through the songs of the Fox.

4. William James, *The Varieties of Religious Experience: A Study in Human Nature,* 440, 449.

5. Thomas Merton, *Seeds of Contemplation,* 31–32.

6. From chapter 14; quoted by Bryant in *Jung and the Christian Way,* 50. For a modern translation, see *The Cloud of Unknowing,* ed. James Walsh, 150.

ing, as the Fox implies. The phrase "swink [toil] and sweat" suggests physical effort; "canst" (know how to) and "mayest" (have power to) suggest the exertion of mental power and determination. The medieval author is emphasizing that the spiritual seeker must work hard, for attaining self-knowledge requires a strenuous effort of the whole person.

Lewis himself struggled with this problem all his life. In *The Screwtape Letters* (1942), one of his earliest books on the spiritual journey, Wormwood is advised to let the "patient" see only a "very expurgated version" of his own thoughts (*ScL*, 16). In *Letters to Malcolm, Chiefly on Prayer* (1964), Lewis's last such book, he says one of the prime difficulties in prayer is to get beyond "the idea I call 'me'"—the phantasmal self that one has created "in the vaguest way from all sorts of psychological odds and ends" (*LM*, 78). What the *Cloud* author calls "swink and sweat" Lewis calls the effort to remember that there is a "real I" under the tragic mask or theatrical makeup. As a tragic heroine Orual is the mother grieving for her lost child, the victim of a hopeless love for Bardia, and the unloved daughter of the Fox, who (in her mind) cared for Psyche more. And in all these tragic roles she rejects her true life and her true self.

Chapter 20. The Queen's Resumé

A. The Art of Story:
To Strengthen Glome and Weaken Ungit

With remarkable brevity, Orual's list of accomplishments sets out her reign in terms of the sovereign's "two bodies"—her public and private persons.[1] "The Queen"'s reign is glorious, but beneath the surface Orual suffers, a mere mortal. Her deeds fall into three major categories: the completely wise and just ones, the ones intended to destroy "Orual," and the attempts to weaken Ungit. As narrator, Orual lists them in roughly chronological order; as author, Lewis leaves the responsibility of understanding the categories to the reader.

The following actions show Orual as a wise and just ruler:

1. She reduced the number of slaves, making the operation of the palace more efficient. She freed the best ones and gave them "land and cottages" so that they could be truly independent.

2. She reformed the operation of the silver mines so that they became a source of wealth rather than punishment or a futile expression of anger.

3. She revised the laws and had them posted in the center of the city, so that all the people could know them. In effect, she turned an irrational autocracy into a constitutional monarchy.

Two actions show her repeated efforts to destroy "Orual":

See *TWHF*, pp. 226–37.
1. See chapter 17, section B, above.

4. She changed her quarters to different parts of the palace, seeking to be free of the swinging chains of the well, which sounded like a girl weeping. When the sound woke her up at night, she went to the Pillar Room and worked.

5. But the chains continued to disturb her, and she stifled the sound by enclosing the well in thick stone walls. It must have solved the problem, for the year after that she defeated Essur.

Three other sensible and efficient actions can be seen as a weakening of Ungit:

6. She developed the river Shennit to make it more serviceable to trade.

7. She built cisterns to store water.

8. She improved Glome's breeds of cattle and sheep, thus lessening the chances of another famine.

These actions weaken Ungit's hold on the people's lives by insuring them against political isolation, drought, and famine. No longer are they dependent on Ungit's favor to protect them from the sort of disasters that made it necessary to sacrifice Psyche.

Two other actions, intended to strengthen Glome spiritually and intellectually, weakened Ungit, or at least so Orual hoped.

9. She supported Arnom in the purchase of a Greek-style statue of the goddess to stand in front of the ugly, shapeless stone. (See section D below.)

10. She had the Fox collect books for a national library, providing the noble youth with an opportunity to substitute enlightenment for superstition. (See section B below.)

One of her actions, condemning Batta to death, combines all the previous motivations. It is narrated second, and the mixture of motives, as well as a certain false openness about the decision, guides the reader in evaluating the other deeds. First, hanging Batta was a sensible, efficient way to cleanse the palace of discord. However, it was also a way of killing "Orual" and putting "the Queen" in her place. By getting rid of the substitute mother who had bullied her as a young child, Orual establishes her own adulthood. She has lost her place as Psyche's Maia, but as queen she is the mother and nurturer of Glome. Finally, by carrying out the destruction of Batta during the fig harvest, Orual symbolically weakens Ungit, because of the fig's sacred and sexual associations. (Even today this association is preserved in the obscene gesture called "making a fig.") Thus hanging Batta is one way to deny Ungit's sexuality, to make a fig at the goddess.

Orual's description of the hanging is a clue to her mixed motives. On the surface, it all sounds perfectly reasonable: "Following up a chance word which one of the horseboys said in my hearing, I found that she had long been the pest of the whole palace," spreading gossip and bullying other slaves (*TWHF*, 230). But why does Orual imply that she made an accidental discovery of something previously unknown? Surely the "chance word" of the horseboy is unnecessary, for the reader has already seen several examples of Batta's wicked tongue. Early on, she tried to frighten Orual and Redival by saying the tutor would whip them. She carried the rumor that Psyche's healing touch actually spread the plague. After Psyche was gone she became "very familiar" with the king and "tattled and whispered and flattered" him while also "snuggling up [with Redival] for gossip and bawdy" (*TWHF*, 182). When the king became bedfast, she took him plenty of wine and shared it with him, even though no one else in the palace had enough. "Orual" knew all about Batta. Why is "the Queen" dependent for information about Batta's activities on "a chance word" from one of the other slaves? And why is the narrator of "the Queen"'s deeds (i.e., Orual) so eager to justify this particular decision?

B. Context: The Glome Library

The list of "the Queen"'s accomplishments is focused on Glome and her inner conflicts; the catalog of the royal library expands this narrow focus. It places Glome within the larger ancient world, recalls the theme of disordered love, reviews "the Queen"'s encounter with Greek wisdom, and suggests the relationship between classical myth and the coming of Christ, the myth become fact. In addition, it points to the next chapter, in which Orual is forced to confront herself in a new way.

How can one paragraph mean so much? Orual identifies only seven of the eighteen volumes by content, and says they were all "what we could get, not what we chose" (*TWHF*, 232). However, the seeming randomness is Lewis's artistically created illusion, and each identified book implies something about love, Orual's lack of self-knowledge, or both.

The paragraph is so intricately designed that we as readers must walk a fine line between missing implications and overreading. As Lewis wrote to Kilby, "Much that you take as allegory was intended solely as realistic detail" (*Let,* 462). For example, Orual's listing of the books is quite different from the way a modern person would do it. She describes contents instead of citing titles, and highlights features different from the ones we would choose. It has been suggested that Orual's descriptions of the books indicate that her knowledge was secondhand, that she as queen was too busy to read the books for herself, and her erroneous naming of Stesichorus as "Hesias" rather than "Teisias" is cited as evidence.[2] But when we remember her chronic insomnia, it is hard to believe that she did not have time to read. Two alternate historical explanations occur: since a manuscript is more likely to be damaged at the beginning and the end than in the middle, identification by content is more informative than by title; "Hesias" rather than "Teisias" is quite plausible as a scribal error.

The fact that three of the books—*Andromeda,* Stesichorus's *Helen,* and the book on agriculture—are no longer extant is Lewis's subtle reminder that we really know very little about the ancient world and what books were considered important. The book on agriculture cannot be identified; Varro, the Latin scholar whose prose work on agriculture, *De re rustica,* was published in 37 B.C., says that he knew more than fifty Greek works on the subject. Also, a Punic work on agriculture by Mago was translated into both Latin and Greek in the late Hellenistic period.[3]

The details ascribed to historical realism also serve the literary purpose of involving the reader in recognizing titles and puzzling out the implications. The list is roughly chronological, beginning with the *Iliad,* the prototypical epic of disordered love, and ending with Aristotle's *Metaphysics,* a work of philosophy based on the assumption that "all men by nature desire knowledge." Identifying the Aristotle by its opening words results in a subtle irony. Do all people really desire knowledge? Even Achilles? Even Orual? Neither

2. Schakel, *Imagination,* 27–28.
3. *OCD* 3, s.v. "agricultural writers."

Orual nor Achilles can be called wise in love. Orual stabbed her own arm to defend Psyche's honor, and Patroclus died because Achilles sulked in his tent instead of going out to fight. Both Orual and Achilles are immoderately possessive—Orual in wanting Psyche to remain her baby forever, Achilles in demanding that Agamemnon return the girl Briseis. Significantly, Glome's fragment of the *Iliad* ends when Patroclus comes into Achilles' tent, begging that he be allowed to don his friend's armor and help the Greeks. It omits the result of his request, when Achilles, mourning over his death, exclaims, "Ah, how I wish that discord could be banished from the world of gods and men, and with it anger."[4]

The reference to Euripides is equally laden with implications. First, it reminds us of the much younger Orual who missed being Iphigeneia, for Euripides wrote two versions of that story. Glome acquired neither of them, but rather *Andromeda* and *The Bacchae*. Andromeda's situation was like Psyche's: taken as a propitiation to an offended deity, chained up to be devoured by a monster, and rescued by a winged hero. (Psyche's Eros is usually portrayed as a winged god.)

The Bacchae presents a more subtle parallel with *Till We Have Faces*. Dionysus (Bacchus), the prologist, speaks of himself in language that reminds us of Christ: "Behold, God's Son is come into this land," come "to be God manifest to men."[5] Like Psyche's god-husband, he is a precursor of Christ. Orual's reference to the "wild women" (Maenads) reminds us of what the Old Priest said about blood sacrifice, for the Maenads worship Dionysus by tearing wild animals apart and eating their raw flesh, a propitiary rite like the sacrifices of Andromeda and Psyche.

The reference to Stesichorus, like the *Andromeda*, suggests a parallel with Glome. In Stesichorus's poem, the real Helen did not go to Troy at all, but stayed in Egypt while her eidolon, or airy image, committed adultery with Paris in Troy. We remember that the god told Orual, "You also shall be Psyche," and the two sisters are in

---

4. In *The Symposium*, Phaedrus praises Achilles as an ideal lover, since he "gave his life to avenge his friend" (180a). Apparently it escaped Phaedrus that Achilles also caused his friend's death. Achilles' speech: Homer, *Iliad*, 18.110, tr. E. V. Rieu.

5. Line 1 is from Gilbert Murray's translation, line 22 from that of Arthur S. Way.

some sense mirror images of each other. Psyche wanders the earth while Orual stays in Glome, and in book 2 we learn that each sister's actions affect the other one.

According to Plato's *Phaedrus*, Stesichorus first related the same story as Homer, and like Homer was struck blind. He regained his sight after he made the alternative version vindicating Helen. In fact, the only surviving passage of Stesichorus's *Helen* consists of three lines quoted in the *Phaedrus:*

> That story was not true;
> Neither did you step into the well-oared ships,
> Nor did you come to the citadel of Troy.[6]

Perhaps it is too far-fetched to see in the reference to Stesichorus a hint of the retraction to come in Book 2 of *Till We Have Faces*. If so, Lewis's fascination with the story of the alternate Helen is sufficient reason for the inclusion of Stesichorus in the Glome library, for Lewis's fragment "After Ten Years" was the beginning of a retelling of Helen's story in realistic, modern style.

By what Orual emphasizes and what she skips over, we get a hint of her deepest concerns with Greek wisdom. The great Plato, founder of Western philosophy, is dismissed as "some of the conversations of Socrates."[7] Heraclitus and Aristotle are mentioned very briefly; and her highest praise goes to the "very good, useful book" on agriculture. In part 2 of the novel, Plato's ideas will become more important.

C. Love: Love Unreceived

"The Queen" calls Bardia and the Fox her "first" great "strength" as a ruler. She realizes that they care for her unselfishly: "[N]either cared a straw for his own dignity or advancement when my needs were in question." She says that they loved her without flattery—that is, honestly—but she downgrades the integrity of their love by the reason she gives for it: "they did not think of me as a woman."

6. Plato, *Phaedrus*, 243b.
7. Although it is theoretically possible that "the conversations of Socrates" could be those of Xenophon rather than Plato, such an identification would destroy the ironic implication of Plato's banishment from Glome. See "Plato," 210.

Her passion was amply expressed in a battle with Essur; Bardia was ambushed, and Orual dashed in to save him, so fiercely that "they say I . . . killed seven men with my own strokes" (*TWHF*, 227–28). Since she has just been speaking of her fear of battle, her experience is reminiscent of Plato's *Symposium*, in which it is said that "the veriest coward," or even a woman, will become "an inspired hero" when the beloved is in danger.[8]

Of course it is not likely that the two men did not think of her as a woman. When she proposed to fight Argan, the Fox was shocked by the impropriety of sending a woman into battle. And is it really believable that Bardia, a married man and the father of eight children, should have been completely unaware of her intense passion for him? Perhaps. The passage in which she describes her relationship—or lack of it—with Bardia's wife, Ansit, is contradictory and confused. Orual says she wanted to love Bardia's wife, but she is pleased when Ansit seems jealous of her closeness to Bardia. She analyses the different ways she and Ansit possess him and concludes, "I have known, I have had, so much of him that she could never dream of." But then her self-pity surfaces again. She assumes (without evidence) that Bardia is completely unaware of the competition between herself and Ansit; they suffer, he does not. And she concludes bitterly, "The one sin the gods never forgive us is that of being born women" (*TWHF*, 232–33). Orual's passion is not, somehow, single-minded; if Bardia is unaware of it, perhaps that is the reason.

As for the Fox, in the confusion of old age, he calls Orual "Karmides" and "Crethis," a sign that his longing for Greece and its philosophical discussions never left him. Orual's response to his sacrifice is indicated in one sentence: "But I was too busy to be with him much" (*TWHF*, 235).[9]

D. Faith: Enlightened Religion
("The Holy," 168; "Pagan Religion," 204)

During the Old Priest's regime, the religion of Glome was analogous to that of the Greeks during the Age of Ignorance. When Arnom

8. Plato, *Symposium*, 179 b, c.
9. Charmides, son of Glaucon, was a young man beautiful in soul and body and a member of the Socratic circle. I have not been able to locate a reference for "Crethis."

became chief priest, he set about to bring enlightenment. The first steps were to add more windows to Ungit's House and to keep it cleaner. Physical light brings a rationality to the mind. But does it also bring enlightenment to the spirit? According to Otto, overemphasis on the rational shuts off one's experience of the aspects of God that are beyond conceptual understanding.[10] As the Old Priest had said, "Holy places are dark places" (*TWHF*, 50). And the cleanliness reduced the holy smell that had frightened Orual as a child.

The second project was to bring in a Greek-style statue of Ungit. We have only to visualize the stone, strangely pushed up from the underground and sitting in her dark, smothery house, and then contrast her with an Olympian Aphrodite standing in a pillared, breeze-swept temple, to see what Arnom was trying to do: he wanted to bring clear-eyed Hellenism to Glome. But if he desired a breeze-swept temple (the book says nothing of it), it was certainly beyond his grasp. Indeed, he did not even dare to get rid of the stone and substitute the statue.

"The Queen" believes that Arnom's modernizations have indeed weakened Ungit, and she turns her back on "Orual's" holy fear. The new statue is beautiful to her eyes, but it is not holy. The new statue, made by human hands, is under human control in a way that the Ungit-stone is not. Perhaps Lewis is reminding the reader that the ancient Jews used to mock such statues, "gods" that had to be shaped and painted and dressed, who had eyes but could not see and ears but could not hear. Despite the crudity of Glome's religion, the old Ungit sitting in darkness is closer to the profound spirituality of the Hebrew Ark of the Covenant, which sat empty in total darkness. As for the beauty of the new statue, Gregory of Nyssa seems almost to be echoing Otto (though Gregory lived in the fourth century) when he wrote, "It would seem that the attractiveness of the divine beauty has something terrifying about it, and this is characterised by qualities which seem the exact opposite of bodily beauty. . . . [D]ivine, incorruptible Beauty is at once something stern and terrifying."[11] In Glome the holy darkness has been lessened, while divine beauty has not been attained: the Fox laughs at the statue.

10. Otto, *Holy*, 1, 4.
11. See Ps. 115:4–8 and 135:15–18; Isa. 44:9–17. Gregory of Nyssa is quoted by Kenneth Leech, *True Prayer: An Invitation to Christian Spirituality*, 124–25.

Chapter 21. What Happened in Essur

A. The Art of Story: Inclusions

The previous chapter concludes with Orual's decision to go traveling. She says, "I could no longer endure to see these same things every day till I died. The very blisters of the pitch on the wooden walls of the byres seemed to be the same ones I had seen before the Fox himself came to Glome" (*TWHF*, 237). There is just enough repetition of vocabulary to remind one of the day the Fox came, when Orual and Redival were sliding on the ice "at the back of the oldest part of the palace, where the walls are wooden" and where "[t]here was ice enough all the way from the byre-door to the big dunghill" (*TWHF*, 5–6). This verbal technique is called an *inclusio*. It marks the beginning and ending of a narrative unit and is especially common in older literature. It is a signal that chapter 21 is going to begin a major change of subject. A film, of course, could use a pictorial version of the *inclusio*, by showing Orual looking at the wall and flashing back to the children playing in the same place.

Orual's meeting with the priest of Istra is the high point of the chapter. Everything builds toward this point, at first very slowly. First Orual tells us, in effect, that the journey would be irrelevant if not for the thing that happened at the very end of it. But instead of skipping the irrelevancy and immediately dealing with the meeting, she embarks on an unhurried account of their visit to Phars. Then she describes the scenery on the way to Essur and the three-night stay in the royal house, leaving the reader to wonder what happened at the end of the journey.

See *TWHF*, pp. 238–50.

Even so, it almost did not happen at all. If they had turned home-ward as Orual originally intended, she would not have met the priest. But to please young Ilerdia, she agrees to go one more day's journey to see a marvelous hot spring before turning back to Glome. They decide to camp near the spring, and while the young ones are working, she wanders idly away from camp. Her relaxation, her complete unawareness of what awaits her is shown by her leisurely description of the calm autumn evening and the perfect little temple.

Meeting the priest destroys her calm and frees "Orual" to re-member the story of Psyche that "the Queen" has suppressed. On the trip home, the leisurely narrative gives way to short, abrupt sentences.

Another *inclusio* ends the chapter. At the beginning of chapter 1, Orual

1. asked the reader to judge the gods,

2. suggested that the gods might send "terrors and plagues" on her,

3. complained that the god of the mountain will not answer her.

At the end of chapter 21, these thoughts are repeated even more emphatically in reverse order:

1. "But will not all the world then know (and the gods will know it knows) that this is because they have no answer?"

2. "[Perhaps] they'll strike me mad or leprous or turn me into beast, bird, or tree."

3. "I say, therefore, that there is no creature . . . so noxious to man as the gods" (*TWHF*, 249–50).

B. Context: The Collective Unconscious ("The New Psychology," 192)

Orual is shocked to hear "the sacred story" as told by the priest of Psyche. After all, no mortal other than herself knew about the palace and what took place between herself and Psyche. She theo-rizes that the gods "dropped [it] into someone's mind, in a dream, or an oracle, or however they do such things" (*TWHF*, 243). This is almost an overt reference to Jung's theory of the collective uncon-scious, for he believed that human beings do learn from each other on this level. Outside the context of Jungian psychology, the fact that the priest knew the story seems magical, a break in the gritty realism of the novel to this point. But if Jung's theory is correct, the priest's story simply adds realism to what has gone before, for reality is more complex than it previously seemed.

Up to this point Orual has believed—or at least acted as if she believed—that she knew her own mind and her reasons for doing things. From this point on she will begin to learn differently. A reader who is sensitive toward Jungian symbolism will have seen images of the unconscious already. For example, in the night before the sacrifice Psyche says, "[The Fox] calls the whole world a city. But what's a city built on? There's earth beneath. And outside the wall? Doesn't all the food come from there as well as all the dangers?" (*TWHF*, 70–71). This is an excellent picture of the human personality as perceived by Jung. The city is the conscious self; the earth beneath is the unconscious, the source of human creativity, and the source of the human experience of God. As Bryant says, "God is to be found in the lowest depths of the soul, [for] the soul is grounded in God."[1]

It is not surprising, then, that one important symbol of the unconscious is the underground; caves, wells, and springs are entrances to the world below. Thus, Orual spends a prodigious amount to tame the well outside the palace, to build a thick stone house around it. Her mason protests the extravagance, but her action brings peace and success: "I heard Psyche weeping no more. The year after that I defeated Essur [and saved Bardia's life]" (*TWHF*, 235). But not for good. In Essur is a marvelous hot spring, and the young people persuade her to add this one side trip to their itinerary. And there near the spring the little temple and the priest of Psyche await her.

Attempts to break off communication with the unconscious always fail in some way. In dreams Orual used to have "an ugly fancy" that "[she] had walled up, gagged with stone, not a well but Psyche (or Orual) herself" (*TWHF*, 235). The defeat of Essur was only temporary.

C. Love: Love Withered

Two brief passages suggest that "the Queen" has succeeded in hardening her heart against love. First, she says that she could have

1. Bryant, *Jung and the Christian Way*, 48.

loved her nephew, the son of Trunia and Redival, "if I had let my-self and if Redival had been out of the way. But I would never give my heart again to any young creature" (*TWHF*, 238). Second, when she has returned to Glome and is trying to catch up with her ad-ministrative work, she learns that Bardia is ill. Her first reaction is to be annoyed at the inconvenience of not having him to help her; then she surmises that he is really not very sick, but his wife is mag-nifying the illness to keep him from coming to help her. It is as if her love for Bardia is swamped by her urgent need to write her book and accuse the gods.

However, there is a hint of human feeling in her friendship with the young people in the traveling party and in the way her heart lifted at the beauty of nature, when "[t]he eagles wheeled above us and the waterfalls roared" (*TWHF*, 239). We remember that she strug-gled against delight, against "freshness and wetness," when she and Bardia were on the way to the Grey Mountain. Perhaps we also remember her comment about it: "The gods never send us this in-vitation to delight so readily or so strongly as when they are prepar-ing some new agony. We are their bubbles; they blow us big before they prick us" (*TWHF*, 96, 97).

D. Faith: History, Myth, and Anthropology

Orual is infuriated when she realizes that the priest knows Psy-che's story, but he has gotten her part in it all wrong. She says, "I wondered how many of the other sacred stories are just such twisted falsities as this" (*TWHF*, 244). A more objective look, however, sug-gests that "the sacred story" tells the real truth. Orual was jealous of Psyche; sometimes she even hated her beautiful sister. The dif-ference between the priest's version and Orual's shows that a his-torical account may be true even though it contains some factual errors. Perhaps one can see in this a sly parallel with biblical scholars and the search for the historical Jesus.[2]

---

2. The questioning of the New Testament was part of a larger movement doubting the historical existence of, for example, Troy, and Lewis as a special-ist in the classics was concerned with it. See "Modern Theology and Biblical Criticism," in *CR*, 152–66. See also Myers, *Context*, 203–4.

There may also be a gentle poke at the methods of anthropology as Lewis knew them. Anthropologists have often explained the content of myths and folktales as ways of accounting for the tribe's worship customs. They imply that it would be ridiculous to think the stories contained any element of historicity. The method, at least in the case of the priest of Psyche, leads to an egregious error. It never occurs to him that Psyche might really have been a mortal girl. The idea that something historical could come to be regarded as myth or legend, or that a physical reality might be considered metaphorical by people who never experienced it, fascinated Lewis, and he uses it in both fiction and nonfiction.

Book Two
What Really Happened

Chapter 1. Reality Check

A. The Art of Story: Reality by Measurement ("Time," 219)

Book 1 is Orual's book as she wrote it, word for word; book 2 is about what happened after she finished it. Book 1 is written in a completely realistic mode. When "the Queen" decided to "kill Orual," she devoted herself to outward things: to science, what she calls physical philosophy; to war when necessary; and to the nuts and bolts of running the kingdom. As she recounts what happened to her in book 1, her way of writing creates an impression of scientific, objective reality. She provides measurements of time and space that are based on bodily movements and observations—heartbeats, walking, the movement of the sun—and thus, as I have previously noted, "involves the reader through kinesthetic images."[1] The same is true of her hate and fear of Ungit, which she describes in physical terms—in her sensory response to "the Ungit smell," the "temple-smell of blood ... and burnt fat and singed hair and wine and stale incense" (*TWHF*, 11). Most important, she reminds us repeatedly that she intends to nail the gods for their injustice, and, therefore, she must make her story perfectly truthful.

But that which can be measured, smelled, or objectively observed is just a small part of a human being. There is also the transcendent, the world of dreams, the divine urgings that come through the subconscious mind. Book 2 is about how "the Queen"'s suppression of Orual was reversed and how the unseen divine called to her from the unseen world.

See *TWHF*, pp. 253–76.
1. Myers, *Context*, 196.

117

In the four chapters of book 2, Lewis gradually diminishes the reality of the seen world and increases Orual's response to the other world. In this first chapter there is nothing supernatural. Orual learns about herself by experiencing two ordinary events (conversations with Tarin and Ansit) and having one important dream. In subsequent chapters, the world of dreams will become more vivid than the everyday world of the senses.

B. Context: Reality by Comparison ("Glome," 163)

Part of Orual's reality check comes from the greater world outside Glome. She had lived in Glome all her life, and the pleasure trip that ended in Essur did not, after all, cover a very great distance. The direct route from Essur to Glome took "seven or eight days," and the average distance covered per day was probably not more than twenty miles. Then comes Tarin from the realm of the Great King to the South and East. His urbane sneer makes us realize how small Glome is: to him the fierce King Trom was only "a little barbarous king whose whole kingdom could be put into one corner of my master's hunting park and never be noticed!" (*TWHF*, 248, 255).

Relating Glome to the Hellenistic world suggests a parallel between Orual and Jesus. Jesus lived at the edge of nowhere, in an unimportant little province of the Roman Empire. But in his life all the myths of the ancient world came into focus, became fact. Orual lived in a tiny, barbarous country outside the Greek trading area and the territories opened by Alexander the Great, but she saw and heard Psyche's god-husband. She learned that the story of the marriage of Ungit's son had become fact within Psyche's experience. (And as the god tells her, she also is Psyche.) By suggesting this parallel, Lewis prepares the reader for the account in book 2 of how Psyche and Orual are guided "towards the true God" (*Let*, 462).

C. Love: The First Unveiling

Tarin and Ansit remember Orual's feelings for Redival and Bardia quite differently from her description in book 1. Tarin, the eunuch who was once Redival's boyfriend, remembers that Redival was lonely: "She used to say, 'First of all Orual loved me much; then the

Fox came and she loved me little; then the baby came and she loved me not at all.' So she was lonely" (*TWHF*, 255). Orual realizes that she has been too self-centered to understand that she is not the only person in the world with troubles.

As for Bardia, while Orual was writing her book she "hardly gave [him] a thought." Anyone who has done even a little writing understands how the "rage of it" (*TWHF*, 257) can take over the mind so that nothing else exists. On the other hand, it looks very much as if Orual's self-defense against the gods is more important to her than Bardia's well-being.

Again, anyone who has loved knows how natural it is to wish that one could have said "I love you"—more plainly, more often, or, like Orual, at least once. But a less self-centered person would gladly suppress her own need lest she hurt Bardia.

Her condolence call on Bardia's wife, Ansit, brings out still another facet of Orual's insensitivity to Bardia and his needs. Ansit accuses Orual of having worked him to death; it is the fault of "the Queen" that he is dead. And when Orual tries to transfer some of the blame to Ansit—"Why did you not tell me?"—Ansit responds, "I was his wife, not his doxy. He was my husband, not my house-dog. He was to live the life he thought best and fittest for a great man— not that which would most pleasure me." It reminds us of what Psyche said when Orual demanded that she test her god-husband: "I am his wife. I know" (*TWHF*, 264, 161) and defended his right to do as he thought best.

At the god's palace Orual was offended by Psyche's wifeliness: "You fling my virginity in my face again, do you?" (*TWHF*, 162). Similarly, Ansit puts her wifeliness up as a barrier, a shield, against the queen when she says, with some irony, "I was only his wife. He was too well-mannered, you know, to nod and yawn in a Queen's house" (*TWHF*, 260). Orual responds more humbly to Ansit than she had done to Psyche, but still with self-pity. She has had no husband, no child; Ansit has had both. She pulls aside her veil for the first time since she became Queen. What Ansit pities, however, is not her ugliness, but her barren, hopeless love of Bardia.

Orual's humility is momentary; at Ansit's accusation that Orual has devoured the lives of the Fox and her sisters as well as Ansit's and Bardia's, she literally sees red: "The air in her room was shot with crimson." But riding homeward, she admits to herself that she overworked Bardia to keep him beside her, asked unnecessary questions "for the mere pleasure of hearing his voice," and in her fantasies in which he sought her love always wanted him to begin "by imploring my forgiveness" (*TWHF*, 265–67). She realizes the sickness of her fantasies about him but does not yet see how much it resembles the love she had for Psyche.[2]

D. Faith: Objective Justice

"The Queen" had pretty well succeeded in suppressing Orual. She had developed objectivity and control of her emotions, but at the expense of living almost completely in her conscious mind. There comes a time, though, when the spiritual, transcendent part of a human being can no longer be neglected. Jung's description applies well to Orual: "Among all my patients . . . [all secure, comfortable people] in the second half of life, there has not been one whose problem . . . was not that of finding a religious outlook on life." He continues, "[N]one of them has been really healed who did not regain his religious outlook."[3] "The Queen," having passed youth and middle age, thinks to flee boredom in her own land, only to encounter in Essur the "religious outlook"—a story about love, loss, and reunion with the divine beloved. In response she embarks on the project of telling the truth about her life; it is a strenuous spiritual search.

Writing her book is the first stage. In it, she is trying her best to tell the exact truth as she perceives it. In her waking hours she tries to classify, to pass judgment on her motivations, and to separate her real motives from the lies she told herself. When she sleeps, her labor continues symbolically, in dream language, as an effort to separate and classify different kinds of seeds (since motives are the seeds of actions). The kind of judgment pictured in the dream is that of absolute law. Her classifications must be completely perfect, for they constitute the case she hopes to bring against the gods, showing that they were wrong and she was right. Later she will encounter a different kind of judgment.

2. Compare her craving for dominance with the abuses of courtly love in book 3 of *The Faerie Queene*.
3. *CW*, vol. 9, para. 509, cited in Bryant, *Jung and the Christian Way*, 14.

Chapter 2. Who Is Ungit?

A. The Art of Story: Ungit in the Temple

The previous chapter ends with the words, "I thought I had come to the very bottom and that the gods could tell me no worse" (*TWHF*, 267). But what she learned in the previous chapter came from Tarin and Ansit, people she met in the course of everyday life, and what they told her was received by her conscious mind. The task of this chapter is to begin the exploration of the unconscious, of what lies beneath the "bottom" in Orual's selfhood.

Lewis uses the visit to the temple of Ungit to move the story from conscious, everyday events to the events of dream and vision. The realistic method of narration is maintained, and a plausible reason is given for the visit: it is required by Orual's status as queen. The activities, personnel, and furnishings of the temple belong to everyday life, since they can be observed; in fact, we see them through Orual's objective account. Nevertheless, the temple is holy ground, sacred space. The worship is real. The peasant woman praying to the stone Ungit received consolation, and the crowd responded to the ceremony of the Year's Birth with joy and brotherhood.

Orual is apparently oblivious to the holiness of the temple and the Ungit stone. She scorns Arnom's allegorical explanation of Ungit as a fertility goddess with the sarcastic rationality of a Mark Twain: "It's very strange that our fathers should first think it worth telling us that rain falls out of the sky, and then, for fear such a notable secret should get out . . . wrap it up in a filthy tale so that no one could

See *TWHF*, pp. 268–80.

understand the telling" (*TWHF*, 271). She finds the ceremony of the Year's Birth equally silly: "a man dressed up as a bird had walked out of a door after striking a few blows with a wooden sword" (*TWHF*, 273). However, the experience inspires her to ask, "Who is Ungit?" (*TWHF*, 270), and her scorn contrasts ironically with what she will soon be experiencing in her dreams.

B. Context: Ungit in the Unconscious
("The New Psychology," 192; "The Holy," 168)

Up to this point, Orual's growing self-knowledge has come from external sources such as hearing home truths from Tarin and Ansit. This chapter moves into the part of her personality that cannot be reached by the scientific method or observed by the behavioral psychologist. Jung calls it "the unconscious," but it may also be called "the transcendent," because it is the receptor for experience of the divine, as opposed to knowledge about the divine. It is not conceptual and language-bound, but intuitive and wordless. It exists outside, beyond, or below the conscious mind. On those occasions when it touches everyday life, it gives meaning and radiance for those with eyes to see.

Lewis was aware of the Jungian elements in *Till We Have Faces*, but he insisted that "the main conscious prosework is Christian, not Jungian" (*LetChil*, 107). However, "conscious prosework" is not imagery; certainly it is not a sufficient explanation of the vividness of Orual's journey into the transcendent. Her dream of digging into the depths of the Pillar Room, for example, is reminiscent of the image of the human personality in Jung's "Mind and Earth."

The structure of the personality, says Jung, is like a building. Its upper story was built in the nineteenth century. It is the conscious level, the place we live, "only dimly aware" that the ground floor is "somewhat old-fashioned." It dates from the sixteenth century, but it is actually a reconstruction of an eleventh-century dwelling tower. Although Jung does not explicitly say so, the ground floor seems to depict the unexamined assumptions that are the basis of one's habitual thoughts and actions. It is a mixture of some concepts from the beginning of modern science and others from the medieval Age of Faith. Under the ground floor is a Roman cellar, and under that a "choked-up cave" with stone tools lying on the floor; below the cave are geological layers containing fossils from glacial times. "As to what lies beneath the earth's surface," says Jung, "we remain totally unconscious."[1]

Lewis uses similar language in discussing the difficulty of coming to prayer, placing oneself in the presence of God: "And what am I? The façade is what I call consciousness.... [But] my thinking ... turn[s] out to be the thinnest possible film on the surface of a vast deep." The deep is the source of "[d]azzling lightness as well as dark clouds," of creativity as well as the "monotonous and claustrophobic material" of sexuality postulated by Freud. It includes the "depths of time too. All my past; my ancestral past; perhaps my pre-human past." He concludes, "Here again, if I could dive deeply enough, I might again reach at the bottom that which simply is" (*LM*, 78–79).

In the digging episode, Orual does not reach "that which simply is," but she gets below the false self-image she has maintained on the surface. As "the Queen" she has been living in Jung's upper story, behind Lewis's "façade" of consciousness. Even the condemnations she received from Tarin and Ansit affected only her conscious mind. However, in the dream her father comes to her with godlike authority. Just as the cold, rejecting god was the only way she could experience the divine on the mountain, so also at this point she can experience God only as angry and domineering.[2] He forbids her to wear her veil, her second unveiling. (The first occurred when she revealed her face to Ansit.) They go to the Pillar Room, the place where she has ruled Glome consciously and rationally, and begin to dig up the floor. It is "Orual," not "the Queen," who digs, for the moment her father addressed her as "girl," her many years as queen "shrank up small like a dream" (*TWHF*, 273).

The digging uncovers an opening like the mouth of a well. "The Queen" had once imprisoned a well in stone so that she would not hear the calling of the well chain. Like that well, the hole in the Pillar Room is an entry into the lower world, the realm of the unconscious.

1. Jung, "Mind and Earth," in *Civilization in Transition*, 31; standard citation *CW*, 10.54.
2. Bryant, in *Depth Psychology*, 2, says Jung and Freud reached opposite conclusions from the same data: "For Freud God is a father-substitute, for Jung a child's father is a God-substitute."

What Orual and the king find below is another Pillar Room, smaller and made of clay, like all the descendants of Adam. It is a more fleshy, more childlike version of Orual's self-centered personality. It is smothery, like Batta's affection for the child Orual and Orual's for Psyche. The third Pillar Room has walls of bedrock. It is even smaller and more smothery, and in it is the mirror, another entrance into the world of the unconscious, the world of both creativity and "monotonous and claustrophobic" cravings. There the god-like father-king forces Orual to look at herself, forces her to confess, "I am Ungit" (*TWHF*, 276).[3]

Like the conscious mind itself, this annotation of the passage in Jungian terms is only a small part of its total meaning. A rereading of the digging episode with close attention to the physical sensations—digging, falling, being smothered, being helpless in a large hand, then finally coming out of that dark warmth into "the cool daylight"—these sensations communicate complex levels of significance that we cannot articulate in logical sentences.

The image of the large hand, "soft and clinging as Batta's arms, or as the tough clay [they] had been digging, or as the dough of a huge loaf" (*TWHF*, 276), combines the possessiveness of the personal feminine (Batta's arms), the inexorable demands of the goddess, the human awareness of being mortal clay, and finally, the very materiality of being nourished by bread, for the loaf, too, is an image of femininity, its yeasty swelling like the swelling of the female belly.

The profundity and complexity of this image were prepared for by what Orual saw in the temple. She saw Ungit, the goddess with a thousand faces or no face at all, with a face such as one might see in a loaf of dough, a feminine being like Batta with her "huge, hot, strong yet flabby-soft embraces, the smothering, engulfing tenacity of her" (*TWHF*, 270). Coming from down under, from the earth that is also the mortal clay, the Ungit stone embodies the human condition. It is feminine, not in contrast with human masculinity, but as all mortals are feminine in relation to the divine.[4] It is powerful as the Greek-style statue of the goddess cannot be, and that is the rea-

3. A deeper significance of the confession, "I am Ungit," comes in the Fox's instruction, "All, even Psyche, are born into the House of Ungit" (*TWHF*, 301).
4. Lewis refers to the femininity of human beings in relation to God in "Christianity and Literature," *CR*, 4–5; and dramatizes it in fiction in *THS*, 315–16.

son the peasant woman always prayed to her rather than to the statue.

In wailing, "I am Ungit," Orual is responding to the Holy with "'creature-feeling' or creature-consciousness." Otto describes it as "feelings of submergence and prostration and of the diminution of the self into nothingness," like Isaiah's response to the vision in the temple or Peter's response to Jesus.[5]

Thus, by digging for self-knowledge Orual has encountered the Holy, and she reacts with self-revulsion. In the second episode, the attempted suicide at the river, she encounters the Holy aboveground, and the imagery is more intellectual, more rational, and closer to the familiar style of Lewis's earlier, explicitly apologetic works.

C. Love: A Little Compassion

No one that Orual has ever loved appears in this chapter. Nevertheless, she shows an unself-centered, queenly compassion for the woman who comes to pray to Ungit, for the wasted lives of the temple prostitutes, for the common people who are lifted from their cares and sorrows by the joy of the New Year's celebration. Her feelings echo, however faintly, the compassion of Psyche for the people who demanded her healing touch.

D. Faith: Dreams and Drenchings

Orual's growth in faith begins with her required visit to the temple for the Year's Birth ceremony. The temple is holy ground, sacred space; it partakes of the transcendent. Orual seems unaware of its spiritual power, but she is impressed enough to ask, apparently for the first time in her life, "Who is Ungit?"

Back at the palace a partial answer comes to her in the dream of King Trom and the Pillar Room. That is, she calls it a dream, but she adds "that from this time onward" she is unable to "discern dream from waking nor tell which is the truer." Likewise, she cannot tell whether her attempted drowning was something that an

---

5. Otto, *Holy*, 50, citing Isa. 6:5a; Luke 5:8.

observer (if there had been one) could have seen or whether "the whole journey had been a dream" (*TWHF*, 276). She realizes that truth (or fact) is not dependent upon the results of a vote, for she says, "[W]hat many see we call a real thing, and what only one sees we call a dream," and then goes on to explain that the perceptions of the many may be of no importance, "while things that are shown only to one may be spears and water-spouts of truth from the very depth of truth" (*TWHF*, 280, 277). It is too bad that she did not know this years ago, in the valley of Psyche's palace.

Her open-mindedness indicates that she is changing her perception of the gods. She is also changing her resistance to divine commands. When she recognizes the voice of the god her response is, "There was no rebel in me now. I must not drown and doubtless should not be able to" (*THWF*, 280).

That the changes are coming from divine grace is indicated by the phrase "drenched me with seeings" (*TWHF*, 276). "To wet thoroughly," the most common meaning of "drench," is appropriate because water is a common image of grace. An older meaning, "to force an animal to drink a draught of medicine," is also appropriate, for it implies that Orual is experiencing a healing. Finally, the mystic Ruysbroeck speaks of divine revelation in terms of drenching: "Their bare understanding is drenched through by the Eternal Brightness even as the air is drenched through by the sunshine."[6]

---

6. See discussion of "drench" in the glossary; Ruysbroeck is quoted by Leech, *True Prayer*, 48.

Chapter 3. The Book at the Bottom of the Soul

A. The Art of Story: Into Another World

This stage of Orual's spiritual journey consists of two dreams and two periods of meditation. The meditations take place in what we would call her real life, but the dreams seem more important. In a film, the difference could be shown economically by lighting and color. The golden fleece of the rams in the first dream and the bright sunlight of the desert in the second one would contrast dramatically with the drabness of Orual's room in Glome. Still another mood, another level of existence, could be represented by the gray light of the judgment hall.

In the second dream, the contradictory images fully engage the physical senses. The brilliant desert sun contrasts with the "sunless country" of death; the heat, with the coldness of death's water. Orual's thirst, and the sand that roughens her throat, makes her long for another drenching, for the wetness of the water of death, however bitter it may be. The solid mountain surface and the sharpness of its pinnacles contrast with the slithering movement of the serpents and scorpions. Orual feels that she has walked "for a hundred years," but the sun with its "terrible light" is motionless overhead (*TWHF*, 285–87).

Most important is the nightmarish helplessness. It comes partly from the contradictory images, but even more from the way objects turn into something else. What seems at first to be a cloud is really an eagle; a black hole appears in the solid rocks of the moun-

See *TWHF*, pp. 281–93.

tain; the empty bowl is really a book; and Orual's great book is really an old, bedraggled, poorly written little manuscript. In addition, there is the unwelcome attention that she is unable to escape in the repeated cries of "Here she is" and "She's come at last" (*TWHF*, 288). Finally, there is the shame of nakedness, another common motif in nightmares. Orual's conscious mind is dormant, and all she can do is to read her book compulsively, over and over, before the judge and the ghosts.

After all this confusion and uncertainty, the judge's question, "Are you answered?" comes as a welcome breath of sanity. In contrast with the continued obsessive reading and the silence of the multitudes, the brief question seems solid as a rock. The whole vision/dream/nightmare has been artistically constructed to lead to this point.

B. Context: Myth and Ordinary Life ("Apuleius," 145; "Time," 219)

When Psyche's palace was destroyed, the god laid two divine pronouncements upon Orual: that she would come to know herself, and that she would be Psyche. In book 2 we see these two pronouncements coming true. Self-knowledge is accomplished by the indirect reprimand of Tarin and the frank denouncement of Ansit, and in her first dream her father forces her to see herself as Ungit.

In her other dreams, each one more intense than the last, Orual experiences the traditional sufferings of Psyche in a different mode. Instead of telling Orual's dream experiences in the same order that Psyche's trials occur in Apuleius, Lewis rearranges them so that the reader gradually realizes that each dream or vision is a parallel to something that Psyche suffers. The classic myths were, in Lewis's time, well known by anyone with a secondary school education. Thus Lewis could expect readers to react to each of Orual's dreams with increasing recognition and understanding of the spiritual meaning that the "retold" version adds to the original fairy tale. At the same time, the rearrangement forms a logical progression in Orual's journey to self-knowledge.

Her first task, the separation of seeds, is the writing of her book—the analysis of how the gods wronged her, deprived her of Psyche, and brought punishment upon her. In Apuleius, Psyche was not set to separating seeds until after she had surrendered to Venus. Orual's surrender—to her father rather than the female goddess—thus comes after she has acquired some self-knowledge through her own judgment. Orual's next dream, an attempt at suicide, is a logical outcome of the episode with her father, in which she sees that her ugliness is not physical so much as the Ungit in her. She wants to get rid of her Ungit qualities and behavior by getting rid of herself. But she is forbidden to commit physical suicide, and she finds it impossible to commit spiritual suicide by dying to her selfishness. Apuleius's Psyche repeatedly tries to commit suicide; she acts out the role of tragic heroine which for Orual existed only in introspection.

Orual's dream of the rams with the golden fleece follows logically as an effort to mitigate her Ungit-like ugliness by possessing something beautiful—their gold. That, too, is impossible, but the experience teaches her that no effort of her own will ever get rid of her Ungit-nature. For Apuleius's Psyche, it is just another impossible task, and the river reeds tell her how to accomplish it. Like Orual, she could not succeed on her own.

Finally, when Orual attempts to get the water from the top of the mountain, she is instead taken inside the mountain to meet the god of justice. (For Psyche, the eagle simply flies to the top of the mountain and brings the water down to her.) Orual's entry into the mountain is her journey to the Deadlands. It overlaps with Psyche's fourth task, as is seen in the next chapter. Thus the stories of Psyche and Orual are separate in the seed task, together in the fleece task, and separated again in the cold water task.

C. Love: As Possession

When the judge commands Orual to read her complaint against the gods, her book seems so paltry, so petty, so shabby that her first impulse is to tread it underfoot. But it is her obsession, and she finds herself unable to resist reading it over and over. The words are not what she wrote in response to what she learned in Essur about the myth of Psyche, but rather what she has been saying in her heart, over and over, for the last forty years. She reveals that her relationship with Psyche was about possession, about keeping Psyche forever innocent (or rather, ignorant), forever a young child, forever dependent on her. She says repeatedly, "The girl was mine" (*TWHF*, 291–92). In her self-centered possessiveness she is like the father she feared and hated so much, for he also had claimed Psyche: "No one seems to remember whose girl she is. She's mine, fruit of my own body. My loss" (*TWHF*, 60).

Here, in the book at the bottom of her soul, Orual reveals to herself the real reason for her hostility toward the gods and her belief that they are angry at her. As Lewis says in his letter to Clyde Kilby, she is an example of what human affection is like "in its natural condition: true, tender, suffering, but in the long run, tyrannically possessive and ready to turn to hatred when the beloved ceases to be its possession" (*Let*, 462). It is this realization that Orual expresses: "There was given to me a certainty that this, at last, was my real voice" (*TWHF*, 292).

D. Faith: God's Injustice
("Chronology of Lewis's Life," 154)

Orual meditates on what her dreams have revealed to her: she herself is Ungit, and Ungit is told to "Die before you die" (*TWHF*, 279). In chewing over these two concepts, Orual concludes that she truly is Ungit because she is a kind of psychological vampire, a person who has lived by feeding on the lives of others. Apparently she is unable to stop being ugly, and when she tries to obtain the golden fleece, she fails. Some are born graceful (both physically and spiritually), and some are born ugly. She finds that in her world "[The other woman] won without effort what utmost effort would not win for me" (*TWHF*, 284). It is not fair.

Ironically, it is her complaint against divine injustice, the book she reads over and over, her insulting language to the gods, that begins to save her. In her anger she is beginning to trust the bedrock certainty of "the Divine Nature," the God who can handle complaint and insult and respond without anger, "Are you answered?" (*TWHF*, 293).[1] Some critics have spoken of Lewis's book on the death

---

1. Nancy-Lou Patterson in "The Holy House of Ungit," 15, demonstrates the "complexly interlocked meanings of *Till We Have Faces*" by associating the divine question "Are you answered?" with Orual's mortal words, "You are yourself the answer." Then she adds the biblical association in which "Truth stands before [Pilate]" and "He who is asked the question is Himself the answer."

of his wife, *A Grief Observed*, as if his yells of pain and protest, his insults—calling God the Cosmic Sadist, the vivisector, doctor or dentist—meant that he was losing his faith. The fact that he wrote about Orual's trial in these images shows that he already, before he lost his wife, knew what it was like to be angry with God. And the fact that *A Grief Observed* lacks the glorious happy ending of *Till We Have Faces* shows the difference between what can be done in fiction and what must be left undone in nonfiction.

Chapter 4. Face to Face at Last

A. The Art of Story: Bringing Closure

In this last chapter the chief problem, of course, is to bring closure to the conflicts opened up by Orual's life and the book of her life. By reading aloud the inner version of her book in the previous chapter, Orual has come to know that her confrontation is with herself. In the beginning, she taunted the gods for refusing to answer her complaint; at the end, she learned that her answer came from herself.

This chapter takes the closure process one step further. It is a harvesting of the fruits of the self-knowledge previously attained. Orual originally dared the gods to punish her. Now she jumps into the arms of the Fox, who volunteers to take her punishment, who exchanges forgiveness with her, explains her life, and finally leads her to a joyous reunion with Psyche.

The Fox's instruction presents the novelist with a technical problem. Too much uninterrupted explanation will turn the chapter into educational TV—talking heads, and people strolling along empty paths. Lewis solves the problem with the technique used by Dante in the *Purgatorio*: he makes the Fox the guide to pictures displayed along some walls, just as Virgil explained visions and images to Dante on the terraces of Mount Purgatory. In Orual's case, the walls turn out to be Psyche's house and the place of final judgment. Two walls show how Orual suffered for Psyche. The third shows how

See *TWHF*, pp. 291–309.

Psyche suffered for Orual and the other people of Glome. Between views of individual pictures are reactions and questions from Orual and responses by the Fox.

Prepared by instructions and pictures, Orual repents of her possessiveness and is healed of her ugliness. Then the god pronounces judgment on her. It is the same judgment that she received on the mountain, but now she sees it as a reward, not a punishment. The vision fades, but the last two paragraphs show that what she experienced in vision remains true in Glome.

The final note by Arnom is a conventional ending for a novel in which the narrator dies. Lewis's use of it and the picture convention are examples of his approach to fiction writing. He cared nothing for originality in either material or technique, but devoted himself to telling the story as clearly as possible. And this, of course, is the secret of his originality.

B. Context: The Initiation ("Apuleius," 145)

In Apuleius, Psyche's final task is to go to the Underworld and obtain from Queen Persephone a box of beauty, to refresh Aphrodite. Psyche is instructed in what she must do by a speaking tower. She must carry in each hand a sweet barley-cake for Cerberus the three-headed watchdog and in her mouth two coins for Charon the ferryman. She must not stop anywhere along the way, nor speak to anybody (lest the coins drop out of her mouth?), nor take pity on anyone in trouble. There are three tests of her resolution: a lame driver with a lame donkey, struggling with a load of wood; a dead man swimming in "the sluggish stream" and begging to be taken aboard the ferry; and some elderly weavers who ask her to help them set their loom. She follows these complex directions and successfully completes her errand.

The meanings of these details are obscure, although classical scholars have ascertained that it was customary to put a coin in the mouth of the dead for Charon. Psyche needs two coins—one to take her to the Deadlands and one to bring her back. The command to be silent was apparently a feature in initiation ceremonies of mystery religions, and the three trials may suggest ritual ordeals that were part of the initiation into such a religion.[1] Since the rituals were secret, we have no way of deciphering the symbolism.

Lewis shapes the Apuleius version for his own purpose by omitting the details of how to deal with Cerberus and Charon and also the tower's instructions for Psyche's behavior with Persephone in the land of Hades. He then uses the three tasks to recapitulate Psyche's life. Just as Apuleius's Psyche must show no pity, Orual's Psyche must ignore the suffering people of Glome. Instead of taking a dead person aboard the ferry, she must ignore the Fox and his philosophy when he invites her to doubt the reality of the gods. Finally, she must reject the web Orual would weave around her, made of the love that "goes down to [her] very roots and cannot be diminished by any other newer love" (*TWHF*, 165).

In Apuleius, Psyche stupidly opens the box to take a little of the beauty for herself. The box actually contains sleep (beauty sleep?). She is overcome by it, but Cupid rescues her, puts sleep back in the box and sends her to deliver it to Aphrodite. In *Till We Have Faces*, Psyche hands the box to Orual (who has previously realized that she herself is Ungit), and Orual becomes beautiful.

There is a hint that Psyche also must become beautiful, even though, by Orual's account, she has never been anything else. Concerning Psyche's trip to the Deadlands the Fox explains, "All, even Psyche, are born into the House of Ungit. And all must get free from her." This freedom comes from dying to self, as the Fox explains with an unStoic metaphysical wit: "Or say that Ungit in each must bear Ungit's son and die in childbed—or change" (*TWHF*, 301).

Just as Orual suffered in Psyche's place during the first three tasks and Psyche suffered for Orual on the way to the Deadlands, so, too, the sisters share in the transformation, "both beautiful . . . beyond all imagining, yet not exactly the same" (*TWHF*, 308).[2]

Psyche is so beautiful that Orual says, "Goddess? I had never seen a real woman before" (*TWHF*, 307–8, 306). Here Lewis restates in Orual's words the much-quoted sentence of Irenaeus (130–c.202): The glory of God is man [fully] alive, and the glory of man is the

1. E. J. Kenney, Commentary 213–14, notes on "Cupid and Psyche," 6.18.3 and 6.18.4.
2. One reader concluded that Lewis's antifeminism was manifested in the "fact" that Orual could become beautiful only by losing her identity in Psyche. Looking at the phrase "not exactly the same" changed her mind.

vision of God.[3] In *Mere Christianity*, Lewis said it this way: "If we let Him . . . [God] will make the feeblest and filthiest of us into a god or goddess, dazzling, radiant, immortal creature, pulsating all through with such energy and joy and wisdom and love as we cannot imagine, . . . [reflecting] His own boundless power and delight and goodness" (*MC*, 174–75).

At this point Lewis joins myth and what he believes to be reality; the beauty of the original Psyche who appears in myth and allegory is matched by the beauty—spiritual, but thereby completely real, produced by struggle in the everyday world—of Orual the queen of Glome. The god's verdict, "You also are Psyche," is confirmed by Arnom's tribute to Queen Orual—*"the most wise, just, valiant, fortunate and merciful of all the princes known in our parts of the world."*

C. Love: Reunion with Psyche

Having been stripped naked before the dead, having heard and judged her own book, Orual need not describe the reconciliation with Psyche. She says only that she wept "a kind of tears that do not flow in this country" (*TWHF*, 306). Instead of holding on to her superiority as "Maia," Orual now sees that Psyche is far above her. Instead of being jealous of Psyche's beauty and strength, she rejoices in them. Far from wishing to control and possess Psyche, she delights in giving up her own agenda. Thus she is able to receive the beauty that comes from the Deadlands—from dying to self.

D. Faith: Bareface at Last

Orual's first act of faith is to "utter the speech which [had] lain at the center of [her] soul for years" (*TWHF*, 294). By exposing her true thoughts before the whole court of the dead, she relinquishes the drama she had written to display the wrongs of Orual, queen of tragedy. Thus she is enabled to trust in the Divine Nature enough

---

3. Irenaeus, *Against Heresies: The Apostolic Fathers with Justin Martyr and Irenaeus. The Ante-Nicene Fathers*, vol. 1, 490.

to be honest and vulnerable—bareface. Lewis speaks of the difficulty in *Letters to Malcolm:* "For what I call 'myself' ... is also a dramatic construction. ... And in prayer [the] real I struggles to speak, for once, from his real being, and to address, for once ... [the real Thou]" (*LM*, 81).

Her second act of faith is to throw herself off the pillar of rock where she stands isolated. Her action parallels that of John in *The Pilgrim's Regress,* and she does it for the same reason: out of desperation, because she cannot think of anything else to do. Just as the Guide shows John the true nature of his pilgrimage, so the Fox shows Orual. He answers her original demand for justice by introducing her to grace: "Be sure that, whatever else you get, you will not get justice" (*TWHF,* 297).

In his instruction she finds the obverse side of her complaint that the gods are not fair.

She asks, "Are the gods not just?"

And he replies, "Oh no, child. What would become of us if they were? But come and see" (*TWHF,* 297).

Conclusion:
The Soul's Journey

Students often emerge from their English classes with this rule of thumb: "If it's literature, it must be full of symbols." The discourses they handle in daily life, from computer documentation to true romances, seem to have only one meaning—the literal meaning. Lewis wrote *Till We Have Faces* for such moderns, for people who had begun to lose the classical tradition but might be willing to see the story of the Soul's union with Love in literal terms. It is not his fault that his commentators and admirers have frequently gone haring off after myth and symbol and allegory without first establishing the literal meaning. They have apparently forgotten that traditional exercises in interpretation, whether the four-fold method of medieval exegesis or the midrashim of the rabbis, always begin with the plain-prose, literal meaning. In "Chapter by Chapter" we see just how rich, in the hands of a skillful writer, the literal meaning can be.

Till We Have Faces is the story of the soul's journey to love and to God the source of love—a journey that, as the spiritual guides of every tradition agree, can be accomplished only through self-knowledge. But instead of an allegorical landscape like Spenser's Fairyland, Lewis sets the story in a little barbarian kingdom at the edge of the Greek colonies around the Mediterranean. Instead of an abstract figure of Soul, there are two real-life women, Psyche and Orual. And instead of an allegorical journey, there is Orual's literal writing of her autobiography.

The process of writing the book was Orual's first step into self-knowledge. She began by intending to write a complaint against the gods, continued by writing a defense of herself, and finished by hearing herself read—not the book she had written, but the text of her real self, the thought she had been inscribing within herself for forty years.

The inner book took a lifetime to write, but the physical, scroll-and-ink book did not begin to take shape until Orual returned from Essur. There she had encountered the priest of the new goddess (her own sister, of all people!), and learned that the myth of Psyche's union with Love and subsequent exile is quite different from the story she tells within herself. She resolves to write the exact truth. She supplies empirical facts, and the scroll-and-ink book allows the reader to follow her spiritual journey in her narrative.

Her acquisition of self-knowledge begins with the arrival of the tutor. She learns that she is ugly but very intelligent. As King Trom tells the Fox, "See if you can make her wise; it's about all she'll ever be good for" (*TWHF*, 7). Then there is a period when self-knowledge is in abeyance as she seeks external knowledge. Bardia teaches her the arts of war; the Fox teaches her science (called physical philosophy in ancient times); and both teach her the art of politics. She thinks of these skills as belonging to "the Queen," while "Orual" sleeps deep within her. "The Queen" is not a false self; she is one aspect of Orual's total personality, and the whole person's ability to be a good, just, and wise ruler emerges as soon as the king is out of the way. However, "the Queen" ruthlessly suppresses the "Orual" part of herself and thus cannot come to self-knowledge. It takes the encounter with the priest of Psyche to break her open. His story is a myth; it does not conform strictly to historical fact, but it sets forth essential truth. Hearing his interpretation of her actions begins the major leg of her journey to self-knowledge.

Overlapping the journey to self-knowledge is the journey to love. It also begins with the arrival of the tutor, for Orual says, "I loved the Fox, as my father called him, better than anyone I had yet known" (*TWHF*, 7). The Fox returned her affection, loving her as a grandfather. In addition, he taught her the poetry of love, of the sweetness of desire *(eros)* and the bitterness of the strife *(eris)* that comes from self-centered, disordered love. Later she came to love Bardia, first with a schoolgirl crush and later with a woman's unrequited passion. Bardia also loved her, first as a little sister and later as his liege lord and comrade in battle. Orual took what Bardia and the Fox gave without considering what she might offer in return.

In any case, the love that transformed her life, intense as Dante's romantic love for Beatrice, was not her love for either of them, but her mother-love for her orphaned half-sister, Psyche. She called it "the beginning of all my joys" (*TWHF*, 20). It was also the beginning of deep sorrow. As Lewis says of the death of his wife, "[B]ereavement is a universal and integral part of our experience of love. . . . It is not a truncation of the process but one of its phases; not the interruption of the dance, but the next figure" (*AGO*, 41). The same is true of mother love; the child grows up and grows away. Psyche was forcibly taken away to be sacrificed, but if this had not happened, as a nubile girl she would have been married and left Glome anyway.

Orual refused to accept Psyche as an adult woman, a person who belonged to her husband rather than her foster mother. Seeking to retain possession, Orual forced her younger sister to betray the god. The palace was destroyed, and Psyche sent into exile. Afterward Orual arranged Psyche's childhood clothes and trinkets in a locked room, forbade her servants to speak of her foster daughter, and ordered the well to be closed in so that the chains would not remind her of Psyche's weeping. Thus, she refused to seek insight from the most important thing that ever happened to her. And from this point of view she writes all of book 1.

The breaking open of her personality that started with meeting the priest of Psyche in Essur was continued in the process of writing. She had hardly begun the book when she learned from Tarin that she had rejected Redival when Psyche came; the love of her life had brought about a failure in love. Then from Bardia's wife Orual learned that her passion for Bardia had not been truly loving, but greedy and selfish. Thus began the purification of her human loves that would lead to divine love.

Orual's journey to God begins in earnest with the restlessness, the sense of empty accomplishment which moved her to go traveling and brought her to Essur. On another level, however, she has been struggling with the divine all her life. As a child she turned in disgust from the faceless, ugly stone of Ungit and from the "holy" stench of the Old Priest's clothes. Before the encounter with the god on the mountain, her remarks about Ungit and other gods are largely directed toward the external observances and customary sacrifices. At that stage she assumes the gods exist because she fears them.

The Fox tried to free her from Glomish superstition with his rational Stoicism, but her gut-level fear of holiness (in Otto's sense of the word) remained. There was a strong admixture of hate in her fear, and when Psyche was taken to be sacrificed, hate became uppermost. In all her subsequent contacts with the divine—the disgusting sacrificial dress in which Psyche was attired, Orual's desperate attempt to seek the gods in prayer, her terror at the golden voice of Psyche's god-husband, and finally the harsh judgment of the priest in Essur—Orual never lost her fear and distrust.

Just as she turned away from self-knowledge and turned away from allowing her love for Psyche (and for the Fox and Bardia) to mature and expand, so also she turned away from the beauty and justice of the god as revealed to her at the time of Psyche's exile. Just as she locked Psyche's clothes away, she put the memory of the god's voice and face in a "[room] of [her] soul that [she] didn't lightly unlock." Even though she had seen a god, she came "near to believing that there are no such things" (*TWHF*, 245, 244).

She was able to do this because she closed her eyes and ears against the hints she had received throughout her life that the gods were lovely as well as dreadful. Others in Glome saw divinity as beautiful and fascinating. They celebrated the Year's Birth with joy, and the woman with a great sorrow found comfort in crying before the Ungit stone. It is Psyche's beauty that causes them to hail her as a goddess, for they see that she is *"Ungit herself* in mortal shape" (*TWHF*, 32, emphasis added). Both her personal beauty and the beauty her presence brought to everything around her were signs pointing to the loveliness in the Nature of Things.

Even in the midst of sorrow, there were hints of something beyond the gloomy, gritty world Orual lived in. As she and Bardia journeyed toward the sacrificial tree, the landscape gleamed, a lark sang, and there was "huge and ancient stillness" (*TWHF*, 95). She saw beauty in Psyche—more accurately, in Psyche the child whom she chose to adore—but closed her eyes to beauty in anything else. How could she be freed from the cage she built around herself?

Spiritual teachers generally agree that self-knowledge is the path to spiritual fulfillment, but they also agree that the seeker must have help from a source beyond knowledge. And so the divine love came to Orual in dreams, "drenched" her with visions, uncovered what she had been hiding from herself, until at last she stood in Hades, before the judge and all the dead, and heard herself reading her book. Not the book she wrote, but the book at the bottom of her soul.

Hearing herself, judging herself, completes the breaking open and leads to reunion with the Fox, reunion with Psyche, and reunion with the god. In the mountains she had heard the god's voice "unmoved and sweet." In the depths "a great voice," says the same words, "You also are Psyche" (*TWHF*, 170, 308).

The beatific vision Orual experiences is, as all the mystics tell us, indescribable, though Lewis makes use of the common words: bright, joy, quaking, terror, piercing, sweetness. But one detail, easy to miss, shows us that Orual's love for Psyche has attained its final maturity. She loves Psyche enough to die for her (not just pierce her own arm dramatically), but with detachment. She says, "I was no one," for she has sluffed off the egotism that needed to be fed with the possession of Psyche's life. Psyche, paradoxically, is also no one, but she counts "gloriously" because she exists for the sake of the god, "the most dreadful, the most beautiful, the only dread and beauty there is" (*TWHF*, 307). Orual's love for Psyche has been taken up into the love of God.

Part II

Further In

Apuleius and Lewis

Comparison of Authors

Apuleius and Lewis are alike in that both had a striking knowledge of Greek and Roman literature, both were deeply influenced by Platonic philosophy, both were at one time interested in magic, and both were criticized for forming an alliance with the mother of a friend.

Both showed their literary knowledge in a facility for quotation and pastiche. Lewis's best works are heavily influenced by others; for example, his *Out of the Silent Planet* is a virtual rewriting of *The First Men in the Moon.* Indeed, he consciously followed the masters of ancient and medieval literature by never aspiring to originality. Apuleius's *The Golden Ass* derives much of its flavor from literary evocation: the *Phaedras*, the *Iliad*, the "sustained . . . exploitation of the sixth book of the *Aeneid,* and "the rhetorical historians like Sallust and Livy."[1]

As for Platonism, Apuleius has been called "a philosopher without original genius," but he was well known in medieval Europe as a transmitter of Platonic ideas. Lewis has been described as a Christian Platonist.[2] He transmitted the medieval synthesis of these two streams of thought in much-acclaimed and widely read books such

---

The chapters for which this is particularly relevant are 1:9, 14; 2:3, 4.

1. P. G. Walsh, *The Roman Novel: The 'Satyricon' of Petronius and the 'Metamorphoses' of Apuleius,* 56, 57.

2. P. G. Walsh, "Introduction to *The Golden Ass*," xiv; Robert Houston Smith, *Patches of Godlight: The Pattern of Thought of C. S. Lewis,* ix.

as *Mere Christianity, The Problem of Pain,* and *Miracles* as well as the planetary trilogy and the Chronicles of Narnia.

As for alliance with an older woman, Lewis met Mrs. Moore during World War I, and after the war they lived in the same household for the rest of her life. In a letter from the battlefront, Lewis called Mrs. Moore and Arthur Greeves "the two people who matter most to me in the world" (*LAG,* 204). Walter Hooper says, "Whatever Lewis's feelings for Mrs. Moore were at the beginning, over time she became a mother to him and in most letters from about 1940 onwards he speaks of her as his 'Mother.'" At age thirty, Apuleius married a friend's mother, who was seven years older than himself.[3]

Lewis was interested in magic in his undergraduate days and was greatly impressed with occultist and poet William Butler Yeats. Apuleius "firmly believe[d] that magicians exist and wield supernatural powers"; in fact, he was sued by the brother of his wife's first husband for using magic love potions to win her. He defended himself in court and was acquitted.[4] Both men experienced profound conversion in their maturity, Lewis to Christianity and Apuleius to the worship of Isis and Osiris.

Comparison of Contexts

Apuleius's "Cupid and Psyche" is inserted within a larger novel sometimes called *The Metamorphoses* and sometimes *The Golden Ass.* The hero, named Lucius (Apuleius's first name), is an undisciplined young man, obsessed by sex and magic. His dabbling with magic causes him to be turned into an ass while retaining the mind of a human being. He suffers many misadventures until finally he has a vision of Isis. She restores him to human form and calls him into special service in her temple.

The Golden Ass is divided into eleven books. Throughout the first ten it is a picaresque novel, sexy and rambunctious. In book 11, however, it turns serious, and we realize that in describing Lucius's dealings with Isis, the author is really talking about his own profound religious experience. Even in the first ten books, however, *The Golden Ass* is not merely fun, but also moral teaching. It follows

3. Hooper, *Companion,* 714; Walsh, introduction to *The Golden Ass,* xii.
4. Walsh, *Roman Novel,* 184; Walsh, introduction, xiii.

the didactic principle that by making fun of lust and other sins, the writer can influence readers to avoid them. In Apuleius's book the implication is that unspiritual people are asses wandering through a confusing and sometimes cruel world. They are without hope until divine grace gives them rebirth into a new life.

Although most of the book deals with the mishaps of Lucius the ass, the part about Psyche and how she became the wife of the god Cupid (Eros) is best loved and often printed as an independent work. Within the context of *The Golden Ass,* "Cupid and Psyche" is a "digression," a technical term in ancient and medieval rhetoric referring specifically to a story that occurs within a larger story and mirrors it.[5] Lucius's imprudence turned him into an ass and forced him to become a wanderer; Psyche's gullibility turned her into a wanderer. Like Lucius, Psyche cannot rescue herself; and just as he is saved by the grace of Isis, she is saved by grace in the form of such helpers as ants, river reeds, an eagle, and a tower, and finally rescued by Cupid himself. Just as Lucius becomes a priest of Isis, Psyche becomes a goddess.

Lewis's *Till We Have Faces* is one of the many stand-alone retellings of Apuleius's "Cupid and Psyche." In it, Orual's lack of insight into her own passions, especially her possessiveness, leads her to destroy her sister's happiness and turns her into a faceless queen. She suffers and labors and is finally saved by divine grace. The autobiographical elements of *Till We Have Faces* are less obvious than those of *The Golden Ass,* especially book 11. However, in Orual's dismay at Psyche's marriage to a god we can see a trace of Mrs. Moore's reaction to Lewis's wholehearted espousal of the Christian way. Also, Orual's determination, after the loss of Psyche, to study hard things and stay very busy is reminiscent of Lewis's "New Look," which he adopted and later gave up for Christianity, as he relates in chapter 13 of *Surprised by Joy.* And Orual's inner journey to the depths of her soul is analogous to Lewis's own experience, obliquely suggested in letters to his spiritual advisees. Although *Till We Have Faces* is not a digression within a larger novel, Orual's doubts and rebellions mirror Lewis's own.

In addition to the literary and autobiographical contexts, there is in both novels an argumentative edge. In *Till We Have Faces,* Lewis

5. Walsh, *Roman Novel,* 190; *OCD* 1, s.v. "Epyllion."

is writing for modernist skeptics and empiricists who "know" that the supernatural does not happen. He is also demonstrating that the Christian Modernists' effort to strip the faith of the supernatural by sophisticated allegorization, like Arnom's explanation of Ungit (*TWHF*, 270–71), is, in the final analysis, not very convincing.

In *The Golden Ass*, Apuleius is asserting the superiority and rationality of devotion to Isis against the silliness of the old pantheon of Jupiter, Juno, Venus, and the rest. His ostensibly naïve treatment of the gods in "Cupid and Psyche" is meant to appeal to the sophisticated esthetes of the Antonine Age. He is also contrasting his faith with Christianity. To him and most of his educated contemporaries the new faith seemed vulgar and superstitious, and they worried because it was making great inroads in their area (North Africa). Christians were called *asinarii*, and according to Tertullian, many outside the faith believed that they worshipped an ass's head. The ending, Walsh says, "is rightly interpreted as Isis' deliverance of Lucius" from bestiality, but "in Africa it could also bear the additional interpretation of deliverance from Christian superstition."[6]

Comparison of Plots

1. Lewis summarizes the plot of the story in "Note" (pp. 311–13) in the American edition of *Till We Have Faces*. As he says, his biggest change to the story is "making Psyche's palace invisible to normal, mortal eyes" (*TWHF*, 313). This involves sending Orual to the Grey Mountain alone. If both sisters went, they could agree that there was nothing to see, that Psyche's palace was simply her illusion. Sending Orual alone allows Lewis to introduce the philosophical question of whether only empirically verifiable phenomena are truly real.

2. The beginning and ending of Apuleius's version (designated as CAP, for "Cupid and Psyche,") follow several fairy-tale conventions. Lewis's version (designated as *TWHF*) pointedly avoids them:

a. CAP begins, "There were in a certain city a king and queen, who had three beautiful daughters" (4.28.1). In *TWHF*, the girls are stepsisters, and both the queens have died. Orual becomes Psyche's

6. Walsh, *Roman Novel*, 186, 187.

foster mother, allowing Lewis to introduce the theme of possessive mother-love out of control. This complexity in family relationships is more often found in daily life than in fairy tales.

b. In CAP the youngest daughter, Psyche, is unmarriageable because of her goddesslike beauty, while the two older girls have "achieved rich marriages" (4.32.3). In *TWHF,* none of the girls can be married because no other kingdom will ally itself with Glome—a much more prosaic motivation.

c. In CAP, there is a double-speaking message commanding that Psyche be exposed on the mountain, to be wed to a nonhuman bridegroom. Like other such messages, it comes from a supernatural source, in this case the oracle of Apollo. In *TWHF,* the message comes from the priest of Ungit reporting the deliberations of Glome's important citizens, and it is only too clear: Psyche has become the Accursed and must be sacrificed on the mountain as a scapegoat. Even in this detail of plotting, Lewis is careful to stay within ordinary causation.

d. In CAP Psyche's personal need for a husband is a typical fairy-tale problem. In TWHF the whole kingdom is in trouble—rebellion, famine, the plague, threats from other kingdoms. The *TWHF* story has a real-world seriousness lacking in CAP.

e. In both stories Psyche is wafted to the Happy Valley by the West-Wind; in both she finds a luxurious palace and is served by unseen maids. In CAP the building is a fantasy construction of gold, silver, and gems. There is an overall impression of vulgar ostentation. In *TWHF* a few details emphasize comfort and good taste—the exquisite fruit and wine, the delicate pillared court, and the crystalline water of the bath.

f. In CAP Psyche endangers her own happiness in a thoroughly fairy-tale manner by being dissatisfied with perfection, persuading her husband to let her sisters come as guests, and arousing their jealousy by showing off the richness of her household. In *TWHF* none of this appears; the story consists only of what the elder daughter, Orual, can observe with her own eyes.

g. After her happiness has been destroyed, Psyche (CAP) gets a fairy-tale revenge by tricking her sisters into jumping off the cliff without the West-Wind to carry them into the valley. Psyche *(TWHF)* goes off weeping and is not heard from again until Orual meets her in a vision.

h. When Venus assigns Psyche (CAP) her impossible tasks, the girl receives magic aids—from the ants, the speaking river, the eagle, and the speaking tower. In *TWHF*, natural-world analogs of the tasks are performed by Orual. The fairy-tale tasks are seen in dreams and pictures, and it becomes clear that Psyche is the recipient of divine grace, for she comes through her trials "all but unscathed" and "almost happy" (*TWHF*, 300).

i. In CAP, Psyche performs all the tasks given her by Venus but on the last one succumbs to curiosity. She opens the casket from Hades and falls into an enchanted sleep. This is important to CAP's structural role in the novel, for it is a variation on the curiosity that initially got Lucius into trouble. Since Psyche's shortcomings are not at issue, this episode is omitted from *TWHF*.

j. In CAP, Cupid, who has been arbitrarily removed from action by a minor burn from the oil in Psyche's lamp, arrives when she needs him, awakens her, and brings about the happy ending. In *TWHF*, Psyche does not fall into error through curiosity, and the happy ending consists of the reunion between Psyche and Orual and the spiritual transformation of them both.

Narrative Technique

"Cupid and Psyche" is told directly, from an omniscient point of view. The reader hears the conversations between Venus and her son, observes the doings in Psyche's wedding suite, is present at the plottings of the sisters, and follows Psyche through her travels and sufferings. Gods and mortals live in the same world. The gods, despite glorious costumes and other accoutrements, are far from admirable. They engage in political squabbling among themselves and are vain and self-centered. *Till We Have Faces* is told from the viewpoint of a single character. The reader's knowledge is limited to what Orual knows, and sometimes she is wrong. The private lives of the gods remain private; as for the delights of the marriage bed, there are only a few hints from Psyche. Needless to say, the limited viewpoint is more realistic. It is certainly more modern, for twentieth-century authors play on our awareness that knowledge is partial and witnesses often unreliable. Until the great reversal of book 2, Orual lives in the world of empirical fact; from her point of view, the world of gods and wonders, of mysteries and miracles, may exist but probably does not.

Characterizations

1. Since "Cupid and Psyche," is a fairy tale, in fact an old wives' tale, within a novel, consistency of characterization is not a primary goal. The characterizations are much more realistic outside the digression.[7]

Psyche, the major human character, is by turns calm and emotional, stupid and clever—whatever the plot requires. At the prospect of being sacrificed, like a Stoic she calmly rebukes her parents for their pride in her beauty. She is hysterically emotional when her husband forbids her to see her sisters. She combines tears, threats of suicide, and seductive kisses (like any other silly woman) to make him change his mind.

Too stupid to remember her own lies, she first tells her sisters that her husband is young and a hunter, then that he is a middle-aged, prosperous businessman. Finally, she is forced to admit that she has never seen him. Then she naïvely believes her sisters' tale that he is a monstrous serpent who is fattening her in order to eat her. Despite her previous stupidity, when in her wanderings she comes "by chance" to the home cities of her sisters, she tells each one a clever lie that causes her to think the West-Wind will catch her. Thus deluded, each one leaps off the cliff to her death. Finally, when Psyche is sent to Hades to obtain the casket of beauty from Persephone, she follows perfectly the complex directions given her by the speaking tower, only to spoil it all by foolishly opening the box.

Venus and Cupid, the major immortals, are motivated primarily by their symbolic significance. Both are aspects of love: love is a mixed blessing; therefore, their behavior is often contradictory. Venus is naturally jealous of Psyche, since love is accompanied by jealousy. She commands her son, Cupid, to avenge her against Psyche, sealing her command with playful but incestuous openmouthed kisses. Apuleius does not say that she loses interest in her revenge, but she

---

7. Walsh, introduction, xxvi.

leaves and goes on a progress to Ocean and stays out of the story until she is needed to torture Psyche and set hard tasks for her.

Cupid portrays erotic attraction, which is often so great that one feels helpless; thus, when Venus orders him to make Psyche fall in love with a worthless man, he falls in love with her himself. He is described as an immoral, irresponsible boy, but he is also a gentle, generous lover to Psyche, who gives in to Psyche's foolish desire to see her sisters. When Psyche betrays him, he leaves her, but he is so devastated by the loss that he returns to his mother's house and holes up in his room until the plot requires him to rescue Psyche from the sleep induced by the casket from Hades. His behavior is self-contradictory, like the human experience of love.

2. In *Till We Have Faces,* minor characters are consistent; major characters have complex inconsistencies that are carefully made to seem plausible.

Among the minor characters, King Trom is cruel and egotistical, Batta a busybody, Bardia kind and strong, Redival silly, and Arnom smooth and efficient.

The major characters—Orual, Psyche, and the Fox—have the complexity of real-life people. The Fox aspires to Stoic imperturbability but loves literature and is tenderhearted; Psyche is brave and compassionate, but also capable of King Trom-like anger; and Orual's abrasive exterior conceals a deep hunger for love, and she is the one who threatens suicide.

The more complex characterization in *TWHF* leads to a subtler process of persuading Psyche to spy on her husband. Lewis's Psyche does not for a moment believe that her husband is a monster or a villain. She does not quite realize that Orual is falsifying by quoting both Bardia and the Fox out of context, but she stands firmly on her own experience of his goodness. Swayed by her childhood love, she is determined to believe that Orual has her best interests at heart, saying, "You mean—I'll believe you mean—nothing but good" (160). She agrees to spy on her husband only because Orual threatens to commit suicide if she does not.

Lewis's method of characterization is meant to promote the reader's lively sympathy with the Glomians, particularly Orual. The more readers identify with the characters, the more they feel the complex problems of loving well and believing honestly. They see, in an intimate, deeply involved way, the misery of going through life without self-knowledge and at enmity with God.

In contrast, Apuleius's method is meant to produce the detachment of trenchant comedy. The mortals are blind fools; the traditional gods are both immoral and absurd, especially in the "Cupid and Psyche" segment. Thus Apuleius calls his readers to shake off their blindness for Platonic clarity and to reject the officially sanctioned worship of the Olympians for a true relationship with the gracious Isis.

Literary Style

Apuleius heightens his comic effects through swashbuckling rhetorical flourishes and a generous use of parody. In *Till We Have Faces*, Lewis's normal voice is completely submerged in the personality of Orual—her bitterness, her scorn for polite euphemisms, her incisiveness. She is capable of irony but not genial humor. Her sentences fall into the patterns taught by ancient rhetoricians.[8] Part 3, the glossary, provides a closer look at her preference for rural, uplandish, and obsolete vocabulary.

8. See Myers, *Context*, 199–203.

Chronology of Lewis's Life

This chronology is selective, focusing on the incidents that are particularly important in the development of *Till We Have Faces*. To everyone who is fascinated with Lewis the man as well as Lewis the author, the novel offers a new perspective. Because it is so different from his previous work—written in a realistic, modernist mode—and especially because it is written so successfully from a woman's point of view, some people infer that it was almost a collaboration between him and Joy Davidman. The book is dedicated to her, and she became his wife just about five months before it was published. In addition, she also wrote to a friend describing how she helped Jack.[1]

For any author, however, the relationship between life and fiction is very complex. Lewis first tried to write a retelling of the Cupid and Psyche story as an undergraduate, in verse, because he hoped to be a famous poet. From the beginning, he planned to tell it from a woman's viewpoint. The palace would be invisible, because the modernist he was then would not believe in a visible one, and the gods were to be at fault.[2] The following list of events in Lewis's life, most before he met Joy, balances our evaluation of her influence by showing that the book grows out of his many experiences and wide reading up to the time of writing.

The chapters for which this is particularly relevant are 1:5, 6, 16, 17, 19, 21; 2:3.
1. Hooper, *Companion*, 125, 808; Lyle Dorsett, *And God Came In*, 116.
2. Quoted in Hooper, *Companion*, 251.

1908–1917—Mother's Death to Military Service

1908 August 23 Lewis's mother died. Orual's mother also dies in the summer. Throughout the story Orual never offers a single personal memory of the woman who gave her birth. Perhaps this omission can be explained with reference to literary structure, but perhaps it is also personal to Lewis.

September 18 Lewis was sent to Wynyard School, called "Belsen" in *Surprised by Joy.* At this time Lewis "first became an effective believer" through being exposed to a serious teaching of Christianity in the neighboring "high" Anglican Church. He also became interested in historical fiction about Greek and Roman antiquity such as *Quo Vadis*, *Darkness and Dawn*, *The Gladiators*, and *Ben Hur*, but he later said the two things were unrelated in his mind (*SbJ*, 33, 35).

1913 September Lewis enrolled at Malvern College, where he began to learn the difference in "flavor" among Norse, Celtic, and Greek mythologies. He is perhaps referring to this period when he writes "[I]t was through *almost* believing in the gods that I came to believe in God." His appreciation of the "[hard], more defiant, sunbright beauty of Olympus" (*Let*, 322; *SbJ*, 144) appears by implication in its contrast with the gloom of Glome.

1914 September 19 Lewis began study with William T. Kirkpatrick, who started him in Homer (*SbJ*, 141).

1917 January 28 Lewis mentions "my 'Psyche,'" to Arthur Greeves. It was apparently a separate book containing the "Cupid and Psyche" portion of *The Golden Ass* (*LAG*, 158; 158n2). He read it over Christmas.

May 13 Lewis read the entire *Golden Ass.* His letter to Arthur Greeves speaks of its "brooding magic" and "occasional voluptuousness & ridiculous passages." He concludes, "I must get a copy of my own" (*LAG*, 183–84).

November 29 Lewis arrived in the trenches. In *Surprised by Joy* he mentions the first bullet he heard and "[his] little quavering signal that said, 'This is War. This is what Homer wrote about'" (*SbJ*, 196). In the novel this experience becomes Orual's memory about how "when the first enemy arrows came flashing in among us," the peaceful surroundings turned into "a place, a Field, a thing to be put in chronicles" (*TWHF*, 227).

1919–1923—Lewis's Undergraduate Years

1919 January 13 Lewis arrived back in Oxford. Mrs. Janie Moore and daughter Maureen also took rooms in Oxford. Lewis was required to live in his college for his first year, but after that he apparently lived with the Moores. Concerning this choice, he says only that it was "a huge and complex episode" in which his "earlier hostility to the emotions was very fully and variously avenged" (*SbJ*, 198). We now know that he was referring to his relationship with Mrs. Moore.

1919–1920 While "'doing Mods' and 'beginning Greats'" at Oxford, Lewis adopted his "New Look"—an emotional hardness combined with Stoical Monism in philosophy. He found his New Look realism emotionally satisfying; he needed a Nature that was "there" no matter what man thought of it and completely indifferent to human considerations (*SbJ*, 205, 209). This was the beginning of his personal search for "what's *really*," the answer to Orual's question, "[Do] you think there really was a palace in the valley though I couldn't see it?" Her retreat into "physical philosophy," i.e., science (*TWHF*, 135, 184), was her escape from the emotional trauma of losing Psyche.

However, this philosophy left no room for the good, the true, and the beautiful—including the literature and myth Lewis loved so deeply. If "the universe revealed by the senses" was "rock-bottom reality," then nonmaterial, mental entities such as moral judgments, abstract thought, and esthetic experience were nothing but the result of material processes. They were not "what's really." His realism had to be given up (*SbJ*, 208–9).

1922 June As recorded in *All My Road before Me*, Lewis read the psychology of William James, Havelock Ellis, and Sigmund Freud. He mentions Freud's *Introductory Lectures on Psycho-Analysis*, newly published in translation, and Ellis's *World of Dreams*. More influential, perhaps, was William James's *Varieties of Religious Experience*. For example, James uses the term *Sehnsucht* in his chapter on mysticism, which Lewis considered his most interesting.[3] James's concept of once-born and twice-born souls is especially helpful in understanding the religious notions and behaviors of Psyche and

3. William James, *Varieties*, 344–45, 345n2.

Bardia (once-born), Orual (the "sick" soul), and the Fox (twice-born but incomplete).

October Lewis began reading for his degree in English. He learned that the authors he admired most were religious, while the "precursors of modern enlightenment...bored [him] cruelly." He admired George Herbert most for his ability to "[convey] the very quality of life as we actually live it from moment to moment" (*SbJ*, 14). This experience is relevant to *Till We Have Faces* in two ways: first, in the way he juxtaposed the most "religious" of Greek literature with Orual's drab life, and second in his success at conveying the moment-to-moment quality of Orual's life.

1923 Rudolf Otto's *The Idea of the Holy* was published in translation, and Lewis must have read it soon afterward. The special meaning of "holy" as Orual uses it owes a great deal to Otto. (See "The Holy: Lewis and Otto," 168.)

1925 (about) Harwood and Barfield became Anthroposophists. This was the beginning of the "Great War," letters of philosophic argument, between Lewis and Barfield, which lasted until 1929. Barfield helped Lewis to move into a basically Platonic idealism.[4] However, he never came close to accepting Anthroposophy. He reacted to Steiner's thought—perhaps his panoply of angels, astral planes, and two Jesuses—with disgust. The gloom of Glome is partly due to the banishment of Plato and Platonic idealism from the philosophic teaching there.

1929 September 25 Lewis's father, Albert, died. Lewis observes how horrible it feels when someone "one ought to love, but doesn't very much" is ill. He wrote to his brother Warnie what a "consolation" it was to have a light lunch at midday, contrary to his father's custom; however, after his father's death he found that missing him so much made the freedom of the family home hateful (*LAG*, 305; *Let*, 271–72, 277).[5] His feelings are transformed into fiction and perhaps amplified in Orual's reaction to King Trom's death.

1931 September 28 Lewis concluded his often-described process of coming to an adult faith in Christ. The effect this process had on Mrs. Moore (and on Lewis when Barfield became an Anthro-

---

4. See Lionel Adey, *C. S. Lewis: Writer, Dreamer, and Mentor*, 29–30.
5. Hooper, *Companion*, 306n, notes that Lewis served his father for more than a month "with touching devotion."

posophist?) is perhaps revealed in Lewis's letter to Clyde Kilby about *Till We Have Faces:* "Someone becomes a Christian [and the] others suffer a sense of outrage. What they love is being taken from them! The boy must be mad! And the conceit of him! Or is there something in it after all?" (*Let*, 462–63). In chapter 11, we see Orual going through this gamut of emotions.

1932 August 15–29 Lewis writes *The Pilgrim's Regress.* When John, the protagonist, completes his pilgrimage, he finds that his perceptions have been all wrong, and that he must return to his starting place. Things look completely different on the return journey. There is some similarity with *Till We Have Faces* in that Orual finishes her book and finds that she must look at the story of her life with new eyes.[6] It is entirely different from what she had believed. Since there is no time to write it over, she adds the four chapters of book 2.

1939–1945—The War Years

During the war years Lewis began to feel a vocation to defend the faith in simple language, for ordinary people. *The Screwtape Letters*, *The Problem of Pain*, and the radio broadcasts that later became *Mere Christianity* were, like his addresses to the Royal Air Force, war work. Living with bombs, food scarcities, and uncertainty, people accepted his writings as adequate defenses of the faith they had learned as children; but Lewis, as described in "The Apologist's Evening Prayer," asks God's forgiveness for his "cleverness shot forth on Thy behalf" (*Poems*, 129). The weaknesses of defending Christianity in terms of logic, striking similes, and a lucid style were to become more and more obvious to Lewis as time went on. Perhaps this realization was behind the Old Priest's passionate denunciation of Greek logic and rhetoric: "They demand to see such things clearly, as if the gods were no more than letters written in a book. . . . [N]othing that is said clearly can be said truly about them" (*TWHF*, 50).

6. Manlove, in "Caught Up," comments on how *TWHF* returns to "the nature of the first book, *The Pilgrim's Regress*. Both deal with whole lives, both have a god on the mountain, and both are concerned with the issue of self-knowledge" (273–74).

1940 October 18 Lewis publishes *The Problem of Pain*, which integrates some aspects of the Freudian theory of human personality with traditional concepts of the Fall of Man and the Great Chain of Being. (See *POP*, 71–86.)

Between October 24 and November 4 Lewis makes his first confession, to the Rev. Walter Adams of the [Anglican] Society of St. John the Evangelist (Cowley Fathers). He continued with Fr. Adams as his spiritual director until the monk's death in the spring of 1952.[7] Sacramental confession, together with spiritual direction, leads to the kind of self-knowledge that Orual experiences in book 2, chapter 3, when she hears her whining, self-centered attack on the gods.

1942 (exact date unknown) Lewis's "Psycho-Analysis and Literary Criticism" was delivered orally to "a literary society at Westfield College" and later published in *Essays and Studies* 27 and by Walter Hooper in *Selected Literary Essays*.

1948 February Lewis's *Miracles* was attacked by G. E. M. Anscombe, linguistic philosopher and herself a Christian. According to Lewis's friend Hugo Dyson, Lewis described his defeat as having "lost everything" and been brought "to the foot of the cross."[8] He turned to writing his autobiography, *Surprised by Joy*, and children's fiction, the Chronicles of Narnia.

An alternative speculation about the defeat is this: it caused Lewis to realize that his expertise in philosophy was out of date—naturally, since he had been specializing in English studies for decades. Therefore he abandoned defenses of the faith based on Aristotelian logic against the methods of the linguistic philosophers, and, as Medcalf says, moved "from the logic of speculative thought" into "the logic of personal relations."[9]

Seen in this light, Lewis's withdrawal from his previous methods of defending the Christian Gospel was not a defeat, but the next step in his artistic and spiritual development. He began *Surprised by Joy* a month after the debate, and when he came to write *Till We*

---

7. Roger Lancelyn Green and Walter Hooper, *C. S. Lewis: A Biography*, 198; Paul F. Ford, "C. S. Lewis, Ecumenical Spiritual Director: A Study of His Experience and Theology of Prayer and Discernment in the Process of Becoming a Self," 55. See also Hooper, *Companion*, 32.

8. Stephen Medcalf, "Language and Self-Consciousness: The Making and Breaking of C. S. Lewis's Personae," 126.

9. Ibid., 127.

Have Faces, he made it clear that Orual's problem with the invisible palace cannot be solved by speculative logic.

1954 November 29 Lewis delivered his inaugural address, *De Descriptione Temporum*, at Cambridge. In it he described the great gap between modern consciousness and traditional European culture and presented himself as an Old Western Man, a surviving dinosaur from this former world. The address seems to signal another new direction in his writing—an effort to help twentieth-century readers, blinded by dry, mechanistic assumptions, to live briefly in the pre-Incarnational world of the peoples around the Mediterranean. He did this not only in *Till We Have Faces* (with the Fox as the cultured Greek), but also in his *Reflections on the Psalms* (published 1958) and the fragmentary "After Ten Years," which opens with an account of how Menelaus Yellowhead felt while shut up in the Trojan horse (*OOW*, 127–48).

1955 March 23 Joy Davidman wrote to Bill Gresham about how she helped Lewis come up with an idea for a new book.

April 2 Lewis wrote to Katherine Farrer that his Cupid and Psyche story shows what it is like for "every nice, affectionate agnostic whose dearest one suddenly 'gets religion.'"[10]

April 29 Another letter from Joy to Bill Gresham described her editorial role in the creation of *Till We Have Faces*. At this point Lewis was "about three-quarters of the way through [it]."

July 9 Lewis wrote to Katherine Farrer (to whom he had apparently sent a draft of the novel) saying that she had misunderstood, "but that only shows I have failed to get across what I intended." He adds, "I'll try to mend it, but not, I think, in the directions you suggest."[11]

1956 April 23 Lewis and Joy Davidman enter into civil marriage.

May 13 Lewis wrote to Arthur Greeves asking him to proofread the manuscript, which Lewis expected to receive from the publisher in June.

September 10 *Till We Have Faces* published in England.

1957 February 10 Lewis wrote to Clyde Kilby commenting on *Till We Have Faces*.

10. Hooper, *Companion*, 77.
11. Ibid., 250–51.

March 21 Lewis and Joy are united in sacramental marriage at Wingfield-Morris Hospital.

Christmas Lewis finishes *Reflections on the Psalms*.[12] To write it, Lewis needed to exercise the same kind of historical imagination that he did in writing *Till We Have Faces.*

1958 August 19–20 The talks that later became *The Four Loves* were recorded in London. Lewis's comments on affection and the need to be needed apply to Orual.[13] Thus Lewis was continuing to write on the same themes, and from the same motives, as we see in *Till We Have Faces.*

1960 March 28 *The Four Loves* was published.

April 3–14 Lewis and Joy travel to Greece. Lewis sees the places he has loved and studied in books.

July 13 Joy Davidman Lewis dies.

August Lewis writes *A Grief Observed*. His concern with the difference between his image of Joy and the real woman may recall Orual's actual remaking of Psyche as she wishes to remember her.

September *Studies in Words* published. It was partially based on the lectures he gave at Cambridge, beginning in Lent Term, 1955—in other words, at about the time he was writing *Till We Have Faces* with its striking use of vocabulary to establish the setting and the personality of Orual.[14]

1962 Summer Lewis writes *The Discarded Image*, a matter of reworking his lectures on the Middle Ages at both Oxford and Cambridge. Again, his ability to apply historical imagination to the facts and documents of the Middle Ages resulted in a book that has remained useful over the years to both graduate and undergraduate students of English literature.

1963 January Lewis writes *Letters to Malcolm*. The book deals with the struggle to be "bareface" in a different literary form.

November 22 C. S. Lewis dies.

Conclusion: Perhaps the task of writing his inauguration address and personifying himself as Old Western Man, the dinosaur, sug-

12. Ibid., 86.
13. Ibid., 88.
14. See Hooper, *Companion*, 73, for a brief survey of Lewis's lecture topics at Cambridge.

gested to Lewis the idea of writing fiction that would bring old stories to life and present their wisdom to a modern audience. If his health had been better, and if he had not been burdened with the ups and downs of Joy's situation, he might have completed the nonmythic, realistic story of Menelaus Yellowhead. But if there was to be only one novel of this type, it is fortunate for us that it was *Till We Have Faces*.

Glome, A Real Place — More or Less

Note: The items of information in this section are of secondary importance to an understanding of the novel. However, they may be of interest to readers trying to construct their own definition/ description of the term *true to life* and, of course, to people who collect trivia.

As Real as Africa

The description of Glome is based on historical and geographical facts from Lewis's broad knowledge of the ancient world. It is generally correct but not fussily accurate in detail. Lewis never aspired to the precision with which J. R. R. Tolkien constructed Middle Earth. As in all Lewis's fiction, information about the setting is subordinate to what is needed for the story—a twilight kingdom on the outskirts of Hellenistic civilization, deprived of both the enlightenment of the Greek golden age and the Dayspring to come with the birth of Jesus in the Augustan age.

As in John Buchan's Africa, the mood is more important than the details. Lewis's details are more accurate than Buchan's, even though his imaginary country owes at least as much to Herodotus (c. 484 to 430–420 B.C.) as to known facts about the much later Hellenistic period (323 to 30 B.C.).[1]

The chapters for which this is particularly relevant are 1:1, 20; 2:1.
1. The argument in Myers, *Context*, 193–95, assumes a greater accuracy for dates and information about ancient history and geography than actually exists.

Clues to the Geographic Placement of Glome

1. Glome is "a little barbarous state on the *borders* of the Hellenistic world" (*Let*, 462, emphasis added).

2. It is outside the colonies established by the Greek city-states along the Black Sea, for Orual tells us that the statue of Aphrodite bought for the temple of Ungit "had to be brought, not indeed from the Greeklands themselves, but from lands where men had learned of the Greeks" (*TWHF*, 234).

3. Glome lies in a northwesterly direction from the city of "the Great King," which is what the Greeks always called the king of Persia.[2]

4. Tarin is an ambassador from the "Great King" (*TWHF*, 254). Herodotus reports that some Scythians paid tribute to Persia in the time of Darius I (d. 486 B.C.). This is, of course, much earlier than Orual's time (see below). Although Orual makes no mention of tribute, she also does not say anything about the purpose of Tarin's embassy. There are at least two possible explanations: that she was too proud to admit that Glome paid tribute, and that she was too intent on her book to think of the business that had to be done. A literary explanation is that Lewis usually does not incorporate details unnecessary to the story.

5. One can glimpse the sea from the area where the Grey Mountain is located, but Orual says specifically that this is not "the Great Sea [Mediterranean] of the Greeks" (*TWHF*, 95). Apparently it is also not the Black Sea, for Glome could not be remote from Greek colonies along the Black Sea and at the same time close enough for the sea to be visible from the mountains.[3]

6. The reference to Glome's fight with "the Wagon Men" (*TWHF*, 227) or nomadic Scythians perhaps places the little city-state even farther from the Mediterranean. This identification is not very helpful, however, for the Greeks habitually called northern barbarians of eastern Europe "Scythians." Herodotus describes three kinds—

2. From William Beloe, tr., *The Ancient History of Herodotus*, 57n4.
3. The inconsistencies in Orual's descriptions of the country seem less glaring when one looks at the map entitled "The World According to Herodotus, B.C. 440" in vol. 2 of the Loeb Classical Library edition of *The Histories*. Published in 1921, this volume would not have been available to Lewis when he was studying Herodotus as an undergraduate.

nomads, farmers, and "royal" Scythians, but his descriptions of their lifestyles do not fit together, so the term must have covered many tribes.[4] Perhaps Glome itself is a kingdom of agricultural Scythians. Or it may have been farther west, near but outside the area of the Scythians.

7. The references to flora and fauna are inconclusive. Orual refers to pears and wheat, both of which grow best in a somewhat northerly climate. However, she also mentions figs; they are native to the Mediterranean region but can also be grown farther north. The king went on a lion hunt, which sounds like an activity for a southern climate, for modern readers think of lions as being found in Africa and southwestern Asia. However, for what it is worth, there are plenty of lions depicted in the artifacts from south Russia.[5]

Summary of Geographic Placement

It seems plausible that Glome is in Scythia, wherever that is, and this conclusion fits with the thematic unity of *Till We Have Faces,* for "Scythia" had a literary significance for the ancient Greeks comparable to that of Conrad's Africa. It was the Greek "heart of darkness." A representative line from Aeschylus's *Prometheus Bound* is quoted by Minns: "And thou shalt come to the Scyths, nomads who dwell in wattled huts . . . upon their fair-wheeled wains, equipped with far-shooting bows."[6]

In more modern terms, the kingdom of Glome could have been in south Russia, but it could also have been farther west, closer to the Danube. Orual's exactness in describing the relative positions of the river, the palace, the temple, and the Grey Mountain yields to vagueness on locations outside of Glome. This combination is both historically and psychologically realistic.

Clues to the Placement of Glome in Time

1. Glome belongs to "the Hellenistic world" (*Let,* 462), i.e., the time between the golden age of Greek culture—"the glory that was

---

4. Ellis H. Minns, *Scythians and Greeks: A Survey of Ancient History and Archeology on the North Coast of the Euxine from the Danube to the Caucasus,* 36, 47.
5. Ibid., 161, 177; M. Rostovtzeff, *Iranians and Greeks in South Russia,* 111.
6. *Prometheus Bound,* l. 735, in Minns, *Scythians and Greeks,* 50.

Greece"—and "the grandeur that was Rome." The conventional dating of the Hellenistic period falls between the death of Alexander the Great in 323 B.C. and the Roman capture of Egypt, the last segment of his empire, in 30 B.C. Some people prefer to mark the end of the Hellenistic period with the death of Augustus, the first Roman emperor, in A.D. 14.[7] In this system, the Hellenistic period overlaps the birth of Jesus in about 6–4 B.C. The Gospel According to Luke is careful to fix the time of the Incarnation during Augustus's reign (Luke 2:1). The story of Psyche takes place before the Incarnation, for when Orual asks whether the gods will "one day" grow beautiful, the Fox replies, "Nothing is yet in its true form" (*TWHF*, 305).

2. The conquests of Alexander the Great opened the way for Greek commerce, philosophy, language, and the arts to affect the lands on the borders of the Hellenistic world. This influence is shown in King Trom's realization that his heir must be educated in the Greek language and culture, the addition to the temple of a Greek-style statue of the local goddess, and Orual's determination to gather a Greek library for the kingdom.

3. The most recent book mentioned by name in the Glome library is Aristotle's *Metaphysics*, which would not have become available to the Glome market until after the philosopher's death in 322 B.C. The story that Aristotle's works were hidden in a cellar and not available in Athens until the first century B.C. is not generally believed by recent classical scholars.[8]

4. Information about the Fox allows us to narrow the time frame a little more. Since he was a Stoic, and this school of philosophy was founded by Zeno in 310 B.C., the events covered by the novel could not have happened much before 300 B.C., and they probably occurred later. When he is freed and thinks of returning to Greece, there is no indication that his homeland is now a Roman province. This, and the complete absence of any reference to Rome in *Till We Have Faces*, suggests that the story takes place before Greece became a Roman province in 146 B.C. and probably even before the Roman conquest of Greece and Macedonia in 197 B.C. However, an argument from silence is seldom reliable.

7. Simon Price, "The History of the Hellenistic Period," 315.
8. *OCD* 3, s.v. "Aristotle."

Conclusions

If the argument about Rome is accepted, Psyche lived sometime between about 300 B.C. and 197 B.C. Interestingly, if she had been a historical person who came to be worshipped as a goddess, it is plausible that she would have lived in the Hellenistic age, for she is definitely one of the latest immortals to join the Pantheon. Furthermore, the "Cupid and Psyche" of Apuleius is the first treatment of her story in words (as opposed to art) that we have. It seems that if her story had been known earlier it would have been treated by one of the poets of the golden age, and we have no evidence that this ever happened. (Of course, as Lewis was fond of pointing out, we really know very little about ancient history and literature.)

Although many accurate clues are provided, Orual's basic lack of knowledge or interest concerning events outside her own territory prevents a truly precise dating. The dating we do have, however, is exactly what is needed to produce the literary effect of surprise and recognition when the reader realizes that Psyche's husband, the pagan god of love, is somehow akin to, perhaps the same as, the Christian God of Love, Jesus, the "myth become fact."

The Holy—Lewis and Otto

The connection between Lewis and Otto is graphically illustrated by a brief passage in *Surprised by Joy*. Lewis reports that there was a time when he began to ask, "Where has religion reached its true maturity? Where, if anywhere, have the hints of all Paganism been fulfilled?" (*SbJ*, 235). Otto answers this question specifically in *Das Heilige (The Idea of the Holy):* "[Christianity] is a more perfect religion ... than [its predecessors] in so far as what is potential in religion in general becomes in [it] a pure actuality."[1] Or, as Lewis later put it, when Christ died and was resurrected, all the myths of death and rebirth, all the foreshadowings of a savior god in paganism became historical fact.

Otto's *The Idea of the Holy* is one of the most significant religious books of the early twentieth century. Like the work of William James and Carl Jung, it explores religion as a psychological and anthropological phenomenon, asserting the reality of religion against the denigrations of some social scientists. First published in 1917, it was translated into English in 1923 and was therefore available to Lewis soon after he completed his postgraduate studies in English literature. It became part of his personal synthesis of religious tradition and modern thought. When asked by the journal *The Christian Century* for a list of the ten most influential books in his life and thought, one was *The Idea of the Holy;* and he made use of it throughout his career.

The chapters for which this is particularly relevant are 1:4, 7, 11, 12, 20.
1. Otto, *Holy*, 56.

In Lewis's first full-fledged book of Christian apology, *The Problem of Pain*, the introductory chapter consists of a summary of *The Idea of the Holy*, illustrated with his own inimitable examples and analogies. In each book of the planetary trilogy, written in the middle of his career, there are sequences in which characters respond to the holy; and the saying, "Aslan's not a tame lion" in the Chronicles of Narnia is the same response on a childhood level.[2] Lewis was still drawing on Otto in one of his last books, *Reflections on the Psalms* (1958), as he compared two kinds of pre-Christian religious experience as expressed in Hebrew and classical pagan poetry.[3]

Lewis's most fully realized and dramatized presentation of the Holy, of course, comes in *Till We Have Faces*. In a key passage Orual asks in vain, "Why must holy places be dark places?" (*TWHF*, 249), and Otto supplies an answer: when we try to deal with human religion using nothing but ordinary reason we are bound to miss the point, for the nonrational is a necessary element of the human experience of God. Light is a common symbol of enlightenment; thus, in saying that holy places must be dark places, Lewis is using a visual symbol of Otto's principle.

At several points Orual speaks of a place as "holy," and the context shows that she is not using the word in its ordinary sense, but rather in the sense of Otto's *heilig*—something dangerous, frightening, uncanny. We ordinarily think of holiness in connection with moral goodness, but Otto coins another word, "numinous," to designate the kind of holiness he is describing.[4] He wants to emphasize that it has nothing to do with moral goodness. It is important to remember, then, that Orual's "holy" means "numinous."

Otto's book is a complex, precise description of the numinous and its role in human religion. He begins by asserting that three kinds of thinkers—theologians, psychologists, and anthropologists—have misunderstood religion because they have ignored the importance of the numinous.

First, theologians have inadvertently overemphasized the role of

2. Paul F. Ford finds Otto's influence in all seven of the Chronicles. See "Numinous" in *A Companion to Narnia*.
3. See Medcalf, "Language."
4. Lewis does connect holiness with goodness in the Chronicles of Narnia. See *LWW*, 80.

the rational in religion. Theology, or god-talk, "consists of words," and words "convey ideas or concepts;—that is what language means." Thus god-talk inevitably emphasizes the "'rational' attributes of God." This is unsatisfactory because God is a "supra-rational subject" that eludes understanding in terms of concepts. Otto is not asserting an anti-intellectual, all-feeling attitude toward God. On the contrary, he insists that belief is more than feeling and that Christianity does possess intellectual propositions about God "in unique clarity and abundance." In fact, he considers it "a very real sign of its superiority over religions of other forms. . . . The contrast is not between rationality and a faith based on feeling, but between rationalism and profounder religion."[5] God-talk that does not take the numinous into account sanitizes religious experience.

Second, some psychologists misunderstand religion by deriving it from childhood feelings toward the all-powerful parent. As the popular expression has it, "God is like Santa Claus. It's really just your father dressed up." In *The Silver Chair*, the Green Witch ridicules the children's talk of Aslan by saying, "You've seen cats, and now you want a bigger and better cat, and it's to be called a *lion*" (*SC*, 180). It is, of course, true that people's ideas of God are influenced by their early experiences of their parents. At first it seems that much of Orual's hatred and fear of Ungit comes from her experience with her bullying, abusive father. However, Orual specifically says that her fear of the Old Priest (who has an aura of the numinous) is "quite different from my fear of my father" (*TWHF*, 11).

The idea that religion comes from imagining a bigger and better father, or "a bigger and better cat," is not new to modern times. In refuting this theory of religion as psychological projection, Otto does not mention Freud, but rather goes back to Xenophanes, who said, "If oxen could paint, they would depict the gods as oxen." But Otto replies, men are not oxen, and actual religion developed not from "the homely" but "the uncanny." Depicting the divine in terms of bigger and better men, he says, was "an accretion" that occurred when belief in the gods was in decline.[6] In *Till We Have Faces*, Lewis follows Otto's principle. It is dramatized when Arnom, the New

---

5. Otto, *Holy*, 1–2.
6. Rudolf Otto, *Religious Essays* 78–79. Lewis's copy of this book with his underlinings is available at the Wade Center.

Priest, brings a Greek-style image of a woman—bigger and better femininity—into Ungit's temple. Arnom's belief in Ungit is pallid at best; he, unlike the Old Priest, has apparently had no experience of the numinous.

Third, theorists of anthropology who study mythology and comparative religion have contributed to an erroneous view of religion by deriving it from the fear of physical dangers in nature. Primitive people had very little control over what happened to them, and to these thinkers, it was plausible to account for the origin of religious rituals as an effort to attain control, to assure the food supply and the tribe supply. This theory underlies Harrison's excellent research on the non-Olympic Greek gods (see "Pagan Religion," 204). But according to Otto, these thinkers misunderstand the direction of the fear. What is at the heart of religious experience is not a fear of natural phenomena such as thunder and lightning, but of the unnatural, the numinous—the Holy.

"The numinous," says Otto, is an "absolutely primary and elementary datum [that] cannot be strictly defined."[7] It is something objective, something felt outside oneself. For example, when Lewis's Orual hears the voice of the god, she feels "a swift wave of terror" and calls it "the salute that mortal flesh gives to immortal things" (*TWHF*, 171)—that is, to the numinous. In the effort to describe without defining, Otto turns to the interaction between the human being's subjective feelings and the objective numinous. He calls it the feeling of the *mysterium tremendum*. The Latin phrase does not mean "a tremendous mystery," as the resemblance in words tempts us to assume, but rather refers to the qualities of a hidden, unknown something that arouses shuddering. *Mysterium* means "the unknowable," and *tremendum* means "causing to shudder."

But what characteristics of the unknowable arouse the shuddering? What are the elements of the *tremendum*? Otto takes several chapters to analyze them, and Lewis uses many passages in *Till We Have Faces* to dramatize them. Here are the elements of the *mysterium tremendum* isolated by Otto along with a few examples from the novel. The reader will doubtless discover others for himself:

1. Religious dread, awe. It is manifested physically in shuddering, creeping flesh, the feeling of hair standing on end and verbally

7. Otto, *Holy*, 7.

in the phrase, "the Wrath of Yahweh."[8] For example, when the Old Priest describes the mystery of sacrifice, "[t]he holiness and horror of divine things" fill the room, and the king's forehead becomes "clammy." And on the mountain, when Bardia and Orual first see Psyche, Bardia cries out. Orual says, "A quivering shock of feeling that has no name (but is nearest terror) stabbed through me from head to foot" (*TWHF*, 49, 101).

2. The feeling of being overpowered, of littleness and creature-hood. Otto calls it *majestas*.[9] It is what causes Psyche to feel ashamed of being a mortal when she sees the West-Wind.

3. Energy, urgency. It is perceived as wrath and described symbolically as "vitality, passion, emotional temper, will, force, movement, excitement, activity, impetus." Mystics speak of the "consuming fire" of love, of a hardly bearable burning strength.[10] When the West-Wind takes Psyche up to carry her to the god's house, his touch seems to burn her. When Orual and Psyche meet in the last vision, one sign that Psyche has become a goddess is that her touch burns Orual.

Orual experiences both the energy and the wrath when the golden rams knock her flat. She observes, "[T]he Divine Nature wounds and perhaps destroys us merely by being what it is. We call it the wrath of the gods," but that is as absurd as to say that a waterfall is angry with "every fly it sweeps down in its green thunder" (*TWHF*, 284).

Having analyzed *tremendum*, Otto turns to *mysterium*. The distinguishing quality of the numinous is that it is "Wholly Other." This quality is manifested in "stupor," blank wonder, and astonishment at something "beyond the sphere of the usual, the intelligible, and the familiar." Otto observes that science is not mysterious in the same way; anything that is in principle understandable is "not a 'mystery', but merely a 'problem.'"[11] Orual's glimpse of Psyche's palace with its Gothic pinnacles and buttresses is an experience of architecture intended to hint at, to suggest, the wholly other. "A labyrinthine beauty," it "brought [her] heart into [her] throat" (*TWHF*, 132). Otto says, "To us of the West the Gothic appears as the most

8. Ibid., 18.
9. Ibid., 19.
10. Ibid., 23, 24.
11. Ibid., 26, 28.

numinous of all types of art," and the palace has some of the qualities he ascribes to the Gothic cathedral: semi-darkness, silence, and sublimity.[12] (In contrast, non-Western art often achieves an impression of the numinous by emptiness and empty distances.)

There is, or can be, something repellent about the wholly other, but at the same time it may hold great fascination. The human creature feels the numinous as gracious and wonderful, as bliss and comfort, as "the object of search and desire and yearning"; the joyous other side of the "'wrath' of God."[13] In *The Problem of Pain*, Lewis exemplifies the awed response of both fear and fascination by quoting the passage from Kenneth Grahame's *The Wind in the Willows* in which Rat and Mole approach Pan, the god of the animals, on the island: "'Rat,' he found breath to whisper, shaking, 'Are you afraid?' 'Afraid?' murmured the Rat, his eyes shining with unutterable love. 'Afraid? of Him? O, never, never. And yet—and yet—O Mole, I am afraid'" (*PoP*, 18).

This passage, combining childhood freshness with complex adult spirituality, is perhaps the seed of several encounters with the holy in the Chronicles of Narnia. In *Till We Have Faces* Lewis attempts an equally difficult feat, that of showing how one who has lost her innocence and blinded herself to the numinous may come to experience it. When Psyche speaks of the one who comes to her only in the "holy darkness," Orual sees "unspeakable joy" in her eyes. But instead of responding with sympathy or even curiosity, Orual replies, "loud and stern," that Psyche's life with the god does not exist. Throughout book 1, she experiences only the wrathful side of the numinous, and little of that; but beginning with the story of the priest of Psyche, the divine gradually breaks down her denial until she finally meets "the only dread and beauty there is" and dares to look up at him (*TWHF*, 123, 307).

Conclusion

These specific passages in *Till We Have Faces* do not begin to exhaust the influence of *The Idea of the Holy* on the novel, much less

12. Ibid., 67.
13. Ibid., 32, 31.

the influence on Lewis's life and thought. Otto's work is unique in the way he describes God as "inconceivable and incomprehensible" while simultaneously insisting that the meaning of God for Christians is "profoundly rational" and "the basis indeed of all reason."[14] The structure of the novel dramatizes the careful, convoluted inquiries of Otto throughout. Orual struggles with the contrast between rationality and the numinous, and the relationship of both to moral law, the law of love. The Old Priest expresses God's incomprehensible side, the Fox, God's rational side, and on the eve of her sacrifice, Psyche praises both. *Till We Have Faces* is both an autonomous work of art and in some sense a commentary on Lewis's own spiritual struggles to reconcile within his own personality the opposing elements of twentieth-century reason, the timeless numinous, and the law of love.

14. Ibid., 185.

James and Conversion

In William James's *Varieties of Religious Experience,* Lewis found a clear description of religious life in general, a relatively complete description of the religious personality, and examples from the diaries and journals of religious persons, often those undergoing a process of conversion. Although the material was highly congruent with his interests, he omits any reference to James's influence on him in *Surprised by Joy,* the account of his own conversion. According to his diary, *All My Road before Me,* however, he was reading James's book in June of 1922 and called it "a capital book" (*AMR,* 48).

Several of the basic intellectual convictions that became part of Lewis's adult Christianity can be found in James. First there was the fallacy Lewis called "Bulverism," the twentieth- century habit of assuming (not proving) that someone is wrong and then proceeding to "[explain] how he became so silly." James specifically applies the fallacy to arguments against religion, inveighing against the common "assumption that spiritual value is undone if lowly origin be asserted." His examples include "Alfred believes in immortality so strongly because his temperament is so emotional" and "Eliza's delight in her church is a symptom of her hysterical constitution."[1] Lewis's first demonstration of Bulverism occurs in *The Pilgrim's Regress,* in which the Spirit of the Age instructs John that the proper answer to an argument proving the existence of God is "You say that because you are a Steward [clergyman]" (*PR,* 62).

The chapters for which this is particularly relevant are 1:5, 12.
1. Quoted from Hooper, *Companion* 552; James, *Varieties,* 18, 223.

Lewis also shared with James the conviction that materialism is self-refuting. James says it this way: "[T]here is not a single one of our states of mind . . . that has not some organic process as its condition. Scientific theories are organically conditioned just as much as religious emotions are."[2] Lewis uses this idea, along with the Bulverism argument, in his *Miracles* (1947), but rather than James he quotes J. B. S. Haldane's *Possible Worlds*: "If my mental processes are determined wholly by the motions of atoms in my brain, I have no reason to suppose my beliefs are true . . . and hence I have no reason for supposing my brain to be composed of atoms" (*Mir,* 22). Lewis then goes on to show that "the reason" of reasoning is ground-consequent, not cause-effect. Though something material causes the process of reasoning, the conclusion of the process will be correct if it conforms to the laws of reason, of which ground-consequent is one.

Another shared conviction is James's assertion that the "nucleus" to all religions is an "uneasiness" that "there is *something wrong about us* as we naturally stand" and a sense of being *"saved from the wrongness* by making proper connection with the higher powers."[3] In *Mere Christianity* Lewis states it this way: human beings naturally have a sense of right and wrong, and we have "put [ourselves] wrong" with the "Power behind the law" (*MC,* 39).

Finally, although there is "a great variety of thoughts" in "the whole field of religion," James finds that people's feelings and rules of conduct "are almost always the same, for Stoic, Christian, and Buddhist saints are practically indistinguishable in their lives."[4] The universal agreement of various cultures concerning right and wrong is, of course, a controlling idea of Lewis's *Abolition of Man.*

In addition to these major convictions, there are interesting parallels between James and Lewis on the level of simile and image. For example, James says the "spiritual grubs and earthworms, the Crumps and Stigginses," might have been "much less ideal still if conversion had not touched them."[5] In *Mere Christianity,* this becomes nice Dick Firkin and awful Miss Bates, and the phrase "spiritual grubs and earthworms" might have inspired Lewis's compar-

2. James, *Varieties,* 21.
3. Ibid., 454, James's emphasis.
4. Ibid., 451.
5. Ibid., 221.

ison of Christ's Incarnation to "becom[ing] a slug or crab" (*MC*, 163, 140) On the other hand, perhaps such similes are commonplace among philosophers and theologians. James quotes Al Ghazzali as follows: "Being drunk, the [drunken man] knows nothing; whilst the physician, although not drunk, knows well in what drunkenness consists."[6] Lewis's version is, "You can understand the nature of drunkenness when you are sober, not when you are drunk. Good people know about both good and evil; bad people do not know about either" (*MC*, 87).

Finally, in James's description of "the simplest rudiment of mystical experience," Lewis may have found insight into his own life. James listed the following examples: a "deepened sense of the significance of a maxim" or even a single word; "effects of light on land and sea, odors and musical sounds"; "the strangely moving power of passages in certain poems read when we were young, irrational doorways . . . through which the mystery of fact, the wildness and the pang of life, stole into our hearts and thrilled them."[7] James called it *Sehnsucht.*

Lewis experienced it at age six when he looked at Warnie's toy garden, and again when he read,

> I heard a voice that cried,
>   Balder the beautiful
> Is dead, is dead—— (*SbJ*, 16, 17).

And he called it *Sehnsucht.*

James's Religious Typology

James's classification of people into once-born and twice-born personalities applies to the inhabitants of Glome and indeed increases one's appreciation of the realism with which they are portrayed. The once-born are the healthy-minded; they tend to ignore or discount evil. The twice-born begin as "sick souls," but when

6. Al-Ghazzali, fl. 11th c. James cites D. B. MacDonald, "The Life of Al-Ghazzali," *Journal of the American Oriental Society* (20:71) 1899 (*Varieties,* 363).
7. James, *Varieties,* 344, 345.

they are transformed they often experience a rapturous happiness that is unavailable to the once-born. James does not exactly equate the sick souls with those who become twice-born, but neither does he spell out just how the two categories overlap. Orual, the center of the story, is a sick soul. She suffers deeply but then becomes transformed by her visions. When she thinks she has come "to the utmost fullness of being which the human soul can contain," she finds that there is still more (*TWHF*, 306).

The other major characters contrast with Orual and are once-born to a greater or lesser degree. They can be placed in a continuum with Bardia as the most completely once-born and the Fox the most nearly twice-born. Indeed, James remarks that Stoics are resigned rather than optimistic or joyous; "[they hope] for no results, and [give] up natural good altogether."[8] (Or, like the Fox, they take refuge in poetry.)

The most important characteristic of the once-born is the absence of a sense of sin, both in terms of personal wrongdoing and evil in the world. They are not introspective, do not think about metaphysical problems, and are not disheartened by their own failings. When they meet evil in the world, they ignore it as much as possible or (without mental anguish) do what they can to relieve the suffering of others. As a "contemporary example" of this type, James cites Walt Whitman. The sick soul, who has the potential to become twice-born, is plagued by a deep-rooted pessimism, which James attributes to three sources: a sense of sin, awareness of the vanity of mortal things, and a fear of the universe. He cites Goethe, Luther, and the author of Ecclesiastes as examples.[9]

The following applications of James's principles are brief and suggestive rather than comprehensive.

Bardia

Religion is just one of the "water-tight compartments" of his mind.[10] He is pious and offers the customary sacrifices, but lets the

8. Ibid., 135.
9. Ibid., 82–85, 151, 128–31.
10. Ibid., 308.

gods alone as far as possible and hopes they will let him alone. He mostly ignores the evil of King Trom, telling Orual that the king does well enough as a leader of men. He shows compassion toward suffering by standing guard over Psyche in person and by letting Orual in to see her. He is sorry for the cruelty of war and remembers what it was like to kill a man for the first time; nevertheless, he enjoys the excitement of war and seems not to regret the killings he has done.

However, he is not completely once-born but has himself experienced depression and deep sorrow. He tells Orual, "I have been as you are now; I have sat and felt the hours drawn out to the length of years" (*TWHF,* 90). Then he teaches Orual to combat her depression with physical exercise.

James calls the method of ignoring evil (Bardia's method) "splendid as long as it will work," but he points out that "evil facts" may provide "the best key to life's significance," possibly the only path to deepest truth.[11] James's observation may suggest the reason why Bardia does not appear to Orual in the Underworld. On an artistic level, the structure of the fiction calls for Orual to learn about her self-seeking love of him from his wife, Ansit; but aside from the artistic structure, one cannot quite imagine an Underworld meeting between Orual and Bardia. His once-born nature would have nothing to contribute to her problem; sword fighting is not theology.

King Trom

The characteristics of the once-born, lovable in Bardia, are despicable in Trom. He, too, leaves the gods alone as far as possible. He sacrifices to Ungit and expects her to take care of his interests—the things required to keep him in control of the kingdom—in return. Almost completely lacking in self-reflectiveness, he complains bitterly when Ungit does not keep her side of the bargain but never wonders whether the situation is partly his fault or whether the nature of divinity is different from his conception of it. He says, "What have I done that all these miseries should fall upon me? I've been a god-fearing man all my life" (*TWHF,* 41).

11. Ibid., 152.

He lacks a sense of sin. When the Old Priest confronts him, his forehead becomes "clammy," not with the sense of inadequacy with which mortals meet the numinous, but with the self-seeking, almost animal fear that he is the one to be sacrified (*TWHF,* 49). After beating Orual, he is momentarily ashamed, and when he picks her up, she finds his "hands were gentler than [she] expected" (*TWHF,* 57). Nevertheless, when she meets him in the Underworld she finds that he has in no way developed or changed his mind (as the Fox has done). Instead he volunteers to teach her a thing or two, perhaps out of sheer pleasure in dominating and bullying.

Arnom

Once-born Arnom is not interested in the gods except as one more center of power to be factored into the political balance. Orual was glad to help set up the statue of Aphrodite because she thought it would reduce Ungit's power and terror; Arnom's motives were quite different. Just as he lacked the "holiness" of the Old Priest, so also he lacked Orual's fear of Ungit, and the text gives us no reason to believe he was troubled by a sense of sin. Perhaps, desiring enlightenment and sophistication, he saw the worship of the shapeless stone as old-fashioned and countrified, not Greek. So he brought light and cleanliness into the temple and taught the young nobles to interpret the deity allegorically.

Psyche

Her once-born lack of self-reflectiveness is admirable. It causes her to think nothing of being worshiped by the people, even though as a child she had dreamed of being a great queen and living in an amber-and-gold house. Her lack of guilt is justified, for her behavior is so good "that in her (the Fox said) Virtue herself had put on a human form" (*TWHF,* 26). She has some imperfections, but they do not bother her; she calls herself "only [her god's] simple Psyche" (*TWHF,* 163). She reacts to evil with compassion for the suffering, but she flees from it when possible, as she ran from the men who threw rocks at her. As a pupil of the Fox she could hardly avoid thinking about metaphysical problems, but she improves on his Stoic cheerfulness with hope. She says, perhaps the gods "don't really do these [evil] things," or perhaps the seeming evil is really good (*TWHF*, 71). When Orual pushes her to the limit, she faces death with agnostic optimism: "We don't understand. There must be so much that neither the Priest nor the Fox knows" (*TWHF*, 72). Because she is so at one with herself, she is able to accept the strange, supernatural things that happen to her with poise and simplicity.

Redival

Because Redival is a minor character and one against whom Orual is biased, there is not enough information to classify her. She seems to lack interest in ultimate questions, and certainly she lacks a sense of sin, but she also lacks the sunny disposition of many once-borns.

The Fox

In comparison with Orual, the Fox cannot be called a sick soul; however, he is not nearly as sure of his religious stance as Psyche—or King Trom. He is cheerful, even heroically cheerful, but his manner comes from a resolved and disciplined faith in the goodness of the Divine Nature rather than a carefree perception that all is well. He is a divided self; he calls the poetry about the gods, which he truly loves, "lies of poets," while trying to embrace the Stoic philosophy that cannot comfort him for the loss of Psyche. His aggressive impatience with Glomish superstition suggests that his trust in the rational is not as solid as he thinks.

As far as we know—a knowledge confined to what Orual tells us—he does not undergo a conversion, as Orual does in the last few days of her life. However, his kindness and compassion, along with his fidelity toward the Divine Nature, apparently enable him to meet the judge in the afterlife, accept the mistakes in his philosophy, and be a tutor to Orual in her last vision.[12]

---

12. See "Stoicism: The Faith of the Fox," 214, for a discussion of the Fox's Christlike nature.

Orual

In book 1, Orual's sickness of soul is fully explored. She suffers from her deep-rooted perception of the vanity of mortal things, her guilt—unsuccessfully papered over with accomplishment and cease-less activity, and her fear of the universe. She is different, however, from most of James's cases in that her pessimism leads to defiance of the gods rather than submission. Even when the priest of Psyche accuses her of destroying Psyche's happiness out of jealousy and Orual realizes that she has not successfully cheated the gods after all, she reacts with defiance, not surrender. She is strong even in her sickness of soul, but her strength is a veneer over the inner divided self.

The last part of the novel recounts her conversion according to the stages outlined by James: "the divided self and the struggle," "the change of personal centre . . . and surrender of the lower self," the union with "the helping power," and finally, "feelings of secu-rity and joy."[13] Her new twice-born status is expressed in her phys-ical loveliness as she sees it reflected in the pool, just before her vision fades.

13. James, *Varieties*, 465.

Myth — A Definition

Lewis's last novel is subtitled *A Myth Retold.* Is a myth retold still a myth? Certainly *Till We Have Faces* does not fit Lewis's own definition of myth in every respect. In *Experiment in Criticism*, published about five years after the novel, Lewis listed these six characteristics of myth:

1. It is extraliterary—i.e., independent of the literary genre or style in which it is conveyed and the touches of vivid imagery supplied by an individual author. This characteristic is derived from the original Greek word, *mythos,* which designated any narrative or story. At first there was no distinction between fact and fiction; later *mythos* was applied only to fiction, whether tale, story, legend or myth in the sense of a special kind of narrative.[1] As Lewis says, the mythic story has a very simple narrative shape, "like a good vase or a tulip" (*Exp,* 42). Often it can be summarized in one or two sentences. Different authors may tell different versions of it, but the narrative shape abides. *Till We Have Faces* and the "Cupid and Psyche" of Apuleius fit this definition in that they belong to different literary genres (modern novel and fairy tale) and use entirely different literary styles, but one can make a plot summary that fits each story equally well.

2. A myth is not dependent on "suspense or surprise." Whether we read it as a completely developed story or just a synopsis, the outcome "is felt to be inevitable," and we make it "a permanent

---

The chapters for which this is particularly relevant are 1:6, 10; 2:3.

1. Frederick William Danker and Walter Bauer, *Greek-English Lexicon of the New Testament and Other Early Christian Literature,* 660b.

object of contemplation" (*Exp*, 43). In "Cupid and Psyche" we realize immediately that no good can come of someone's effort to control and manipulate the wonder of love. Thus we are not surprised
that Psyche loses her happiness when she brings the lamp into the
bedroom, and we contemplate what the lack of respect for the mystery can do to love.

As Lewis says, a mythic story does not cause us to ask "Will the
hero escape?" but rather to feel, "I shall never escape this. This will
never escape me. These [narrative] images have struck roots far
below the surface of my mind" (*Exp*, 48–49). Perhaps we realize
most vividly that Orual is living within a myth when she visits
Psyche on the night before the sacrifice and sees her sitting on the
bed with a lamp beside her. Though it was "only in a flash," Orual
says, "the picture . . . is everlasting" (*TWHF*, 67).

3. In a myth "Human sympathy is at a minimum," for the characters are "like shapes moving in another world" (*Exp*, 44). This
characteristic does not fit *Till We Have Faces* at all, since the psychology of the characters is a major interest. The royal family, for example, with slight changes of costume and circumstance, would fit
perfectly well in the modern world: Redival, the rebellious, slightly
slutty daughter; Psyche, the saintly one; Orual, the misfit; and Trom,
the abusive father.

It is true that human sympathy is at a minimum in Apuleius's
"Cupid and Psyche." However, the reason is not that the characters
come from another world; on the contrary, most of the time they
are bound by Roman customs and marriage laws. We fail to sym-
pathize precisely because they are denizens of this world, but ones
whose actions are comical, sometimes even farcical.

4. Myth always deals with the fantastic, "with impossibles and
preternaturals" (*Exp*, 44). *Till We Have Faces* departs from this criterion in that the sisters' experience with the god of the Grey Mountain is treated as something real, though miraculous, while the trips
to the Underworld at the end of the book take place as dreams and
visions. Apuleius's "Cupid and Psyche" describes the supernatural
life of the gods as something beyond everyday life, but the comic
treatment prevents us from taking it seriously.

5. Thus Lewis's fifth criterion, that the story is always grave, never
comic (*Exp*, 44), applies to *Till We Have Faces*, but not to Apuleius's

version, which is as ludicrous as the whole novel in which it occurs (see "Apuleius and Lewis," 145).

6. The experience is "not only grave, but awe-inspiring," that is, "numinous." A myth reminds us that there is more to life than daily existence, more to ourselves than our petty concerns, more to our world than can be seen with scopes and instruments. I call it "mythic radiance." It is simple and well known, yet beyond our grasp. Lewis says, "[We feel] as if something of great moment had been communicated to us." We may try to tame it by analyzing it intellectually in terms of symbol and allegory, but "after all allegories have been tried, the myth itself continues to feel more important than they" (*Exp*, 44).

Lewis does not probe more deeply into this point, because *Experiment in Criticism* is a broad survey of many different types of literature. However, I believe the feeling that "something of great moment [has] been communicated to us" is due to the special kind of events found in a myth. The myth deals with universal anxieties, life crises, and choices, but by putting the story in a context of "impossibles and preternaturals," it involves the readers or hearers in meaningfulness far beyond the ordinary.

For example, the Cupid and Psyche myth deals with everyday life and its anxieties in that every person's marriage is a union with a more or less unknown partner, and every love relationship involves vulnerability and lack of understanding. In a culture of arranged unions, the partners are even more likely to be unknown to each other. The story of Cupid and Psyche probably stems from a story about such an anxiety. No definite source is known, but a similar story appears in several cultures; Apuleius was not the creator, but the transmitter of the story.[2] As a matter of history, Herodotus tells of a harem woman who learned that her partner was not the true king by feeling of his ears as he slept.[3] On her wedding night, Psyche's mother was placed in bed with King Trom, a man she did not know. This was ordinary life. But when Psyche sleeps with an

---

2. As Lewis says, Apuleius was "its transmitter, not its inventor" (*TWHF*, 313). Incidentally, one of the most familiar stories of an unknown marriage partner is Jacob's bedding of Leah, Gen. 29:16–27.

3. Herodotus, 3.68–69.

unknown partner, the story goes beyond everyday life, for the marriage partner is a god rather than a mortal man.

What Lewis says about old stories in "The Anthropological Approach" bears out this interpretation. The old stories, he says, were not unrelated to the real world; however, they were "invented by and for men who felt the real world, in its rather different way, to be also cryptic, significant, full of voices and 'the mystery of all life'" (*SLE*, 310). He goes on to suggest that modern people in general cannot view the real world in this way. In *Experiment in Criticism*, however, he recognizes the existence in modern times of mythic stories. Just as there are folk ballads and art ballads (songs by individuals composed in the ballad style), so also with myths. Lewis mentions as art myths Stevenson's *Dr. Jekyll and Mr. Hyde*, Wells's *The Door in the Wall*, and Kafka's *The Castle* (*Exp*, 42).

There is some doubt as to whether the "Cupid and Psyche" versions of either Apuleius or Lewis can be called art myths. Apuleius blurs the story's mythic radiance by making it into a comedy, and Lewis by making it into a modern novel. However, the retelling of the story by the priest of Psyche recovers the mythic radiance, and the judgment of Orual in book 2 completes the process. Throughout most of book 1, we readers are protected from the mythic radiance by the skepticism of the narrator, but at the end the reader can truly say, "I shall never escape this."

No definition of myth permits one to make an absolute division of all possible stories into on-off, zero-one, myth or not-myth, and certainly Lewis's definition-description does not. Many stories that are not myths have touches of the mythic radiance, and as Lewis says, "the same story may be a myth to one man and not to another" (*Exp*, 45).

Two Final Notes

1. The common meaning of the word *myth* is "a nonfactual story." Although this meaning is related to the kind of story Lewis is describing, in many contexts it is misleading. For example, people who know "myth" only in the sense of "nonfactual" may be confused when Lewis calls the story of Jesus Christ "myth become fact." He is saying that many stories in classical mythology dealt with hero-

saviors who died and arose to new life. Because they expressed the deep longing of ancient hearts and shone with mythic radiance, they are myths in Lewis's sense. They are also myths in the sense of "nonfactual." But Lewis asserts that at one point in history there was in fact a hero-savior who died and rose again.

2. A myth (as Lewis defines it) is not merely a phenomenon of the social sciences. What interests him is the myth as a source of joy and awe. Therefore he separates himself from the anthropological study of myths in terms of origins—as primitive explanations of scientific phenomena, as fictions that explain the origin of rituals and customs, as "the fabrications of medicine men," and as the expression of psychological anxieties and insights from the collective unconscious (*Exp*, 44–45). In fact, he gently ridicules the anthropological approach in *Till We Have Faces*. The priest of Psyche sees "the sacred story" as the explanation of the temple ritual, and Arnom sees the story of Ungit and her male consort as an explanation of meteorology. In both cases Orual is displeased, for both priests have missed the point.

Names in Glome

Lewis sometimes made inaccurate statements about small details in his own novels. For example, in one unpublished letter he mis-names one of the characters in the Chronicles of Narnia. Similarly, in a letter to a fan he says that the names in *Till We Have Faces* "are just 'made up'" (*LetChil*, 107). This is obviously not true of Psyche, whose name is traditional. Neither is it true of Psyche's name for Orual, "Maia." It is an equally traditional name meaning "mother/ grandmother" or "nurse." Known only as one of the Pleiades and the mother of Hermes, she may have been a goddess of the *kouro-trophos* (child-nurturing) type. The name, then, signifies Orual's chief relationship with Psyche. Earlier critics identified "Maia" with the Hindu word "Maya," "illusion."[1] This significance is not, of course, impossible: it is a loose pun, and certainly Orual lived under illusion for most of her life. However, the Greek meaning is arguably more important to the novel as a whole, since Orual's role as mother to Psyche is her chief justification for her decision to force Psyche to betray her lover.

"The Fox" is a nickname given to the slave by King Trom, suggested by his reddish hair and his sly Greek cleverness. His true Greek name, "Lysias," is the name of a noted Athenian orator. It is appropriate for the Fox because of his skill with words. Orual and Istra used Greek names for each other as a form of intimate address, and Arnom probably used "Lysias" rather than "the Fox" for the

---

The chapter for which this is particularly relevant is 1:2.
1. *OCD* 3, s.v. "Cybele," "kourotrophos." "Earlier critics" are listed in Schakel, *Reason and Imagination*, 188n4.

same reason. The choice of name probably has no significance beyond plausibility, since it is mentioned only once (*TWHF*, 186).

"Batta" is the feminine form of "Battus," a peasant who tattled about a theft. Hermes stole Apollo's cattle, and Battus broke his promise not to tell. Graves's *The Greek Myths* also lists Battus as the nickname of a King Aristeus. "Battus," amusingly enough, means "tongue-tied." It is probably irrelevant that "Battus" is also the name of three kings mentioned in Herodotus.[2] The name also has many possible word associations; see below.

Linguistic Technicalities

Other names are made up, but they resemble each other and thus create the vague impression that they belong to the same language. For example, "Arnom," "Trom," and "Gram," male names, end in the letter *m* preceded by a nonfront vowel. A person with some linguistic knowledge might assume that -om/-am was a masculine suffix for names in Glomish. The names of outsiders such as Argan of Phars, Orual's nephew Daaran of Phars, and the eunuch Tarin also end in a vowel plus a nasal consonant, so that all these names are related.

Another apparent masculine suffix for both Glome and Phars is -*ia*, as in Bardia, Ilerdia, and Trunia.

Three feminine names, "Ungit," the goddess, "Ansit," the wife, and "Alit," the young girl (Poobi's daughter) seem to have the feminine suffix -*it*. This suffix may be suggested by the Babylonian "Belit," consort of the male god Bel.

The -*val* in "Redival" and the -*ual* in "Orual" can be seen as variant pronunciations of the same suffix, and perhaps "Orual" should be pronounced "Aw'val" or "Aw'wal," in accordance with the British dialects' dropping of *r* in this position.[3] This similarity would emphasize the two girls' relationship as sisters. However, I have found no letter from a fan asking Lewis about the pronunciation of "Orual,"

2. Hamilton, *Mythology*, 325. (The name appears in the Hamilton index without a page reference.) See also Graves, *Greek Myths*, 82.1; Herodotus, 4:319.

3. On the other hand, Doreen Anderson Wood, "The Pattern in the Myth: Archetypal Elements in C. S. Lewis's *Till We Have Faces*," 84, believes that Orual is a "written variant" of Orval, the French name for the herb Salvia Clerea.

and most people seem to say either "Or'-u-àl" (last syllable rhyming with "call") or "O-ru'al."[4]

Word Associations

Some of the names carry subtle connotations through their resemblance to known words.

"Ansit" resembles "Anat," the goddess who is the sister and consort of Baal.[5] "Anat" is also a mother goddess. Thus the syllable *An-* suggests femininity and is appropriate for Ansit, a mother of eight, and *-it* is a feminine ending.

"Bardia" suggests "bard," from French, meaning "defensive armor for a horse," or "bards," armor made of metal plates and worn by men-at-arms. His name also suggests "barði," an Old Norse word meaning "a beaked ship," and metaphorically, "a shield." Thus the name has military connotations. Also, Bardia is always a shield to Orual, physically in battle and politically in the conduct of royal business.

"Batta" sounds like English "bat." It is a word of many meanings, but the most relevant one is "a lump, a piece of certain substances; a mass, dull-sounding, or formed by beating."[6] Thus Orual compares the face she sees in the Ungit-stone to Batta's—"a face such as you might see in a loaf, swollen, brooding, infinitely female" (*TWHF*, 270). "Bat" can also mean "a felted mass of fiber, a sheet of cotton wadding." What Orual says about Batta's "hot, strong yet flabby-soft embraces" first suggests bread dough, but perhaps also cotton or wool batting.

"Batta" can also be associated with "batten," especially the definitions "to grow fat," "to feed gluttonously," and "to prosper at the expense of another." These meanings point to her drunkenness and her nipping at King Trom's wine in his illness and the way she preyed on the other slaves. Finally, "Batten" means "to fasten," and Orual complains of feeling confined by Batta (*TWHF*, 230, 276).

4. The instructor of a course entitled "In Search of Cupid and Psyche" at Rutgers University recommends the pronunciation "OR-RULE." (http://www.scils.rutgers.edu/special/mjoseph/html).
5. Marvin H. Pope, tr. *Song of Songs*, 668.
6. *Oxford English Dictionary*, 1st ed.

Lewis is reported to have suggested "Trom" might be "Mort," i.e., "death," spelled backward. Since Trom was constantly so angry and aggressive, the backward spelling "Mort" might suggest Mortdant, who represents the irascible passions in book 2 of *The Faerie Queene*. Mortdant literally means "death giver," and the dramatic scene in which Trom stabs the pageboy certainly shows him capable of such action. Adey sees a bookish jest in the name "Gram," a short form of the Greek "gramma" or "letter." Gram's silence suggests "silent letter."[7]

"Istra," Psyche's Glomish name, is similar to "Ishtar," the Babylonian goddess, who is also identified with the planet Venus.[8] The Fox said Ungit was an Aphrodite who was like the Babylonian goddess (Ishtar), and Psyche, like Ishtar, makes a descent to the Underworld. This leads to an interesting set of equivalencies. The god said to Orual, "You also shall be Psyche" and in the process of becoming self-aware Orual realizes, "I am Ungit" (*TWHF,* 174, 276). Thus, in a sense Psyche is Ungit is Aphrodite is Ishtar.

The name Ungit has two parts, the (postulated) feminine suffix and *Ung-*. The sound seems evocative, but of what? The name "Ugarit," a city in Syria (fl. 1450–1195 B.C.), sounds exotic and non-Greek, but it is hard to see any connection with Glome. Uruk is Ishtar's city, but the two names do not resemble one another very closely.[9] How about "ungulate," a cowlike mammal? Ishtar, like other mother/fertility goddesses, is of course the Cow of Heaven. Still another association is with "Ugh," the exclamation of disgust. Lewis's muse may have brought any or all of these associations to light. At any rate, the name "Ungit" seems strange at first but more and more inevitable as the story goes on.

7. Carol Ann Brown, cited by Adey, *C. S. Lewis,* 162n113. For "gamma," see p. 160. For "Mortdant," see Myers, "Spenser," pp. 90–91.
8. Gwendolyn Leick, *A Dictionary of Ancient Near Eastern Mythology,* 87.
9. Ibid., 87.

The New Psychology

In his undergraduate days, Lewis eagerly read Freud and Jung—what was called "the New Psychology."[1] It was so called to distinguish it from faculty psychology, a traditional model of the human mind that goes all the way back to Plato. Lewis's familiarity with this traditional model is especially seen in "The Human Soul" section of *The Discarded Image,* and in chapter 2 of *The Abolition of Man.* He used the old psychology almost exclusively in the rest of his fiction. Although few readers are aware of it, his use of the new psychology in *Till We Have Faces* may be what differentiates it most sharply from the others.

This "Further In" essay discusses only Freud and Jung. Lewis also read William James's *The Varieties of Religious Experience* and Rudolf Otto's *The Idea of the Holy* during his undergraduate years, but James and Otto are discussed in separate essays.[2]

This reading did not directly prepare him for his final examinations in "Greats"—ancient history, philosophy, and literature—but

The chapters for which this is particularly relevant are 1:5, 7, 21; 2:3.

1. That psychology was a lifelong interest of Lewis's is shown by the books in his personal library, now found in the Wade Collection: Carl Jung, *Answer to Job;* William James, *Textbook of Psychology* and *The Varieties of Religious Experience;* E. Howe, *Motives and Mechanisms of the Mind;* F. W. H. Myers, *Human Personality;* C. H. Mowrer, *Crisis in Psychiatry and Religion* (a gift from Clyde Kilby); Karl Stern, *The Pillar of Fire, The Third Revolution,* and *Through Dooms of Love.* List compiled by Leigh C. Bishop.

2. In chronological order, these contributors to the rising human sciences are as follows: William James, psychologist-philosopher, 1842–1910; James G. Frazer, anthropologist, 1854–1941; Sigmund Freud, psychologist, 1856–1939; Rudolf Otto, theologian, 1869–1937; Carl Jung, psychologist, 1875–1961.

it was not irrelevant to his field of specialization. At this point in the early twentieth century the anthropologists were reporting new parallels to ancient myths in the cultures they studied, and the classicists were finding new confirmations of their philological and historical researches in the reports of anthropologists. At the same time, the new psychologists were beginning their research on the human soul with the categories of thought descended from the ancients. We remember immediately Freud's work on the Oedipus complex, but it was not the only psychological theory inspired by ancient literature and philosophy. It is difficult now to realize that psychology was originally a branch of philosophy, but William James, whose ideas influenced both Freud and Jung, preceded the other two men just enough to be considered both a philosopher and a psychologist, and he is listed under both headings in modern encyclopedias.

Lewis Reads Freud

In *Surprised by Joy,* Lewis remembers that "the new Psychology was sweeping through us all" (*SbJ*, 203). In a June 1922 entry in his diary, published under the title of *All My Road before Me*, he mentions picking up Freud's *Introductory Lectures in Psychoanalysis,* which he inadvertently calls *Introductory Letters.* He and his literary friends were especially concerned about distinguishing "fantasy" and "imagination" in Coleridge's philosophy from "fantasy" and "wishful thinking" as used by Freud (*AMR*, 44).

It is important to note that Lewis was not treating the new psychology as an isolated body of knowledge, but as something that had implications for him as a literary scholar. He also applied it to his search for personal truth. At this time he was adopting his "New Look," and part of it was rejecting joy on the ground that his "delectable mountains and western gardens" were nothing but wishful thinking as expounded by Freud, and that his fantasies always degenerated into "erotic reverie or the squalid nightmare of Magic" (*SbJ*, 203–4).

Later Lewis began to be more critical of Freud. Neville Coghill's remark that Lewis regarded the new psychology as "the quirks of fretful foreigners [word play: geographical foreigners, mentally foreign people] to good sense, sound poetry, and the known stuff of the soul" apparently comes from the postgraduate year when Coghill and Lewis were studying for the English school together.[3] This period also culminated in Lewis's return to traditional Christianity.

In his first book as an adult Christian, *The Pilgrim's Regress*, he vehemently attacked the New Psychology, especially Freudianism. One character, a henchman of the Spirit of the Age, is named Sigismund (Freud's original first name). Sigismund causes the hero, John, to see his own insides—"his lungs panting like sponges, and the liver, and the intestines like a coil of snakes" (*PR*, 61). This is, of course, a metaphorical description of what happens in psychoanalysis. John says despairingly, "If we are really like that inside, whatever we imagine must be abominable however innocent it looks." But Reason, who has rescued John from the Spirit of the Age, explains, "[I]f you take . . . a longing out of the dark part of a man's mind and give [it] the self-consciousness which [it] never has in reality," it is bound to look horrible (*PR*, 69, 71). Since Lewis says in the preface that the heresies we hate most are those we believed most fervently, his forcefulness is good evidence that Freudianism once meant a great deal to him.

By the time Lewis came to write *The Problem of Pain* (1940), his attitude toward Freudian psychology was more moderate. Indeed, he integrated it into his account of the Great Chain of Being and the Fall of Man. He describes how God raised physical and chemical processes to support vegetable life, used vegetation to support animal life, and then called humanity with its rational consciousness out of animality. (He later dramatized this process in *The Magician's Nephew*.) When humanity fell, human reason lost control of itself and became subject to the influences of biochemical and environmental conditions. Since reason no longer had control, "the will . . . had no resource but to force [unwanted thoughts and desires] back by main strength, and these uneasy rebels became the subconscious as we now know it" (*PoP*, 82).

This integration of the new psychology with old ideas is somewhat simplistic, and the same is true of the psychological material in "Christian Behavior," a section of *Mere Christianity*. In it he affirms psychoanalysis as a medical theory compatible with Christianity

3. Neville Coghill, "The Approach to English," 60.

but rejects it as a "general philosophical view of the world" that (in Freud's version but not in Jung's) specifically denies the validity of Christianity. He concludes with the mild observation that the psychoanalyst has no special expert knowledge about philosophy. However, his willingness to accept the New Psychology as science and medicine but not as philosophy is somewhat questionable, given the origin of psychology as a branch of philosophy.

As a professional scholar Lewis worked to define the applicability of the New Psychology to literature. In "Psycho-Analysis and Literary Criticism" (1942), he attacks Freud's assertion that wish fulfillment is a source of literature—either the author's motivation to write or the reader's pleasure in reading. He grants Freud's assertions about infantile sexual experiences, that everyone uses certain standard symbols (e.g., "house" equals the human body) "in dream, imagination, or literature," but insists that these principles of psychological theory have nothing to do with the actual enjoyment of literature (*SLE*, 291–92). In this he is fighting against the tendency to use Freudian theories to reduce the dignity of both literature and the human intellect that enjoys literature.

In private, especially in letters of spiritual direction to his intellectual equals, Lewis's treatment of the New Psychology is nuanced rather than naïve or disparaging. For example, in a 1940 letter to a former student he admits that his "partly pathological hostility" to anything fashionable has "betrayed" him into negative, somewhat indefensible statements about psychoanalysis. (He is perhaps referring to *The Pilgrim's Regress*.) He adds that the psychiatric field "merely defines" what we have always known, that moral choices "operate inside a complex non-moral situation" (*Let*, 343–44).

He warns another directee against non-Christian psychiatrists, lest the therapist "start with the assumption that your religion is an illusion and try to 'cure' it." He uses the same idea in *That Hideous Strength:* Grace Ironwood, a medical doctor, says to Jane Studdock, "[the therapist] will proceed on the assumption that the dreams merely reflect your own sub-conscious" and warns that the results of such treatment would be ineffective (*Let*, 383; *THS*, 66). Perhaps reflecting what Lewis found for himself, the instruction Jane receives about her problems comes not from a secular psychiatrist, but from the director, the literature she reads at St. Anne's, and her vision of the Renaissance-style Venus. Despite Lewis's doubts about certain aspects of the New Psychology, the characterizations in *Till We Have Faces* are based on it. However, he maintains his own view that the supernatural exists, making it quite clear that Orual and the Fox are wrong in dismissing Psyche's palace in the mountains as a delusion or Freudian wish fulfillment.

Although Lewis rejected much of what Freud taught, it was not because he was defending himself against self-knowledge. In *Letters to Malcolm*, written during March and April 1963, before his death in November, he expressed much gratitude to the Freudians for exposing our "cowardly evasions of really useful self-knowledge." A careful reading of the whole passage shows that his objections to the New Psychology are largely based on its weaknesses and abuses, for he warns that psychoanalysis may lead to an obsessive self-centeredness, "a merely morbid and fidgety curiosity about one's self" (*LM*, 34).

An important, but seldom-discussed, reason for Lewis's partial rejection of Freud was his conviction, formed not too long after his conversion, that Christian spiritual disciplines provided a safer, more effective route to healing the human personality. For example, in a pre–1939 essay on Shelley he remarked, "If a man will not become a Christian, it is very undesirable that he should become aware of the reptilian inhabitants of his own mind" (*SLE*, 198).

In late 1940 he discovered a powerful tool of healing and self-knowledge when he made his first sacramental confession to the Rev. Walter Adams, an Anglican monk. Afterward he wrote jubilantly to his pen friend, Sister Penelope, "Well—we have come through the wall of fire and find ourselves (somewhat to our surprise) still alive and even well," adding that he planned to continue the practice. He continued to see Fr. Adams until the old man died in 1952.[4] Soon afterward, he offered to find a confessor for one of his advisees but warned, "[R]emember it's not the psychoanalyst over again" (*Let*, 357). As Kenneth Leech explains, both the psychologist and the Christian spiritual director seek to promote self-knowledge and greater maturity in the client, but the spiritual director's goal is to help the client use this maturity to discern the

4. Green and Hooper, *C. S. Lewis*, 198. Fr. Adams was a member of the Society of St. John the Evangelist, popularly known as the Cowley Fathers. See also Hooper, *Companion*, 32; and Ford, "C. S. Lewis, Ecumenical Spiritual Director," 55.

will of God.[5] Judging from the understanding reflected in his later works, this discipline apparently helped Lewis to attain a healthy attitude toward his own inner self.

For example, he points out that the medical model of mental functioning is misleading: while medical normality involves the near-perfect functioning of bodily organs, mentally normal people are tempted to commit, and do commit, abuses of themselves and others in the way they love. In *The Four Loves,* he says that the "greed, egoism, self-deception and self-pity" that spoil *storge,* or affection, are "not disease, but sin" and concludes, "Spiritual direction will here help us more than medical treatment" (*FL,* 80–81). And in *Reflections on the Psalms* (1958), he is both genial and self-aware when he imagines that one of our pains in purgatory will be to "see our own faces and hear our own voices as they really were" (*Refl,* 8).

There is no spiritual director for Orual in Glome; but in her visions, her father forces her to see her own face, and the judge forces her to hear her own voice.

Lewis Reads Jung

In his July 1922 diary entry Lewis mentions obtaining Jung's *Analytical Psychology* for Arthur Greeves, who was visiting him at the time. This entry suggests that he himself had read it quite soon after its translation into English. Much later, when Lewis was going to Fr. Adams for spiritual direction, he may have been exposed to a synthesis of Christian ascetic theology and Jung's theories through Christopher Bryant, one of the monks who was a special student of Jung. Although Bryant did not publish his first book on the subject until 1972, it is natural to assume that Fr. Adams and the other monks living at Cowley would have benefited from Bryant's studies and used the information in their own ministries. At any rate, Lewis's study of Jung was lifelong. Jung's *Answer to Job* (English translation published in 1954) was among the books in his personal library; Lewis may or may not have read it before he began writing *Till We Have Faces* in early 1955 (see "Chronology," 154).

Lewis found Jung's thought more congenial than Freud's. First, Jung treated religion more sympathetically than did Freud. Whereas

5. Leech, *Soul Friend,* 105–6.

Freud spoke of religion as an illusion, Jung called it a psychic fact, one found in all cultures. As Bryant observes, "Freud and Jung came to diametrically opposite conclusions from the same psychological data. For Freud God is a father-substitute, for Jung a child's father is a god-substitute."[6]

In addition, Jung's work contained some of the same ideas and qualities that, as an adolescent, Lewis had loved in George MacDonald's *Phantastes* and Spenser's *Faerie Queene*. He first read *Phantastes* when he was sixteen and started *The Faerie Queene* at about the same time. George Sayer remarks, "A list of the themes of *Phantastes* would read like chapter headings to a book by Carl Jung," and A. N. Wilson calls MacDonald's book "the missing link between Spenser's *Faerie Queene* and the writings of Freud and Jung."[7]

Most important, Jung's approach to the human mind was more literary than Freud's. His explanations of the role of symbols in psychology showed a broader, more literary understanding of metaphorical language than Freud's. Jung criticized Freud for assigning fixed meanings to symbols in dreams based on their psychological causes in the past. Jung himself believed that a dream was "a spontaneous self-portrayal . . . of the actual situation in the unconscious," so that the meaning of the symbols varied along with the dreamer's psychological situation. He was conscious that he was dealing with metaphor, whether he found it in dreams, religion, alchemy, myth, or folklore.[8] For this reason, Jung's theory of archetypes was established as a fruitful approach to literary criticism by E. M. W. Tillyard and Maud Bodkin, and in a 1942 essay Lewis said wryly, "Indeed I have slipped into it at times myself" (*SLE*, 296). By 1955, when *Till We Have Faces* was being written, Lewis was suggesting the theory of archetypes as a critical tool for dealing with *The Faerie Queene* in his Cambridge lectures. The lectures, on which his unfinished book, *Spenser's Images of Life*, is based, did not begin until January 1955, but he had also lectured on Spenser at Oxford. While counseling modesty about the results of the archetypal approach to literature, he pointed out that Spenser's epic includes the Hero as

6. Bryant, *Depth Psychology*, 2.
7. Sayer, *Jack:*, 57; A. N. Wilson, *C. S. Lewis: A Biography*, 46.
8. Samuels, Shorter, and Plaut, *Critical Dictionary*, 48, citing Jung, *CW* 8, para. 505; ibid., 12 (alchemy), 93 (metaphor).

Deliverer, the Wise Old Man, the Anima, the Terrible Mother, and the Persona (*SIOL*, 117).

Jung in Glome

As Lewis himself admitted in his letter to a young reader, there are "some Jungianisms," in *Till We Have Faces*, "but the main conscious prose work is Christian" (*LetChil*, 107). He understates the case. The integration of two ways of talking about the unconscious, the Old Priest's way and Jung's way, plus the story's placement in everyday, historical life, creates a novel of striking depth and subtlety. Certainly there are too many "Jungianisms" to list with any completeness, although Lewis scholars have studied the topic extensively.[9] This discussion will touch only four: dreams, the personal unconscious, the collective unconscious, and individuation.

Dreams

Whereas Freud was primarily interested in dreams as caused by past conflicts and repressions, Jung was interested in them for their purpose and usefulness—what they could reveal about the present state of the soul, and indeed its future state. He believed that in dreams the unconscious brings home important facts that might otherwise be overlooked.[10] Orual has her first informational dream when she falls ill after Psyche has been taken away. Orual dreams

9. Jungian studies of *TWHF* include the following: M. J. Anastasi, "King of Glome: *Pater Rex.*" *Lamp-post of the Southern California C. S. Lewis Society* 19.1 (1995): 13–19; B. E. Atkinson, "From Facelessness to Divine Identity," *Lamp-post of the Southern California C. S. Lewis Society* 15.1 (1991): 21–30; H. M. Luke, *The Way of Woman, Ancient and Modern* (Three Rivers, Mich.: Apple Farm Paper, 1947), 2:19–88; S. Okiyama, review of *Till We Have Faces, Lamp-post of the Southern California C. S. Lewis Society* 15.1 (1991): 15–20; Laura A. Ruskin, "Three Good Mothers: Galadriel, Psyche, and Sybil Coningsby," *Mythcon I Proceedings,* ed. Glen GoodKnight (Los Angeles: Mythopoeic Society, 1971), 12–14. These items are cited from "An Annotated Bibliography to C. S. Lewis: *Till We Have Faces: A Myth Retold,*" comp. by H. Lesfloris and I. C. Storey (Trent University) http://www.trentu.ca/ahc/materials/lewis-bib.html.

10. Samuels, Shorter, and Plaut, *Critical Dictionary*, 48; Bryant, *Jung and the Christian Way*, 21, 25.

that she is beautiful and has a lover of her own, but just before the union can be consummated Psyche appears, doll-sized and dressed like a temple girl, and takes Orual's lover away. This dream could have shown Orual her Ungit-like possessiveness and jealousy, her treatment of Psyche as a doll rather than a person, but at that point it did not. Many years later, however, after Orual begins to write her book, she understands her dreams better, and through them she gradually comes to self-understanding and healing.

The Personal Unconscious

Jung, like Freud, uses the term "unconscious" to describe aspects of the mind which are hidden from the ego.[11] If the ego is strong, it can receive a kind of knowledge from the unconscious. As Psyche says, "[The Fox] calls the whole world a city. But what's a city built on? There's earth beneath. And outside the wall? Doesn't all the food come from there as well as all the dangers?" (*TWHF*, 71). This is a metaphorical expression of Jung's conviction that the unconscious is a creative force, one that serves both the individual and society. As Austin Farrer says, "The human imagination has always been controlled by certain basic images in which man's own nature, his relation to his fellows, and his dependence on the divine power find expression."[12]

The Old Priest's explanation of how to get along with Ungit describes metaphorically the need for the individual to come to terms with the unconscious: "[Ungit's] anger never comes upon us without cause, and it never ceases without expiation" (*TWHF*, 45). Orual's struggles to stop up the well come from her desire to block messages from the unconscious, for wells are openings into the underground. When she succeeds in imprisoning the well, she is able to defeat the kingdom of Essur in battle, but during her tour of Essur she comes to the hot spring (also an opening into the underground), and this leads to her meeting with the priest of Psyche.

11. Discussion of the unconscious is based on Samuels, Shorter, and Plaut, *Critical Dictionary*, 155–57.

12. Quoted by Bryant, *Jung and the Christian Way*, 30. Incidentally, both Farrer and his wife, Katherine, were friends of Lewis.

What she had done was not expiation, and stopping the well did not stop the anger of Ungit in her unconscious.

The Collective Unconscious

The turning point of the story comes when Orual finds out from the priest what happened to Psyche in exile, for it is the breaching of her defenses against her personal unconscious. Orual's surmise that the gods dropped the information "into someone's mind, in a dream, or an oracle, or however they do such things" (*TWHF*, 243) shows that this is a message to her from the collective unconscious. This Jungian notion had been part of Lewis's mental furniture at least since 1943, when he published *Broadcast Talks;* concerning the pagan precursors of Christ he said, "[God] sent the human race what I call good dreams" (*MC*, 54).[13]

Bryant says God speaks to the conscious mind "through the unknown heights and depths of our [whole] personalities." The unconscious, a "shared possession of mankind" and storehouse of archetypal images, is a large part of the personality.[14]

Without this context of Jungian psychology, the transmission of the Psyche myth might seem unlikely, a break in the literary realism that has dominated the novel to this point. But in a Jungian context, the priest's story simply adds psychological realism to what has gone before, showing that realism is more complicated than it originally seemed.

Individuation

Finally, individuation, the Jungian theory of personality development, is the basis of Orual's whole story.[15] According to Jung,

---

13. *Broadcast Talks* were first published as three short books in 1943–1945, then combined into *MC.*

14. Bryant, *Depth Psychology,* 33; *Jung and the Christian Way,* 33.

15. This convenient thumbnail sketch of individuation was presented by Barbara (Sophie) Eurich-Rascoe, lecture at Southern California C. S. Lewis Society Workshop, July 31, 2002. Needless to say, any errors are due to my mishearing.

the first half of life is about developing an ego. It is motivated by the desire to be liked, to meet expectations. But this effort, says Jung, invariably brings about consciousness of the "shadow," "the thing a person has no wish to be."[16] In *Till We Have Faces* the internal shadow is externalized as the Shadowbrute, the monster (or god) of the mountain to whom Psyche is sacrificed.

Awareness of the shadow is the first step of individuation, the process by which one comes into a more objective relationship with the ego and "regain[s] [one's] religious outlook."[17] In order to integrate the Jungian model with the original myth, Lewis moves the sighting of the shadow to the beginning of the story, but Orual's individuation does not actually begin until she goes on the journey at the end of her life. After she becomes queen, she works very hard at meeting expectations, and she succeeds beyond all expectations. But her work on the rational level produces more shadow—the weariness and ennui of her daily life. It causes her to decide to go traveling, which leads to hearing the priest's story. The awareness that comes from writing her response to the story is the real beginning of her individuation.

The story is complicated by the integration of the Jungian process with Christian spiritual wisdom. An important turning point comes when Orual realizes that she is Ungit and attempts to repent, to stop being Ungit. But trying to become good and wise by one's own effort is an operation of the ego. It shuts off access to the unconscious, God's means of communicating with the self. To succeed Orual must give up, stop striving after virtue. The psychological law known to both Jung and Christian spiritual directors then comes into play: as she no longer depends on her ego, her queenly judgments become even better than they were before. As Bryant says, "Only when ego feels itself weak and defenceless is it prepared to throw down its defences against the influences of the unconscious and open itself to the reinforcing energy from within.... This is perhaps the commonest of all experiences of God."[18]

Orual's struggle toward individuation is motivated by "God's wrath," which Bryant describes as God's "unrelenting opposition

16. *CW*, 16, para. 470. Cited in Samuels, Shorter, and Plaut, *Critical Dictionary*, 138.
17. *CW*, 9, para. 509. Cited in Bryant, *Jung and the Christian Way*, 14.
18. Bryant, *Depth Psychology*, 48.

to everything that is damaging a man." It is not punishment, but rather a corrective built into an individual's nature.[19] Orual first experiences "God's wrath" on the mountain, as "passionless and measureless rejection," as a voice saying "You also shall be Psyche" (*TWHF*, 173, 174). She hears that wrath expressed again in the judgment hall, in the form of her whiny inner voice, and finally meets it for the last time in the portico after Psyche has given her the casket. In the last scene the god is terrible because he is all in all: "The earth and stars and sun, all that was or will be, existed for his sake. And he was coming. The most dreadful, the most beautiful, the only dread and beauty there is, was coming" (*TWHF*, 397). As Orual lowers her eyes before him, her individuation is complete, and she sees her true self.

19. Ibid., 38–39.

Pagan Religion

The knowledge about pagan religion that is relevant to *Till We Have Faces* comes from research in archeology and anthropology pursued in the late nineteenth and early twentieth centuries, largely by scholars trained in the Greek and Roman classics. Although many of their hypotheses and conclusions are now discredited by scholars, Lewis read their works as an undergraduate, and they shaped his historical imagination. Therefore in the following discussion, what they say will be treated as authoritative. James G. Frazer and Jane Ellen Harrison will be taken as the primary authorities; in addition, we will use Gilbert Murray's very accessible synthesis of Harrison's work and Robert Graves's reference guide to the Greek myths.

Frazer's *Golden Bough,* first published in 1890, broke new ground by finding relationships between customs recorded in the classics, customs of primitive lands as reported by world travelers, and customs followed by European rural people. According to Church, his work "was one of the first triumphs of the new science of anthropology," causing "the cultured readers of his world" to see that "the doings of backward and primitive peoples were comprehensible, even rational by their own lights." He provided a rational structure for the course of mankind's mental development: "from a primitive faith in *magic*, through *religion*, to the growth of modern *science*."[1]

A less famous, more narrowly focused, but equally groundbreaking study along the lines set out by Frazer was Harrison's *Prolego-*

The chapters for which this is particularly relevant are 1:1, 2, 5, 7, 9, 20.
1. Curtis Church, foreword to Frazer's *Golden Bough* (1890), vii; quoted in Mary Beard and John Henderson, *Classics: A Very Short Introduction*, 63.

mena to the Study of Greek Religion, first published in 1903 (thirteen years after *The Golden Bough*). Harrison approached the subject in a new way: instead of looking to literature for primitive myths and customs, she focused on the actual rituals of the people, deriving her information from illustrations on vases and other artifacts. She found that the attitudes toward the gods expressed in art were "more primitive and more permanent" than those in mythology seen through literature. She concluded that the Homeric gods arise from "a story-telling instinct," rather than actual human experiences of worship, and that Homer's treatment of the gods was not primitive, but subtle and sophisticated.[2]

In portraying the benighted superstitions of Glome, Lewis no doubt drew on his knowledge of Frazer and Harrison as well as his own reading of the classics. He also heard the lectures of Gilbert Murray, one of Harrison's pupils. Murray provided a useful overview of Greek religious development in his *Four Stages of Greek Religion* (1912). The stages correspond roughly with stages in the external history of the Greek peoples as understood in his day:

1. The Age of Ignorance—about 1100 to 776 B.C. When Murray was writing, very little was known about the Minoan and Mycenaean civilizations that preceded the Homeric period; therefore, it seemed appropriate to call the pre-Homeric centuries "The Age of Ignorance." The religious practices of Glome are most like those of this period (as imagined by classicists), for Glome is a very backward place, more or less untouched by the conquests of Alexander the Great.

2. The Olympian or classical age—from 776 B.C. (the Panathenaic Festival established for public recitation of Homer) to about 404 B.C., the defeat of Athens by Sparta. The Olympians replaced the mysterious god-forces that were worshipped in the Age of Ignorance. Portrayed and honored in exquisite literature, they were "cleaner and more warlike and lordlier, though in actual religious quality much less vital" than the tribal or local gods they replaced.[3] This period is represented in Glome by wonderful poetry the Fox taught to the girls, even though he always hastened to assure them that it was only "lies of poets."

2. Harrison, *Prolegomena*, 274.
3. Gilbert Murray, *Four Stages of Greek Religion*, 79.

3. The Failure of Nerve—from Plato (d. 347 B.C.) to St. Paul (d. ca. A.D. 64).[4] This is basically the Hellenistic period, just a little expanded past the traditional dates (323 to 330 B.C.) on either end. Marked by scepticism about the traditional gods, this period is represented in Glome by Arnom's allegorizing and philosophizing about the gods as the Fox taught him to do. He also set up the beautiful female statue of Ungit in the temple, but Orual found that she was less powerful than the old, ugly stone, just as the Olympians were less powerful than the frightening gods of the Age of Ignorance.

4. The Last Protest—This period recognizes the effort by Julian the Apostate (b. A.D. 331, d. 363) to reverse Constantine's favoritism toward Christianity and bring back paganism. This period is, of course, not represented in Glome, since *Till We Have Faces* takes place before the birth of Christ.

In 1925 Murray published a new edition called *Five Stages of Greek Religion*. The fifth stage comprised the great schools of philosophy—Stoicism, Epicureanism, and Aristotelianism (the Peripatetics) of the 300s B.C. (Glome's contact with philosophy is discussed below in "Stoicism, the Faith of the Fox" and "Plato—Banished from Glome.")

The Greek stages of Olympian gods, disbelief, and turning to philosophy play only minor roles in the religious situation at Glome. Only the Fox, Orual and Psyche, his pupils, and Arnom ever consider these three attitudes. The worship practiced by the general population of Glome comes exclusively from the Age of Ignorance.

In Glome, as in other primitive cultures, the primary requisite for survival was fertility—"the Food Supply and the Tribe Supply." The purpose of worship was to promote fertility and to purify the community and to protect it from evil influences that would hinder fertility. According to Harrison, the rites were marked by fear, anxiety, and guilt. The most primitive sacrifices were holocausts rather than a meal shared with the gods. In some rituals a *pharmakos*, or scapegoat, was killed or driven out of the community. Sometimes the scapegoat was tortured horribly, because the greater the suffering, the stronger the power of the sacrifice.[5]

---

4. Ibid., 18; exact date assigned to death of St. Paul is from Raymond E. Brown, *An Introduction to the New Testament*, 428.

5. Murray, *Four Stages*, 81; Harrison, *Prolegomena*, viii–ix, 95–105.

These rites, says Harrison, were "more primitive and more permanent," and vestiges of them persisted even in the classical age, along with the "cheerful sacrificial feast[s]" offered to the skyborn Olympian gods. In those ceremonies the worshipper said, in effect, *"Do ut des"*—"I give this sacrifice to you so that you will give me what I want." Then the god's portion of skin, bones, and fat was burned and the rest of the meat cooked and eaten by the worshippers in a banquet shared with the god. Murray describes the Olympian gods as "conquering chieftains, royal buccaneers [who] live on the revenues and blast with thunderbolts the people who do not pay."[6]

The sacrifices of Glome were (at least according to Orual) motivated by fear, anxiety, and guilt. And since these emotions are potentially endless, the House of Ungit is a bottomless pit; into it drains "the seed of men that might have gone to make hardy boys and fruitful girls" and "the silver that men had earned hard and needed" (*TWHF*, 269–70). As Orual remarks bitterly, "Food for the gods must always be found somehow, even when the land starves" (*TWHF*, 79). Apparently those sacrifices that were not holocausts provided food for the temple personnel, as is shown in Bardia's words concerning the bull sacrificed at the beginning of the battle between Orual and Argan: "Ungit must let us have a share of the bull; I'll speak to Arnom of it" (*TWHF*, 221). The only cheerful ceremony she records is the celebration of the Year's Birth, and even then the wasting of resources occurs the night before. As a virgin Orual is barred from attending this sacrifice, good evidence that it is meant to assure fertility.

Besides the gloom and anxiety of the rituals, the religion of Glome is shown to be primitive by the vagueness of the deity. Harrison says, "[T]he beings to whom these rites were addressed" were not "completely articulate gods," but more like "sprites, ghosts, and bogeys." The consort of the goddess was "somewhere half-way between [Son] and Lover, with a touch of the patron saint."[7] Thus Glome's Ungit is an undifferentiated power of fertility, and her form is a faceless, featureless stone. There is no myth, no coherent story about her and her consort. The Shadowbrute is either Ungit

6. Harrison, *Prolegomena*, viii; Murray, *Four Stages*, 65.
7. Harrison, *Prolegomena*, x, 273.

herself, Ungit's consort, her husband, or perhaps her son, but neither goddess nor god is clearly visualized as a personality. Ungit is
a chthonic, or earth, goddess; she has pushed her way upward
from under the earth, just as Persephone, the maiden earth goddess, and earlier, Pandora, are pictured undergoing the "*Anodos*"
or way upward. Later on "the great figure of the Earth-Mother
re-emerges . . . as Aphrodite."[8]

Since Ungit underwent *Anodos*, she must be a local version of
Aphrodite. The Fox accounts for her strangeness by observing that
she is similar to the Babylonian rather than the Greek Aphrodite. In
Greece, Aphrodite was worshipped as the goddess of sexuality and
reproduction, and in many cities brides sacrificed to her so that
their first sexual experience would be salubrious. Temple prostitution was not a Greek practice, although the Greek Aphrodite was
the protectress of prostitutes. Babylonia, however, was associated
with temple prostitution, on the basis of information coming from
Herodotus, and it is historically plausible that the Fox would have
known his work.[9] Thus Lewis's smooth melding of mythology, history, and anthropology in the creation of Ungit provides reasons
for the ugliness of her cult: greediness, facelessness, and temple
prostitution. Psyche's journey to the Deadlands to get a potion to
make Ungit beautiful brings together the datum from Apuleius and
an occasion for reflection on God and the unconscious (see "The
New Psychology," 192 above.)

Ungit's egg-shaped temple and the priest's bird mask may remind
those who have read the Chronicles of Narnia of Tash, the Calormene
god with the bird head, but Lewis probably chose those symbols
to demonstrate the non-Olympian, primitive character of Glomish religion. Bird and egg are part of both the Pelasgian and the
Homeric-Orphic creation myths. The Pelasgian tells how "Eurynome,
the Goddess of All Things," took form as a dove and "laid the Universal Egg." Out of it hatched everything that exists. The Homeric

---

8. Ibid., 276, 284, 285.
9. Regarding temple prostitution, see *OCD* 3, s.v. "Aphrodite"; and *Herodotus
with an English Translation,* Loeb ed. 1.199. In addition to the Babylonian Ishtar,
Frazer's *Golden Bough* (3rd ed), 5.34–37, associates the practice with the Phoeni-
cian Astarte, Artemis at Perga in Pamphylia, and Derceto at Ascalon. Beloe, tr. of
The Ancient History of Herodotus, adds Heliopolis, Aphace (between Heliopolis
and Biblius) and Sicca Veneria, in Africa, 61n10.

and Orphic myth says that "black-winged Night . . . was courted by the Wind and laid a silver egg in the womb of Darkness." Out of the egg, Eros (also called Phanes) was hatched, and he "set the universe in motion."[10]

The relationship between the bird-headed priest who fights his way out of the egg-shaped temple in the celebration of the Year's Birth and the (traditionally) winged Cupid (Eros) who was Psyche's husband is unclear. Harrison says, "Given an egg as the beginning of a cosmogony, and it was almost inevitable that there should emerge from the egg a bird-god, a winged thing." But are the cosmic egg and the god who emerged from it really the oldest of all beings? There was an older and a younger Eros. In *The Symposium*, Phaedrus calls Love one of the oldest gods, born out of the great egg of Chaos, but Agathon calls him the youngest god, and in his *Description of Greece*, Pausanias says it is the younger Eros who is the son of Aphrodite.[11] Perhaps it all depends on the weight we give to the epigraph of the novel, from Shakespeare's Sonnet 151: "Love is too young to know what conscience is."

In any case, Lewis has combined various elements of Greek worship to create a satisfactorily primitive religion for benighted Glome.

10. Graves, *Greek Myths*, 27, 30. Incidentally, the riddle "Which came first, the chicken or the egg?" is apparently a way of asking which myth should be accepted.
11. Harrison, *Prolegomena*, 630–31; Plato's *Symposium*, 178 b, c, and 195 a, b.

Plato — Banished from Glome

One thing that we as readers are not likely to notice is that Plato is never mentioned in book 1 of *Till We Have Faces*. Though the Glome library contains some of his work, it is dismissed in a phrase: "Also, some of the conversations of Socrates" (*TWHF*, 232). Thus Orual banishes Plato, arguably the most influential philosopher in the Western world, from her attention.

Thematically, Plato's absence is strange: the novel is about love relationships—Psyche's marriage to Cupid, Orual's obsession with Psyche, and her passion for Bardia. And Plato, after all, is the philosopher of love, particularly in *The Symposium* and the *Phaedrus*. Apuleius, Lewis's source author, was a Platonist, and Platonic ideas are important in almost all of Lewis's other works, both fiction and nonfiction. Robert Houston Smith even goes so far as to say that "Platonism, as the mature Lewis perceived it, was a philosophical embodiment of the same absolute truth that was to be found in Christianity."[1] Why, then, has Plato been banished from Glome?

There are two kinds of reasons. The first is historical realism. The Fox, the only philosopher in Glome, is a Stoic and therefore opposed to Platonism. The founder of his school of philosophy, Zeno, entitled his book *The Republic,* and the implication is that it serves as a refutation and correction of Plato's *Republic*.[2] Zeno's philosophy was based on the assumption that everything, even the Divine Nature, is material; Plato posited a world of pure forms and called the

The chapters for which this is particularly relevant are 1:1, 2, 7, 8, 16, 18.
1. Robert Houston Smith, *Patches of Godlight: The Pattern of Thought of C. S. Lewis,* 5.
2. Edwyn Bevan, *Stoics and Sceptics,* 11–14.

material universe we inhabit a "shadow" of the real. An equal incompatibility was a matter of mood: Zeno and his early followers were very much out of sympathy with Plato's poetic style of philosophy.

It is a realistic detail that the Fox makes no effort to instruct the girls in Platonism. To him, Plato's myths must have seemed very similar to the "lies of poets" that he worked so hard to scorn. He did not accept the hope expressed by Socrates in Plato's *Phaedo* that there is another world "of purity, and eternity, and immortality, and unchangeableness"; instead he believed that "[a]t death we are resolved into our elements" (*TWHF,* 17).[3] As readers we learn only indirectly that he has mentioned the possibility of another world to the girls. On the night before the sacrifice Psyche says, "he has sometimes *let out* that there were other Greek masters than those he follows himself," who teach "that death opens a door out of a little, dark room . . . into a great, real place where the true sun shines" (*TWHF,* 73; emphasis added).

This bit of indirection—Psyche's report of the Fox's inadvertent acknowledgment—allows Lewis to introduce Plato into Glome while perpetrating his banishment. The banishment is necessary to maintain the gloom of Glome, for no suggestion of transcendence, of something beyond "Shadowlands," must influence Orual's consciousness until Lewis is ready for her to receive it. This is the second kind of reason for the banishment—the shaping of the novel by the contrast between book 1 and book 2.

In book 1, Orual maintains that the gods are vile or unreal. Her indictment is convincing; Psyche's only rejoinder is, "[Perhaps] they are real gods but don't really do these [vile] things. Or [perhaps] they do these things and the things are not what they seem to be" (*TWHF,* 71).

When the evidence is stronger the other way, the Fox suppresses it. Knowing that she was unable to see Psyche's palace, except for a momentary glimpse, Orual tentatively suggests to the Fox, "there might be things that are real though we can't see them." Instead of responding moderately that Socrates in the *Phaedo* postulated two sorts of existences, the seen and unseen, the Fox "[runs] his hands through his hair with an old, familiar gesture of teacher's dismay." Orual's persistent "But do you, even you, know all?" is answered

3. Plato, *Phaedo,* Jowett's tr., 464, para. 79.

by his hint that perhaps she is out of her mind: "[I]f I can get that hellebore, yours had better be the first dose" (*TWHF*, 141–42).

After the disastrous final encounter with Psyche, Orual turns away from all such inquiries and seeks to "pile up knowledge" of "the physical parts of philosophy" (*TWHF*, 184, 183). By shutting out all but a few hints of something beyond Nature, Lewis aligns Orual with the empiricism and positivism of the eighteenth to twentieth centuries (as well as the Stoic enlightenment of the Fox) and thus preserves the reader's sympathy with Orual's point of view.[4]

In book 2, there is evidence that Orual had read the *Phaedo;* she even says, "Socrates understood such matters better than the Fox" (*TWHF*, 281). However, if *The Symposium* was among the "conversations of Socrates" in the Glome library, Orual either did not read it or did not ponder its wisdom. For example, *The Symposium* contains a speech connecting the god of love with the workings of the cosmos.[5] Orual sees through Arnom's facile allegorization of Ungit (*TWHF*, 270–71), but she does not entertain the possibility that love might be the principle of the universe and continues to hate the goddess of love. The comic myth of Aristophanes in *The Symposium* shows love as the desire for wholeness, certainly a part of Orual's personality, but a desire she suppresses. Finally, Diotima teaches that love is really a search for the good, so that the first attraction to a beautiful person is the beginning step in an ascent to virtue. This is, of course, what happened to Dante, as set forth in *The Divine Comedy*, and perhaps Lewis's use of the Greek letter *delta* to stand for Mrs. Moore is a learned reference to a similar experience.[6] But Orual's love is the domination and possession of others.

For Lewis, Plato was the philosopher of first importance. As Digory says in *The Last Battle*, "It's all in Plato, all in Plato" (*LB*, 170).

4. I believe Lewis is performing a literary maneuver analogous to the one Stanley Fish (*Surprised by Sin*, 1967) attributes to Milton in *Paradise Lost*—seducing the reader into falling when Orual falls, experiencing her wrongness from the inside.

5. In speech of Eryximachus (185e–188e); cited in Cobb, introduction to *The Symposium*, 12.

6. Plato, *Symposium*, 212a. The suggestion that "D" may have stood for "Diotima" is made by Fredrick and McBride, *Women among the Inklings*, 61. This fits with the cryptic reference to the "one huge and complex episode" (*SbJ*, 198). But see Wilson, *C. S. Lewis*, 83, for another suggestion.

Not quite all. As Augustine said, he learned from the Platonists that the Word was God, but not that the Word was made flesh and dwelt among us.[7]

But perhaps it is "all in Plato" after all. In *Reflections on the Psalms*, Lewis reminds us of a startling passage in Plato's *Republic*. It is the image of "a perfectly righteous man treated by all around him as a monster of wickedness." Plato then asks us to "picture him, still perfect, while he is bound, scourged, and finally impaled (the Persian equivalent of crucifixion)." Lewis's point is that Plato did not know that the perfect man he imagined "would ever become actual and historical"; yet he knew that it could happen, just as the "imperfect, yet very venerable, goodness of Socrates" led to the hemlock, "because goodness is what it is, and because the fallen world is what it is" (*Refl*, 104–5). And though the Fox has resisted teaching Orual and Psyche about Plato, he offers to risk being flogged and impaled for the love of them.

No detailed reading of Plato is needed to perceive what Lewis is doing. It is enough to know that Plato philosophized about love and believed in something beyond the world of the senses. By leaving Plato out of Glome, Lewis enables his readers to taste the flatness of a world without transcendence and perhaps encourages them to seek what he regards as basic reality.

7. Augustine of Hippo, *Confessions*, book 7, 130–31.

Stoicism — The Faith of the Fox

The Fox is a Stoic, an adherent to the school of philosophy founded by Zeno of Citium in about 300 B.C. Stoicism continued to be taught in Athens until at least A.D. 260, so that it spans all of the Hellenistic period.

It is impossible to define Stoicism precisely. First, Zeno's original philosophy is known mainly by inference, since only fragments of his writings remain. Furthermore, during its time of greatest acceptance, a wide variety of beliefs, sometimes contradictory ones, became part of Stoicism; and finally, some Stoic principles were taken up into Christianity. The following topics are those most relevant to *Till We Have Faces*.

The Basic Beliefs of Stoicism

1. The reality underlying what we perceive by our senses is itself a *physis*, a material stuff. It is the fifth element, the fiery ether, beyond earth, air, water, and fire. Thus, Stoicism denies Plato's belief that the world of Forms underlies our material world.

2. God is not a person, but rather the Divine Reason, the Logos, the overarching purpose that governs the universe. Apparently the Divine Reason is somehow identified with the fiery ether.

3. The reasonable soul of man is also a particle of this divine fire. In contrast with Plato, who implies that the Soul must leave the material world to find God, Zeno says that everything in its origin is God, in whom man lives and moves and has his being.

4. The human task is to follow the leadings of one's own particle of divine fire and bring one's will into harmony with the Divine Reason.

5. In seeking this harmony, the Stoic strives to live in accordance with Nature, which is governed by the Divine Reason.

6. Although Divine Reason governs everything, human beings have free will. By our will we can make some things happen, but other things happen without our choice, such as the evils done by others. If we remember that evil ultimately serves the divine plan, we can be happy in spite of our circumstances.

7. The mental discipline that makes all this possible is *apatheia*, detachment from everything except harmony with the Divine Reason. However, instead of the radical detachment exemplified by the homelessness of Diogenes, Zeno taught that one should follow human customs whenever possible.[1]

The Influence of Stoicism

Stoicism was so flexible that Cicero the noble Roman orator, Philo the Jew, Origen the Christian, Epictetus the Roman slave, and Marcus Aurelius the emperor could all find what they needed in it. Stoic philosophy was also an important element in Christianity almost from the beginning. The Apostle Paul was reared in Tarsus, an important center of Stoicism. In his sermon on Mars Hill he uses Stoic ideas to establish common ground with his audience of intellectual Greeks (Acts 17:16–34), and in his closely reasoned epistle to the Romans, he uses a Stoic-sounding reference to the law of Nature (Rom. 2:14–15). Stoic elements also appear in other New Testament writings, including 1 Peter, Hebrews, 1 John, and chapter 1 of the Gospel of John.

Thus incorporated into Christianity, Stoicism did not die when the Stoa in Athens was closed down. As Gilbert Murray (one of the lecturers Lewis heard as an undergraduate) says, "[Stoicism] lasts now as the nearest approach to an acceptable system of conduct for those who do not accept [miracles and] revelation, but still keep some faith in the Purpose of things."[2]

1. Vernon Arnold, *Roman Stoicism*, 409, 413–14.
2. Gilbert Murray, *Five Stages of Greek Religion*, 123.

Stoicism in Practice

The Fox's Stoicism is appropriate to the Hellenistic age. At the same time, he sounds very much like many of Lewis's contemporaries, intellectuals who denied revelation but retained some of Christianity's ethical principles. For Lewis to portray the enlightened Fox as a Stoic is ideal for dramatizing the eternal struggle of faith—that is, rationalism versus the human desire for God. It was the obvious choice—after Lewis chose it.

But the Fox's philosophy is not easy to practice. He must fight two ongoing battles: the struggle against the benighted superstition of Glome, and his personal struggle to bring his will into harmony with Divine Reason.

The Struggle for Enlightenment

Several episodes show the Fox struggling for enlightenment against superstition:

1. After telling Orual the scary story of Anchises and Aphrodite, he reassures her that it is not real, just one of the "lies of poets" (*TWHF*, 8).

2. On the night Psyche is born, while the mother screams and the priest sacrifices to Ungit, the Fox soothes Orual with the thought that birth is natural, and "We must learn not to fear anything that nature brings" (*TWHF*, 14).

3. He teaches Orual to look for natural explanations of supposedly supernatural phenomena. Concerning the report that the Shadowbrute has been seen on the mountain he says, "If the man had a torch, of necessity the lion would have a big black shadow behind it," so that he "took a shadow for a monster" (*TWHF*, 48).

4. He accounts for Psyche's survival and good health by surmising that a mountainy man has found her and is caring for her.

In summary, the Fox's belief that Nature is the Divine Nature, and that there is nothing outside it is a remedy for Orual's superstitious fear of the gods. But if it guards against fear, it also prevents a strong, living hope, even though he does teach that the Whole is, in some sense, good. In his deepest self, however, the Fox yearns for love, for beauty, for enchantment. He finds the Stoic ideal of *apatheia*—detachment—very difficult to attain.

The Struggle for Detachment

If, as Stoics believe, all people have a spark of the divine fire, then they are all members of one city, to be respected and served. It is the practical way of conforming one's will to that of the Divine Nature. On the other hand, the Stoic is to practice *apatheia*—indifference to life or death, material prosperity or adversity, the world's praise or blame. But the Fox is a man of intense passion, and he cannot practice detachment consistently:

1. When the king threatens to send him to the silver mines, he struggles to ignore the shaking of his body, even though he says, "At death we are resolved into our elements" and calls Orual a barbarian for mentioning "the land of the dead" (*TWHF*, 17).

2. He speaks *about* the Divine Nature, but when he is deeply moved he speaks *to* Zeus. For example, when he learns that Psyche is alive, in thanksgiving he "make[s] a libation to Zeus the Saviour" (*TWHF*, 140). When he is frustrated about being helpless to save Psyche, he exclaims, half praying and half cursing, "Oh Zeus, Zeus, Zeus, if I had ten hoplites and a sane man to command them!" (*TWHF*, 147). As Lewis remarked in *The Problem of Pain*, "even Stoicism finds itself willy-nilly bowing the knee to God" (*PoP*, 23).

3. He denies the reality of the pantheon of gods while being deeply moved by the beauty of the poetry about them (*TWHF*, 8–9).

4. He praises Psyche for having achieved virtue but is overcome with grief: "She died full of all things that are really good; courage, and patience, and-and-Aiai! Aiai-oh, Psyche, oh, my little one!" Orual observes, "[L]ove got the better of his philosophy" (*TWHF*, 85).

5. He speaks contemptuously of Bardia's passion for his wife. Yet he loves Orual and Psyche with every fiber of his being and is "ready to be a runaway—to risk the flogging and impaling" (*TWHF*, 149) for love of them. His real expression of love for Orual is more beautiful and terrible: as deeply homesick as he is for Greece, he decides to stay in Glome after Orual frees him. What this cost him is revealed by Orual's comment: "But that he did not limp, you

would have thought he had been in the hands of the torturers" (*TWHF*, 209).

The Fox is a forerunner of Jesus, also a deeply loving man who lacked Stoic imperturbability. Jesus expresses emotion frequently; that he was not a Stoic was a very important point to Lewis, and he mentioned it several times.[3] For example, in a 1947 letter he wrote, "God could, had he pleased, have been incarnate in a man of iron nerves, the Stoic sort who lets no sigh escape him. Of His great humility He chose to be incarnate in a man of delicate sensibilities who wept at the grave of Lazarus and sweated blood in Gethsemane" (*Let*, 383).[4]

In conclusion, the Fox is a good man. Although Redival mocks and teases him, he speaks kindly to her, calling her "daughter." He watches patiently at King Trom's bedside, even though his master had scorned him, overworked him, and "addled [his] brains with beating [him] about the ears" (*TWHF*, 28, 144). Zeno taught that Reason—the Divine Nature—was carrying out its purpose in the universe but did not say what that purpose might be. In the Fox's efforts to conform to the Divine Nature, Lewis perhaps is suggesting that the purpose of the universe is love. Thus the Fox is all the better for his inability to be a perfect Stoic. In his loving inconsistency he shows how good paganism can be, and how incomplete.

3. See Mark 1:41, Mark 10:21, Luke 22:15, Mark 14:32, John 19:26–27
4. See also *Let*, 431; *LM*, 42–44; *LAL*, 39.

Time in *Till We Have Faces*

In writing her book Orual aims to tell the exact truth. Her references to times and seasons create the impression of punctilious accuracy, but a closer examination of the text shows that it is an artistic illusion. For example, Orual's age at any particular time seems vague. This is not a flaw, but a psychologically accurate feature, an expression of Lewis's conviction that most people are not particularly aware of their chronological age and that it is a rather insignificant part of one's personality.

The following represents an effort to visualize the ages of people, especially Orual, at certain points in the story, as accurately as possible. The first number is an estimate of Orual's age; the number in brackets is the location in *Till We Have Faces*. The last (approximately) half-year of her life is analyzed in greater detail.

9—Orual's mother dies in the summer. Redival is 6 [5].

9 or 10—The Fox comes. It is late fall or winter, because there was "a bitter frost that day" [5].

10—The following summer, the king announces his marriage [9].

10 or 11—The marriage is not many weeks later [10]. The Old Priest refers to the girls in the bridal chorus as "young women" [11], and logically such a chorus should consist of girls who are at least pubescent (Redival would be only 7 or 8), but Orual calls herself and her sister "children" [11].

The king's second wife quickly becomes pregnant and also becomes "pale and thin" [13].

The chapters for which this is particularly relevant are 1:3; 2:1.

11 or 12—Psyche is born, probably in March or April, since the great hall is cold with the windows open [14]. Psychologically Orual is still a child [16], but she is old enough to become Psyche's foster mother [21].

Orual summarizes the years of Psyche's childhood, probably from birth to 12, since Psyche has to be of marriageable age at the time of the sacrifice. These years seemed to Orual "all springs and summers" [22].

23 or 24—Redival (age 20 or 21) flirts with Tarin. She is ordered to be with Psyche, Orual, and the Fox constantly, and "all the comfort we three had had was destroyed" [26].

24 or 25—Autumn and the first bad harvest. People's worship of Psyche begins [26–27].

25 or 26—Rebellion and the fever. The Fox contracts it in the autumn, the time of the second bad harvest [29]. Psyche, age 13 or 14, nurses him. After his recovery, Psyche goes out to heal the people by touching them. Although it is (apparently) the beginning of autumn, there is a "hot, pestilential glare" [32]. Psyche catches the fever herself, and when she recovers, her "childishness had gone" [33]. In a primitive society, she is old enough to be married.[1]

25 or 26—Psyche is sacrificed. Orual falls ill, recovers, and begins to learn sword fighting from Bardia. The drought breaks while she is ill, reviving the grass and the gardens [83].

When she plans her trip to the Grey Mountain, it is about twenty-five days "before the earliest snow" [87]. Six days later, she and Bardia go to the mountain [93]. This must be late autumn, for when they return in the afternoon of the next day, it is "nearly dark" inside the palace [140].

After she returns from her second trip to the Grey Mountain, Orual assumes her veil permanently, and she defies her father for the first time.

Perhaps just turned 26 or 27—The king, drunk from a midwinter revel (perhaps January 1), slips on ice and breaks his thigh [184–85].

At this point, things happen very rapidly. On the third night of the king's illness [186], Arnom, Bardia, and the Fox hail Orual as queen. She meets Trunia that same night [190], and the duel with Argan is set for three days later [199]. On the first day, Orual frees

1. *OCD* 1, s.v. "marriage ceremonies."

the Fox [207]. On the second day, Redival manages to be seen by Trunia and perhaps seems younger than she is (23 or 24) [211–12]. The king dies [213]. On the third day after Argan falls, Orual's "real reign" begins [216].

26 or 27—Orual has Batta hanged at the time of the fig harvest [230], before she has ruled for a year.

Orual summarizes the years of her reign, which apparently lasted about forty years [291]. She passes over the Fox's decline and death, which occurred sometime after "the first years" [227] of her reign. She says, "I was too busy to be with him much" [235]; he died "about the end of harvest" [236].

66 or 67—Orual begins her "progress" just after harvest [237]. It is probably in October, since the weather is still fine [239].

The Days of the Progress

Unstated period of travel to Phars—eight to ten days? Note that the return trip to Glome took seven or eight days [247].

Ten nights or more in Phars, visiting Trunia and Redival [238].

Unstated period of travel to Essur.

Three nights in Essur [239].

Short day trip to the hot spring [239]. While the young people are setting up camp, Orual finds the little temple, hears the "sacred story," and returns to camp [240–47].

Seven or eight days—quick return trip to Glome [247].

The progress seems to have lasted about a month; therefore, it probably ended in November.

The Writing of the Book

When Orual gets back to Glome, she is hindered from beginning her book by "petty work." Bardia is ill [248]. She works on it "all day, day after day, day after day, while Bardia was dying" [289].

Early in her writing, when she is remembering childhood play with Redival [5], she is forced to entertain Tarin, ambassador from the Great King [254]. His remembrance of Redival is "the first snowflake of the winter that I was entering" [256], but after her meeting with him, she does not record what he said about Redival's loneliness. She says that "the very writing itself" changed her, but she did not write about it at the time, and indeed she does not relate the incident until book 2, in which she "set[s] out to 'mend' her book" [253].

During the writing, she labors by day with her pen and in a dream, sorts seeds by night [256–57].

When the book is finished, she at last understands what Arnom has been telling her: Bardia is dying [257]. For the last nine days, he has been forgetting his responsibilities to her [258].

Adding to the Book

When Orual begins adding to the book, "not many days" have passed since she wrote the last words "no answer" [253]. How many?

Five days after Orual finishes the book, Bardia dies. His body is burned [258].

Three days later, Orual pays a condolence call on Bardia's wife, Ansit [259].

A few days after, Orual is in Ungit's temple at the rite of the Year's Birth [268]. This is in the spring [94], probably March 25, a traditional time for New Year's Day.

At this point there is an enormous discrepancy. While Orual was writing the book, she was burdened by "petty work," and to make the situation worse, Bardia was staying at home because of illness [248]. When she finishes the book, she finally grasps the fact that he is seriously ill, and Arnom says Bardia has forgotten about the government of Glome "these last nine days" [258]. It is conceivable that Orual could have written her book in nine days, especially if she had been as fluent as Lewis; however, if her time after the return from Essur consists of the nine days of Bardia's illness while she writes the book plus five more days until his death, plus three days until her condolence call on Ansit [259], plus "a few days" until the Year's Birth [268], the total is something less than a month. This implies that the Year's Birth was in January, but it was earlier described as occurring in the spring [94]. If the earlier detail about the Year's Birth is correct, Orual started writing the book in late autumn, when she returned from Essur, and continued it until about two weeks before time to celebrate Year's Birth in the spring.

As Donaldson says, in book 2 the reader is "forced to shift attention from . . . plot and sequence of events to . . . character development."[2] Linear time is breaking down; still, Orual continues to analyze what is happening to her and to lay it out with honesty and accuracy. Perhaps the simplest explanation is that Lewis forgot that the Year's Birth was supposed to be in the spring, for Orual's reference to her spiritual winter [256] would be more telling if the Glomish year began in January.

After the Year's Birth ceremony, which occurs at noon [272], Orual returns home and is confronted in a dream by her dead father [273].

When the dream is over, it is daylight [276], either the afternoon of the same day or a new day. She realizes that she does not have the physical strength to kill herself and waits until "the house slept" [277] to go drown herself in the River Shennit. She disguises herself by taking off her veil and going "bareface" "for the first time in many years" [278]. She returns home and sleeps soundly until the new day [280].

For "some days" Orual chews over the problem of what it means to cease being Ungit, to die. She tries to die to self by practicing philosophy [281–82].

Then comes the dream of the golden rams, which shows her that her efforts are ineffective. She gives up and goes about her daily work, using her book as her one pleasure and comfort [283–84]. There is no way to tell how many days elapse.

One day she goes out to the garden. What follows is "vision and no dream" [285]. Orual is taken to judgment and forced to read her book before all the dead [287–93]. She throws herself into the arms of the Fox and is taken to the place where she is instructed by pictures and then meets Psyche. Psyche is transfigured, "a goddess indeed" [306]. Here Orual's interior time coalesces with exterior time, for just as the priest in Essur said, "In spring, all summer, she is a goddess" [246].

After the god comes, the vision ends, and Orual finds herself back in the garden [296–308].

2. Mara Donaldson, "Orual's Story and the Art of Retelling: A Study of *Till We Have Faces*," 162. Her book *Holy Places Are Dark Places* sets forth her theoretical approach.

Four days later she dies [308]. How much of that time is devoted to writing the four chapters of book 2? It is possible that the first two chapters could have been written during the time she was left alone to "chew the strange bread [the gods] had given [her]" [281]. But not until the judgment, when she heard what book 1 really said, was she in a position to write book 2.

Arnom finds the book and stores it in the temple. His added note is both epitaph and directions for the disposition of the book [308–9].

Conclusion: Apparently the time between the words "no answer" and Orual's death is between three and four weeks of ordinary time. In book 1, the chronology is fairly accurate and fairly definite. In book 2, the chronological time of the everyday world begins to overlap with inner and spiritual time. Although Orual continues to reassure the reader with exact time references, they do not quite fit together. As an expression of repentance and progress on a spiritual journey, however, the divisions of book 2 are masterful. "Reality" for a human being is not solely a matter of empirical measurement, but also a relationship to transcendence.

Part III

Glossary

architrave Horizontal beam laid across a column or columns; can also be the molding around a door or window. 132

awful Awe-inspiring. 306

barbarian Originally, in Greek, a person who does not speak Greek. Lewis sometimes uses it in this original meaning, but often with the modern connotations of savagery and superstition. 7, 11, 17

battened Fed on, prospered at the expense of another, fastened down. *See* "Names in Glome," 188. 264, 296

bawd Originally, a pander or procuress; after 1700, used only of women to mean a madam or a prostitute. 191

blubbered A contemptuous expression for weeping. 203

bodkin A small dagger. Listed as obsolete in *OED*, though familiar to most readers through Shakespeare's *Hamlet*. 53

bottom The keel or hull of a ship. King Trom's use of the word seems out of character, since Glome was not on the sea. 13

brat Specifically, an illegitimate child, but sometimes used as a general term of contempt. 146, 209

broils Quarrels or turmoils. 195

burden Theme; related to "melody." 81

byre-door A byre is a cow barn. 6, 237

carrion Dead animal, food for scavengers; today, roadkill. 3, 42

casket Originally, a box. 301, 305

cistern A reservoir or large vessel in which water is stored. A well, in contrast, is a structure around a surface spring or a hole deep enough to tap into a spring. It is a path to the Underworld, or, in Jungian terms, the unconscious. While Queen Orual struggled to wall up the well outside the palace, she encouraged her people to build cisterns. 236

complaint In context, a legal accusation brought by a plaintiff. 3, 4, 287, 294

corn Not the American maize, but wheat, barley, etc. 35

curd-face As milk sours, it divides into curds, the solids of protein and fat, and whey, the remaining liquid. In addition to implying that Orual's face would sour the morning drink (i.e., milk) King Trom may be comparing it to a mass of curds. 18

doxy, doxies Paramour(s), mistress(es), or prostitute(s). Orual may be using it in the softer dialectal meaning of wench or sweetheart. 97, 163

draught Something that is drawn; the action of drinking or drinking in. 202

drench Common meaning, to soak; but Orual uses it in its technical meaning, "to force a large dose of medicine mixed with liquid down the throat of an animal." 232. Orual also uses it in its spiritual meaning. 276.[1]

drought Dryness, lack of moisture. 96, 97, 108

dugs The teats of a female mammal; contemptuous when applied to a woman. 258

dunghill Manure pile, a standard feature of a barnyard. 6

eft Today, newt. 72

faith Fidelity, keeping one's word. 170

ferly Something unexpected, terrible, or wonderful; obsolete except for Scottish or dialectal usage. 134, 142

flock In the episode of the golden rams, "flock" first means "flock of sheep" and then "tuft of fiber." The etymology of the first "flock" is obscure but can be traced to Old English and Old Norse. The second flock comes from Latin *floccus,* and is the word used in Apuleius's "Cupid and Psyche." It connotes indifference; *flocci non facere* means "to think nothing of."[2] 283

fortunate Favored by fortune; lucky, prosperous. 308

gay Lighthearted, exuberantly cheerful, merry, with a connotation of brilliance and showiness; Orual contrasts it with "happy," the emotion she felt when studying with Psyche and the Fox before trouble came. 222, 271

gelding, vb. castrating. *OED:* obsolescent in general literary use, but still used as a technical term in animal husbandry. 29

girdle Belt or sash. 298

gown The Fox's garment is probably an ankle-length tunic; to call it a "gown" reminds one that he is a teacher.[3] 215

1. Leech, *True Prayer,* 48.
2. D. P. Simpson, *Cassell's New Latin Dictionary.*
3. Adkins and Adkins, *Handbook,* 416.

grain *See* in grain.

grandam Grandmother, from grand + dame (woman, lady). 198

graveled Perplexed; no explicit reference to a more literal meaning of a ship being run aground. 155

hauberk A shirt of chain mail. 213, 214

hazard my Queen Bardia is speaking of risking Orual's life in terms of a chess game, an anachronism. Chess may have been invented in India. It was found in Persia in about A.D. 500. When the Arabs conquered Persia in A.D. 600, they brought the game to Spain, and from there it spread throughout Europe. However, a similar game, draughts (checkers) was played in ancient Greece, and it is possible that the Glomites played something like chess or checkers. The rule change that made the queen the most powerful piece became popular after 1475, and Lewis is apparently thinking of this modern version of the game. He may have been influenced to use the expression by the imaginative resemblance of Orual to Elizabeth I.[4] 197

heat Sexual heat, estrus. 137

hellebore A name given to a number of plants native to Europe and Asia and still others found in America. The roots contain a powerful poison that the ancients used medicinally as an emetic or purgative, and also as a cure for madness. 17, 141

hobgoblin "Hob," a rustic or clown plus "goblin," a mischievous and ugly demon; also a bogy; a frightening apparition. 88

holy For Orual, Ungit's temple and any place where a god may be present is holy. A holy place is dark, dreadful, smothering, and probably filthy. 8, 11, 43

hoplite A heavily armed foot soldier of ancient Greece. 147, 219

hummock A protuberance or knoblike swelling of earth, rock, ice, or the like, usually cone- or dome-shaped. 216

impaled Fixed upon a stake thrust up through the body; a slow, cruel death comparable to crucifixion.[5] 146, 149

in grain Dyed into the fabric, as in "tattler in grain." 25

---

4. *OCD* 3, s.v. "Games"; *New Encyclopedia Britannica* s.v. "Chess"; regarding Elizabeth I, see Myers, *Context*, 201.
5. See *Refl*, 104–5.

jostling [and wrangling] To "jostle" originally meant to collide in a joust or tournament. Orual uses it figuratively here. 136

knobbles Small knobs (in the sense of rounded hills or mountains). 97

light Unimportant, not difficult, 260; *compare* "lightly." 294.

lightened Both meanings, "not dark" and "not heavy," apply. 154

lilted his voice "Lilt" is chiefly Scottish or literary, and the transitive usage seen here is obsolete. The Fox raised his voice and used a rhythmic cadence. 8, 9

lissom Supple, limber. 96

make account Hold in estimation, value, esteem. 194

mark Notice. 125

mated *See* hazard my Queen. 236

men Used like German *man* to mean "someone" or "people." 306

mince Literally, to cut in small pieces; "to mince the matter" means to make it small, insignificant. 13

morning drink This is apparently milk. If the Glomians are Scythians (*see* "Glome," 163), it would probably be mare's rather than cow's milk.

mountainy man An Anglo-Irish usage; in this context, an outlaw. Men who hold a marginal position in society have always fled to the mountains.[6] 179

mountebank Originally, an itinerant quack; figuratively, a pretender, one who resorts to degrading means to obtain notoriety. 84

new-hatched Helen was the daughter of Leda, who was impregnated by Zeus, who had taken the form of a swan. It was said that Helen hatched from an egg. 21

none of you A solecism; should be either "none of us" or "neither of you." 199

obol The smallest unit of Greek money. *See* talent. 232

paps Teats or nipples. Archaic term, more common in northern Britain. 42

parrot, n. Reference to the bird may be an anachronism, for most parrots are found in South America, Australia, and other Pacific Rim countries. However, the gray parrot comes from Africa and might have been known to a Greek like the Fox. In verb form, the word has been used since at least 1596 to

6. Buxton, *Imaginary Greece*, 86–88.

mean "repeat mechanically." In the early twentieth century, Ogden and Richards derided as "psittacism" or "the parrot disease" any use of language to designate nonfactual, metaphysical concepts. In *The Pilgrim's Regress*, Lewis, in turn, ridiculed their modernist, positivist attitude toward metaphysical language in the character "Master Parrot." Thus, the Fox is accusing himself of committing a specifically modernist error.[7] 295

passions Motivations common to animals and human beings, which human beings ought to control by reason. 178

pawned Not a chess word, but "wagered" or "gave as security for the performance of an action"; related to pawnbroker, pawnshop. 195

plump A compact body of persons, animals, or things; "a plump of spears" is an obsolete expression revived by Sir Walter Scott. 237

policy, policies Expediency, trickery, 165, 211; political maneuvers. 189

posset A drink made of milk with wine or ale and spices, used as a remedy for colds; now obsolete or dialectal. 182

prince In certain contexts, "prince" does not mean "the son of a king," but "ruler," male or female. The wife of a king is just a queen, but she who holds the throne is prince as well as queen. Cf. Machiavelli's title *The Prince*. 199, 309

progress Used in the special meaning of a state journey of a royal person; somewhat archaic. 237

prophet, prophetess One who speaks for God/the god, 15; also, a person who accurately foretells the future. 157, 217

quean In Scottish dialect, simply a girl or young woman, but in Standard English, an ill-behaved woman, a hussy. 55

quick Living; the sensitive part of a nail. 19

quickened Came to life, as in the phrase "the quick and the dead." 247

ripe In describing a girl as "ripe," Orual means that she has reached puberty. 20

ruin downfall; damage or injury.[8] 152

7. See Myers, *Context*, 5, 18.
8. See Owen Barfield, *Poetic Diction*, 113–26.

salt bitch, the Female dog in heat. "Salt" comes from Middle French *saut* and literally means "on the jump." Compare "saute."[9] 26

savoury Tasty. Both King Trom and Orual use depersonalizing words when speaking of the sexuality of women. 182

shore Old form of "sheared." 5, 19

slug abed, vb. To lie idly or lazily; *OED* lists as "somewhat rare." 88

small beer Weak or inferior beer. 36

stale, n. Urine, obsolete or dialectal usage; last *OED* entry, 1891, 6, 11; adj. something that has lost its freshness. 209.

swill, n. Liquid or partly liquid food for swine (not used in novel); vb. to rinse out. 215

tale Tally or score, from "tell," meaning "count." 223

talent 36,000 obols in Greek money. By weight, a Euboic talent was 57 pounds and an Aeginetan one 95 pounds.[10] 232

tell Count in the sense of "be accountable." 133

terrible Arousing fear mixed with awe. See "The Holy," 168. 8, 14, 114, 117

towsing Tossing, rumpling, rough pulling about, horseplay. (The temple girls, though holy because they were dedicated to Ungit, were prostitutes, after all.) Lewis uses the spelling common in the sixteenth through eighteenth centuries; modern spelling is "tousing." 269

travail Hard work; the modern word *travel* derives from the same root. 9

trull The present meaning is "prostitute"; an obsolete meaning is simply "girl." 55, 148

tunnies Tuna; derived from Greek *thunnos.* 208. The Fox's homesickness includes longing for the food of his homeland.

unchancy Inconvenient, ill-timed, or dangerous. 135. *See also* unchanciest 22.

used, using Treated, 184; treating, 211; ill-used, badly treated, 265; employed for a purpose, 204; employed plus badly treated. 262

vent Opportunity for selling; slightly old-fashioned, since the latest citation in the *OED* is dated 1828. 231

virtue Strength, but suggesting the obsolete meaning of "manliness." 8, 10

---

9. See also "salt lust for the occult" (*SbJ*, 207).
10. *The Greek Historians,* 2.766–67.

weaponed Virile, not castrated. Note the implication that the penis is a tool of domination. 186

wearish Delicate, sickly-looking. 20

win Attain; cf. "won through." 86

with child Pregnant; seldom used today. 13, 20

won through Succeeded in reference to a desired object. In *OED*, listed as chiefly Scottish or northern. 30, 33, 41

Further Reading

Apuleius. *Cupid and Psyche.* Edited with commentary by E. J. Kenney. Cambridge Greek and Latin Classics. New York: Cambridge University Press, 1990.

Beard, Mary, and John Henderson. *Classics: A Very Short Introduction.* Oxford: Oxford University Press, 1995.

Bryant, Christopher, SSJE. *Jung and the Christian Way.* 1983. Reprint, London: Darton, Longman & Todd, 1990.

Herodotus. *The Histories.* Translated by Walter Blanco. Edited by Walter Blanco and Jenniver Tolbert Roberts. A Norton Critical Edition. New York: Norton, 1992.

James, William. *The Varieties of Religious Experience.* 1902. Reprint, New York: Library of America, 1987. Especially valuable chapters are "The Religion of Healthy-Mindedness," "The Sick Soul," and "The Divided Self, and the Process of Unification."

Jung, Carl G. *Memories, Dreams, Reflections,* 2nd ed. Recorded and edited by Aniela Jaffe. Translated by Richard Winston and Clara Winston. New York: Vintage Books, 1989.

Nicholi, Armand M., Jr. *The Question of God: C. S. Lewis and Sigmund Freud Debate God, Love, Sex, and the Meaning of Life.* New York: Free Press, 2002.

Works Cited

Lewis's books have a complex publication history, since they have been published in both Britain and American editions and reprinted many times. See Walter Hooper, "A Bibliography of the Writings of C. S. Lewis," in *C. S. Lewis at the Breakfast Table*, edited by James T. Como (New York: MacMillan, 1979). A less readable but updated bibliography appears in Walter Hooper, *C. S. Lewis, Companion and Guide* (New York: HarperSanFrancisco, 1996).

Adey, Lionel. *C. S. Lewis: Writer, Dreamer and Mentor.* Grand Rapids, Mich.: Eerdmans, 1998.

Adkins, Lesley, and Roy A. Adkins. *Handbook to Life in Ancient Greece.* New York: Facts on File, 1997.

Alighieri, Dante. *La Vita Nuova.* Translated by D. G. Rosetti. In *The Portable Dante*, edited by Paolo Milano. New York: Viking, 1947.

———. *The Divine Comedy of Dante Alighieri.* 3 vols. Translated by John D. Sinclair. New York: Oxford University Press, 1939.

The Annotated Book of Common Prayer . . . of the Church of England. 2nd ed. Edited by John Henry Blunt. London: Longmans, 1892.

Apuleius. *Cupid and Psyche.* Edited with commentary by, E. J. Kenney. Cambridge Greek and Latin Classics Imperial Library. Cambridge: Cambridge University Press, 1990.

———. *The Golden Ass.* Translated by P. G. Walsh. Oxford: Oxford University Press, 1995.

Arnold, E. Vernon. *Roman Stoicism.* 1911. Reprint, London: Routledge & Kegan Paul, 1958.

Augustine of Hippo. *Confessions.* Translated by Edward B. Pusey. New York: Modern Library, 1949.

Barfield, Owen. *Poetic Diction*. 1928. 3rd ed. Middletown, Conn.: Wesleyan University Press, 1973.

Bauer, Walter. See *Greek-English Lexicon*.

Beard, Mary, and John Henderson. *Classics: A Very Short Introduction*. Oxford: Oxford University Press, 1995.

Beloe, William. See Herodotus.

Bevan, Edwyn. *Stoics and Sceptics*. 1913. Reprint, Cambridge: W. Heffer & Sons, 1959.

Bishop, Leigh C. "C. S. Lewis on Psychoanalysis: II. Through Darkest Zeitgeistheim," n.d. Wade Center, Wheaton College.

Boethius. *The Consolation of Philosophy*. Translated by V. E. Watts. 1969. Reprint, Middlesex, Eng.: Penguin Books, 1984.

Brown, Raymond E. *An Introduction to the New Testament*. The Anchor Bible Reference Library. New York: Doubleday, 1997.

Bryant, Christopher, SSJE. *Depth Psychology and Religious Belief*. London: Darton, Longman & Todd, 1987.

———. *Jung and the Christian Way*. 1983. London: Darton, Longman & Todd, 1990.

Buxton, R. G. A. *Imaginary Greece: The Contexts of Mythology*. Cambridge: Cambridge University Press, 1984.

Cavander, Kenneth. See Euripides.

Cobb, William S. See Plato.

Coghill, Neville. "The Approach to English." In Gibb, 51–66.

Cloud of Unknowing. Edited by James Walsh. Classics of Western Spirituality. New York: Paulist Press, 1981.

Danker, Frederick William, and Walter Bauer. See *Greek-English Lexicon*.

Donaldson, Mara E. *Holy Places Are Dark Places: C. S. Lewis and Paul Ricoeur on Narrative Transformation*. Lanham, Md.: University Press of America, 1988.

———. "Orual's Story and the Art of Retelling: A Study of *Till We Have Faces*." In Schakel and Huttar, 157–70.

Dorsett, Lyle. *And God Came In*. 1983. Reprint, New York: Ballantine, 1984.

Dummelow, J. R. *A Commentary on the Holy Bible*. New York: Macmillan, 1927.

Elwell, Walter A. *The Concise Evangelical Dictionary of Theology*. 1984. Abridged by Peter Toon. Grand Rapids, Mich.: Baker Book House, 1991.

Euripides. *Bacchanals [The Bacchae].* Translated by Arthur S. Way. Loeb Classical Library, vol. 3. 1912. Reprint, Cambridge, Mass.: Harvard University Press, 1962.

———. *Hippolytus.* Translated by Gilbert Murray. 1902. Reprint, London: Longmans, Green & Co., 1920.

———. *Iphigeneia at Aulis.* Translated with commentary by Kenneth Cavander. Greek Drama Series. Englewood Cliffs, N.J.: Prentice-Hall, 1973.

Ferm, Vergilius. *An Encyclopedia of Religion.* New York: Philosophical Library, 1945.

Filmer, Kath. *The Fiction of C. S. Lewis: Mask and Mirror.* New York: St. Martin's Press, 1993.

Ford, Paul F. *A Companion to Narnia.* 4th ed. San Francisco: HarperSanFrancisco, 1994.

———. "C. S. Lewis, Ecumenical Spiritual Director: A Study of His Experience and Theology of Prayer and Discernment in the Process of Becoming a Self." Ph.D. diss., Fuller Theological Seminary, June 1987.

Frazer, James G. *The Golden Bough.* 1890. Reprint, with foreword by Curtis Church, New York: Random House Value Publishing, 1981.

———. *The Golden Bough,* 3rd ed. New York: Macmillan, 1951.

Fredrick, Candice, and Sam McBride. *Women among the Inklings: Gender, C. S. Lewis, J. R. R. Tolkien, and Charles Williams.* Westport, Conn.: Greenwood Press, 2001.

Gibb, Jocelyn, ed. *Light on C. S. Lewis.* London: Geoffrey Bles, 1965.

Gibbons, Stella. "Imaginative Writing." In Gibb, 87–101.

Grant, Michael. *From Alexander to Cleopatra: The Hellenistic World.* New York: Charles Scribner's Sons, 1982.

Graves, Robert. *The Greek Myths.* New York: George Braziller, 1955.

Greek-English Lexicon of the New Testament and Other Early Christian Literature, 3rd ed. Based on Walter Bauer's *Griechisch-Deutsches Wörterbuch,* 6th ed. Revised and edited by Frederick William Danker. Chicago: University of Chicago Press, 2000.

Greek Historians, vol. 2. Edited by Francis R. B. Godolphin. New York: Random House, 1942.

Green, Roger Lancelyn, and Walter Hooper. *C. S. Lewis: A Biography.* New York: Harcourt Brace Jovanovich, 1974.

Hamilton, Edith. *Mythology.* New York: New American Library, 1940.

Harrison, Jane Ellen. *Prolegomena to the Study of Greek Religion.* 3rd ed. Cambridge: Cambridge University Press, 1922.

Herodotus. *The Ancient History of Herodotus.* Translated by William Beloe. New York: Bangs, Brother, & Co., 1855.

———. *Herodotus with an English Translation.* Translated by A. D. Godley. 4 vols. Loeb Classical Library. London: William Heinemann, 1920–1924. Reprint, Cambridge, Mass.: Harvard University Press, 1960.

Homer. *The Iliad.* Translated by E. V. Rieu. 1950. Reprint, Baltimore: Penguin Books, 1966.

Hooper, Walter. *C. S. Lewis Companion and Guide.* London: HarperCollinsPublishers, 1996.

Irenaeus. *Against Heresies: The Apostolic Fathers with Justin Martyr and Irenaeus.* Vol. 1, *The Ante-Nicene Fathers.* Translated and edited by Alexander Roberts and James Donaldson. Grand Rapids, Mich.: Eerdmans, 1975.

James, William. *The Varieties of Religious Experience.* 1902. In *Writings 1902–1910,* with notes by Bruce Kuklick. New York: Library of America, 1978.

Julian of Norwich. *Showings.* Translated by Edmund Colledge, O.S.A., and James Walsh, S.J. The Classics of Western Spirituality. New York: Paulist Press, 1978.

Jung, Carl. *Collected Works.* Bollingen Series 20. Princeton: Princeton University Press, 1968–1979.

———. *Memories, Dreams, Reflections.* 2nd ed. Recorded and edited by Aniela Jaffe. Translated by Richard Winston and Clara Winston. New York: Vintage Books, 1989.

Kantorowicz, Ernst H. *The King's Two Bodies: A Study in Mediaeval Political Theology.* Princeton: Princeton University Press, 1957.

Kennedy, George. *The Art of Persuasion in Greece.* Princeton: Princeton University Press, 1963.

Kenney, E. J. See Apuleius.

Leech, Kenneth. *Soul Friend: The Practice of Christian Spirituality.* San Francisco: Harper & Row, 1977.

———. *True Prayer: An Invitation to Christian Spirituality.* San Francisco: Harper & Row, 1980.

Leick, Gwendolyn. *A Dictionary of Ancient Near Eastern Mythology.* London: Routledge, 1991.

Lewis, C. S. *The Abolition of Man.* 1943. Reprint, New York: Macmillan, 1947.

———. *All My Road before Me.* San Diego: Harcourt Brace Jovanovich, 1991.

———. *Christian Reflections.* Edited by Walter Hooper. Grand Rapids, Mich.: Eerdmans, 1967.

———. *The Chronicles of Narnia.* 1950–1956. New York: Collier-Macmillan, 1974.

———. *The Discarded Image.* 1964. Cambridge: Cambridge University Press, 1970.

———. *An Experiment in Criticism.* Cambridge: Cambridge University Press, 1961.

———. *Fern-seed and Elephants.* Edited by Walter Hooper. Glasgow: William Collins & Co., 1975.

———. *The Four Loves.* San Diego: Harcourt Brace Jovanovich, 1960.

———. *God in the Dock.* Edited by Walter Hooper. Grand Rapids, Mich.: Eerdmans, 1970.

———. *A Grief Observed.* London: Faber & Faber, 1961.

———. *Letters of C. S. Lewis.* Rev. and enl. ed. Edited by Walter Hooper. London: Fount Paperbacks, 1988; rpt. 1991.

———. *Letters of C. S. Lewis to Arthur Greeves.* Edited by Walter Hooper. New York: Collier-Macmillan, 1979.

———. *Letters to Children.* Edited by Lyle Dorsett and Marjorie Mead. 1985. Reprint, New York: Simon & Schuster, 1995.

———. *Letters to Malcolm.* 1964. Reprint, New York: Harvest, 1973.

———. *Mere Christianity.* New York: Macmillan, 1952.

———. *Miracles: A Preliminary Study.* 1947. New York: Collier-Macmillan, 1978.

———. *Of Other Worlds.* Edited by Walter Hooper. New York: Harcourt, Brace & World, 1967.

———. *Perelandra.* 1943. New York: Macmillan, 1965.

———. *The Pilgrim's Regress.* 1933. London: Geoffrey Bles, 1943.

———. *Poems.* Edited by Walter Hooper. New York: Harcourt Brace Jovanovich, 1964.

———. *The Problem of Pain.* New York: Macmillan, 1962.

———. *Reflections on the Psalms.* San Diego: Harcourt Brace Jovanovich, 1958.

———. *The Screwtape Letters.* 1942. New York: Macmillan, 1961.

————. *Selected Literary Essays*. Edited by Walter Hooper. Cambridge: Cambridge University Press, 1969.

————. *Spenser's Images of Life*. Edited by Alastair Fowler. Cambridge: Cambridge University Press, 1969.

————. *Surprised by Joy*. New York: Harcourt, Brace, & World, 1955.

————. *That Hideous Strength*. 1945. Reprint, New York: Macmillan, 1965.

————. *Till We Have Faces*. 1956. New York: Harcourt, Brace, & World, 1957.

————. *The World's Last Night*. 1952. Reprint, San Diego: Harcourt-Brace Jovanovich, 1960.

Manlove, Colin. "'Caught Up into the Larger Pattern': Images and Narrative Structures in C. S. Lewis's Fiction." In Schakel and Huttar, 256–76.

Medcalf, Stephen. "Language and Self-Consciousness: The Making and Breaking of C. S. Lewis's Personae." In Schakel and Huttar, 109–44.

Meilander, Gilbert. *The Taste for the Other*, 2nd ed. Grand Rapids, Mich.: Eerdmans, 1998.

Merton, Thomas. *New Seeds of Contemplation*. 1962. Reprint, New York: New Directions Publ. Corp. 1972.

Milton, John. *Paradise Lost*. Edited by Roy Flannagan. New York: Macmillan, 1993.

Minns, Ellis H. *Scythians and Greeks: A Survey of Ancient History and Archaeology on the North Coast of the Euxine from the Danube to the Caucasus*. Cambridge: Cambridge University Press, 1913.

Murray, Gilbert. *Four Stages of Greek Religion*. New York: Columbia University Press, 1912.

————. *Five Stages of Greek Religion*. New York: Columbia University Press, 1925.

————. See Euripides, *Hippolytus*.

Myers, Doris T. *C. S. Lewis in Context*. Kent, Ohio: Kent State University Press, 1994.

————. "Spenser." In *Reading the Classics with C. S. Lewis*, edited by Thomas L. Martin. Grand Rapids, Mich.: Baker Academic, 2000.

Otto, Rudolf. *The Idea of the Holy*. Translated by John W. Harvey. 1923. Reprint, New York: Oxford University Press, 1958.

————. *Religious Essays: A Supplement to "The Idea of the Holy."* Translated by Brian Lunn. London: Oxford University Press, 1931.

Oxford Classical Dictionary, 1st ed. Edited by M. Cary, J. D. Denniston, J. Wight Duff, A. D. Nock, W. D. Ross, and H. H. Scullard. Oxford: Clarendon Press, 1949.

Oxford Classical Dictionary, 3rd ed. Edited by Simon Hornblower and Antony Spawforth. New York: Oxford University Press, 1996.

Patterson, Nancy-Lou. "The Holy House of Ungit." *Mythlore* 82 (Winter, 1997): 4–15.

Plato. *Phaedo.* Translated by David Gallop. Oxford: Clarendon Press, 1975.

————. *Phaedo.* In *The Dialogues of Plato*, vol. 1. Translated by Benjamin Jowett. 1892. Reprint, New York: Random House, 1937.

————. *The Symposium; and The Phaedrus: Plato's Erotic Dialogues.* Translated by William S. Cobb. Albany: State University of New York Press, 1993.

Pope, Marvin H., trans. *Song of Songs.* The Anchor Bible, 7C. Garden City, New York: Doubleday, 1982.

Price, Simon. "The History of the Hellenistic Period." In *The Oxford History of the Classical World*, edited by John Boardman, Jasper Griffin, and Oswyn Murray. Oxford: Oxford University Press, 1986.

Prickett, Stephen. *Words and "The Word": Language, Poetics and Biblical Interpretation.* Cambridge: Cambridge University Press, 1986.

Pyles, Thomas, and John Algeo. *The Origins and Development of the English Language*, 4th ed. Fort Worth, Texas: Harcourt Brace Jovanovich College Publishers, 1993.

Reilly, R. J. *Romantic Religion: A Study of Barfield, Lewis, Williams, and Tolkien.* Athens: University of Georgia Press, 1971.

Rostovtzeff, M. *Iranians and Greeks in South Russia.* Oxford: Clarendon Press, 1922.

Samuels, Andrew, Bani Shorter, and Fred Plaut. *A Critical Dictionary of Jungian Analysis.* London: Routledge & Kegan Paul, 1986.

Sayer, George. *Jack: C. S. Lewis and His Times.* San Francisco: Harper & Row, 1988.

Sayers, Dorothy L. *The Man Born to Be King: A Play-Cycle on the Life of Our Lord and Saviour Jesus Christ.* Grand Rapids, Mich.: Eerdmans, 1943.

Schakel, Peter J. *Imagination and the Arts in C. S. Lewis.* Columbia, Mo.: University of Missouri Press, 2002.

————. *Reason and Imagination in C. S. Lewis.* Grand Rapids, Mich.: Eerdmans, 1984.

Schakel, Peter J., ed. *The Longing for a Form: Essays on the Fiction of C. S. Lewis.* 1977. Reprint, Grand Rapids, Mich.: Baker, 1979.

Schakel, Peter J., and Charles A. Huttar, eds. *Word and Story in C. S. Lewis.* Columbia, Mo.: University of Missouri Press, 1991.

Simpson, D. P. *Cassell's New Latin Dictionary.* New York: Funk & Wagnalls, 1962.

Smith, Robert Houston. *Patches of Godlight: The Pattern of Thought of C. S. Lewis.* Athens: University of Georgia Press, 1981.

Walsh, P. G., trans. *The Golden Ass.* See Apuleius.

Walsh, P. G. *The Roman Novel.* Cambridge: Cambridge University Press, 1970.

Wilson, A. N. *C. S. Lewis: A Biography.* New York: W. W. Norton, 1990.

Wood, Doreen Anderson. "The Pattern in the Myth: Archetypal Elements in C. S. Lewis's *Till We Have Faces.*" Ph.D. diss., University of Tulsa, 1976. Wade Center, Wheaton College.

Freud, Sigmund, 7, 123, 159, 170, 192n2; criticism of, 193, 194, 195, 196; on God, 123n2, 198; James and, 193; Jung and, 198, 199; on Oedipus, 193; paradigms of, 3; reading, 156, 192, 193–97; religion and, 197–98; unconscious and, 200
Freudians: gratitude toward, 196
"Further In" (Lewis), 192

Garden of Eden, 56
Garden of the Hesperides, 16, 17
Genesis, 80
genres, 5, 6
geographic placement, 164–65
Gethsemane, 20, 218
Gladiators, The, 155
Glome: Africa and, 163; described, 3, 13–14, 15, 28, 88; Fox and, 112; geographic placement of, 164–65; gloom of, 155, 157; Great Offering and, 47; Hellenistic world and, 15, 111, 118; *Iliad* and, 108; names in, 188–91; Orual and, 1, 13–14, 89, 106, 118, 133; paganism of, 14; Phars and, 93, 94; placement in time of, 165–66; Plato and, 210–13; Psyche and, 24, 72, 191; religion in, 95, 96, 110, 111, 207, 209; returning to, 65, 68, 79, 82, 115, 221; sacrifices of, 32, 206–7; Scythians and, 165; superstitions of, 205, 216
Glome library, 106–9, 166; Plato and, 210; Socrates and, 212; Stesichorus and, 109
God: attitude toward, 64, 170; concept of, 29, 57, 73, 170, 174; conscious mind and, 201; disobeying, 53; Freud on, 123n2, 198; goodness of, 135; injustice of, 130–31; journey to, 139; Jung on, 123n2, 198; knowing, 50–51, 102, 123; Lewis on, 102, 131, 135, 174; love and, 137, 141; miracles/Pagans and, 57; as myth-become-fact, 41; Orual and, 118, 139; Psyche and, 118; rational and, 111, 174; soul and, 114; wrath of, 80, 173
goddess of peace: mortal women and, 94

godhood: plain speaking and, 66–67
gods, 96, 115, 120, 121, 129, 150, 186; food for, 207; Greek stages of, 206; Homeric, 205; hostility towards, 73, 130, 216; Orual and, 14, 73, 96, 119, 130, 171, 211; perception of, 126, 206; Psyche and, 211; reality of, 134; seeking, 140; terrors/plagues and, 113
god-talk, 170
Goethe, Johann Wolfgang von, 178
Golden Ass, The (Apuleius), 2, 51, 81, 145, 155; books of, 146; Isis and, 148; moral teaching in, 146–47. *See also* "Cupid and Psyche" (Apuleius)
Golden Bough, The (Frazer), 54, 204, 205
golden fleece, 129
Gospel According to Luke, 20, 166
Gothic, 172–73
Grahame, Kenneth, 173
Gram, 74, 78, 82, 86, 189; gramma and, 191
Grapes of Wrath (Steinbeck), 4
Graves, Robert, 7, 189, 204
Great Chain of Being, 159, 194
Great King, 118, 164, 221
Great Offering, 32, 38, 44, 47
Great Unknown, 73
Greek culture, 5, 15, 36, 165–66
Greek literature, 5, 33, 39
Greek Myths, The (Graves), 189
Green Lady: Ransom and, 56
Green Witch: Aslan and, 170
Greeves, Arthur, 146, 155
Gregory of Nyassa, 111
Gresham, Bill, 160
Grey Mountain, 55, 115, 164, 165, 220; god of, 35, 45, 49, 184; Orual at, 148; palace on, 59; Psyche at, 54
grief: love and, 80–81, 139
Grief Observed, A (Lewis), 131, 161

Hades, 134, 140, 150, 151, 152
Haggard, Rider, 15
Haldane, J. B. S., 176
Happy Valley, 62, 75, 79, 80, 149
Hardy, Thomas, 3, 4
Harrison, Jane Ellen, 7, 204–5, 209; research by, 171; on rites, 206, 207